THE REAL CROWN JEWELS OF ENGLAND

100 PLACES THAT MAKE US GREAT

Clive Aslet

CONSTABLE

CONSTABLE

First published in Great Britain in 2020 by Constable
This paperback edition first published in 2021 by Constable

1 3 5 7 9 10 8 6 4 2

A CIP catalogue record for this book
is available from the British Library.

ISBN: 978-1-47213-374-8

Typeset in Minion Pro by SX Composing DTP, Rayleigh, Essex
Printed and bound in Great Britain by Clays Ltd, Elcograf, S.p.A.

Papers used by Constable are from well-managed forests
and other responsible sources.

MIX
Paper from
responsible sources
FSC® C104740

Constable
An imprint of
Little, Brown Book Group
Carmelite House
50 Victoria Embankment
London EC4Y 0DZ

An Hachette UK Company
www.hachette.co.uk

www.littlebrown.co.uk

For Bevis

Contents

Icons of National Identity

Outstanding Beauty

History

The English Eye

Architecture

Works of Skill, Ingenuity and Art

Things We Do Well

Unconditioned Stimuli

CONTENTS

Introduction
We'll Always Have Paris . . . ?

On 15 April 2019, Notre-Dame de Paris was ablaze. Images of the roof in flames and the crashing of the spire – albeit erected by Viollet-le-Duc in the nineteenth century and not medieval – caused a shock wave that spread far beyond Paris, far beyond France. I felt a connection; the very first place I stayed as a boy, independent of family or school, was the Île de la Cité, a few hundred yards from the cathedral. Everybody had their own reason to mourn. It was one of the most famous landmarks of the world, a symbol of the city in which it stood.

To children, the death of an old person seems not only sad but unnatural; it destabilises the order of their world. They had previously assumed – contrary to the known facts of human life – that the people familiar to them would continue to be there, part of the background to their existence, sometimes visited, sometimes not, but forever present. Notre-Dame had something of this quality. It was even older than the Queen; far, far older than any human being. It had existed for centuries, nearly a millennium . . .

It turned out that the damage, in the way of many fires, was not as devastating as it had seemed at first. The roof had burnt, the nave below was only scorched; many of the treasures can be restored. Still, the erasure of the famous silhouette is cause enough for grief. It knocked the world and left a bruise. 'We'll always have Paris,' says Bogie in *Casablanca*. Well, possibly not. A thing can be of the utmost value – revered as a landmark, precious as a work of art, totemic as a manifestation of national identity – and yet tomorrow, it could have gone.

So it is worth asking the question: what could we not bear to lose, if it disappeared? What would cause national trauma, provoke the same depth of mourning as Notre-Dame?

Life is fragile

This book is not a rant about the death of history or the rise of attitudes that are, in conventional terms, anti-historical. My point is this. Life is fragile. So is beauty. So are buildings, monuments, places that move us. A careless spark – or in the case of a Grade I Elizabethan country house in the West Country that burnt down a few years ago, an unluckily positioned shaving mirror that concentrated the rays of a low November sun onto a curtain – and whoosh, that's it. Gone overnight. A few days before the Notre-Dame fire, proceedings in the House of Commons had to be suspended as a leak of sewage descended into the Chamber from an overburdened pipe. This was just the latest manifestation of a truth well known for years: the Palace of Westminster is clapped out. Pipework, wiring, what in human terms would be the veins and sinews of the building, are completely shot; and no amount of statins, by-pass work or other emergency surgery will fix them. Every time a new run of services has been needed – in this building that is used so intensively it is difficult to close – the wherewithal has been installed next to its predecessor in the large voids that the Victorian architect, Charles Barry, intended as ventilation ducts. Those ducts are now full. The structure has been patched and patched again and now the patches are coming off. When a building degenerates to that extent, but continues to service a busy Parliament, disaster may be just around the corner. The present Palace of Westminster replaced a medieval and Georgian warren, after a fire in 1834. Government, when it comes to failure to husband its estate, has form.

I began this book after the disaster at Notre-Dame. I am completing it under lockdown, during the time of Covid-19. Life is fragile indeed. The places that resonate so strongly, giving solace and inspiration to those who visit them, are now off limits. Some I see from the outside when I take my day's permitted constitutional around our home in London. I may make it as far as Westminster Abbey and the Banqueting House, before turning around at Charles I's equestrian statue at the top of Whitehall. Or I may reach the Royal Artillery Memorial on Hyde Park, with Apsley House on the other side of the now deserted thoroughfare, usually a potential death trap for the unwary pedestrian because of the thundering vehicles – worse than the charge of the Scots Greys at Waterloo. The continuity that these monuments represent gives comfort; they are old friends, reliably present and unaffected by pandemics. I'm still hoping to see a bumblebee although it may be too early in the year for what the American thinker Ralph Waldo Emerson called 'that yellow-breeched philosopher' – and bumblebees aren't as numerous as they once were. Emerson wrote his poem

'The Humble-Bee' after losing money he could ill afford to miss in the banking panic of 1837.

> When the fierce northwestern blast
> Cools sea and land so far and fast,
> Thou already slumberest deep;
> Woe and want thou canst outsleep;
> Want and woe, which torture us,
> Thy sleep makes ridiculous.

Could there be a similar moral to draw from the Crown Jewels? These buildings and places survived other crises: they will survive this one. Which is another reason to treasure them.

What are the roots that clutch?

Life brings with it other risks than fire and disease. Coasts erode, rivers dry up, quiet places become crowded. And this makes it all the more important to value what we have. To bring to mind its special qualities and bang the drum. That is the purpose of this book. Fire officers advise householders to keep a grab-bag of essentials that can be seized by the family as it flees a burning building. I have applied the same principle to England. What are the places that we most cherish, that express qualities that are specially English? What is it that we would like to save at all costs from a general conflagration? What would enable us to rebuild England if all else went up in smoke? This book is England's grab-bag. As grab-bags go, it is fairly large. I have allowed myself one hundred items. That is a good round number, and seemed quite big when I first thought of it. But it does not take long to use it up. There have been hard choices to make. For every entry in the book, a dozen – or far more – potential entries have been rejected. A hundred, for this purpose, is pretty small.

Of course, the whole number could have been occupied by churches and cathedrals. I have included Salisbury Cathedral but not Ely, York Minster (for the east window) but not Southwell, and so on. Chatsworth is the country house of country houses – but how could I have left out Houghton, Arundel, Alnwick, Castle Howard or Blenheim? Only, reader, with a steely determination and a sometimes bleeding heart.

I have had to be ruthless. No National Gallery, no Wallace Collection, no Ashmolean Museum. I wonder at my own brutality. Sometimes a single entry will have to stand for a genus. I struggle with sport. (I have always struggled with sport; at school, my art master persuaded the authorities to let me spend games afternoons visiting art galleries instead. My contribution on the sports field was not missed.) Although an important part of national life, sport doesn't usually take place in buildings that would, in themselves, be greatly missed. The old Wembley Stadium could be regarded as hallowed turf from the number of football matches played there, not least the England–Germany World Cup Final of 1966. But nobody much cared when it was rebuilt. Arsenal survived its move to the Emirates Stadium without trauma. Twickenham is an important venue for rugby – but the place would survive a conflagration. Who cares about the stands? New ones would probably be better. The Hurlingham Club would be deeply mourned by members of the Hurlingham Club but I cannot feel it qualifies. Lord's Cricket Ground . . . yes, that may be different. Some of the buildings are steeped in the traditions of the MCC and the Club has usually done its best for architecture when new ones have been commissioned. But the elephantine Media Centre, built in what looks like white plastic to resemble a gigantic television cabinet, is unforgivable. I have chosen what could be the most beautiful cricket ground in England instead. I admit there is little beautiful about the All England Lawn Tennis Club at Wimbledon, but Wimbledon fortnight is Wimbledon fortnight – inseparable from the place itself.

I have not included the whole of the United Kingdom. Scotland and Northern Ireland have their own manifold wonders but equally their own traditions. Just once do I go fully into Wales, in search of lichens – simply because the fact of its being the lichen capital of the world is too joyous to ignore. I make another foray when following the River Wye, a river that begins in England and tempts me into Wales in its lower reaches. I am unrepentant. Nature does not always respect boundaries.

This is something of a parlour game. But there is a serious undertow. England is a miracle. It is one of the most densely populated countries in the world – not so crowded, on a people per hectare basis, as Singapore, but getting that way. The pressures on it are intense; a ghost returning from, say, two centuries ago would be appalled by the casual ugliness that has been allowed to deflower the land – the shopping centres, the distribution hubs, the acres upon acre of car park (all, incidentally, a shockingly extravagant use of space in these populous islands). There are few hay meadows, almost no farmland wild flowers, few songbirds, less casual beauty; Nature itself is on the retreat.

But he would also be reassured to discover that some things were as he remembered, or better (the fabric of churches, for example). Not everything has been trampled under foot.

Beauty remains. Sometimes in remarkable abundance. Far more people live in the Surrey Hills, not far from London, than they did when William Cobbett made his Rural Rides in the 1820s. They are hugely more prosperous; the inhabitants drive cars. Yet it is possible still to glimpse, just, the landscape that Cobbett knew. Not only have we been successful in preserving large parts of the countryside, our cities are generally far more pleasant to live in than they used to be; the suburbs bequeathed to us by the early twentieth century can still be green and pleasant. We have much that is worth transmitting to future generations. We may, in recent years, have found it difficult to agree on fundamental questions about politics. But not everything of importance in life happens at Westminster. Let us pause for a moment to remember what we have and who we are. Beauty remains and we can all enjoy it. The real Crown Jewels are a common heritage. At a time of social division, remembering the best things about this country can help bring us together.

Let us not neglect to care for our shared patrimony. Let us be thankful for it and rejoice.

Special to Here

We live in a world of increasing sameness. You travel only to find you have arrived somewhere very similar to the place you left; only the climate and the faces are different. Architecture, internet, shops, food – they are all pretty much alike. This puts a special value on the things that can be experienced in one place and one place only. England can boast a few of them. Although other countries have ancient yews and olive trees, nowhere has such numbers of very old oaks that are awe-inspiring in their venerable deformity. Only English Gothic produced the Perpendicular style with its forest canopies of fan-vaulting and daring expanses of stained glass. Bluebell woods do occur elsewhere, but not in such numbers as can be seen here (in the French countryside, some bulbs are eaten by wild boar); the Spanish bluebell – erect, not drooping, and a weaker blue – is an invader we must beware of. The English have made a cult of ruins, partly because Henry VIII left us with a lot to make a cult of, and partly because they were essential to the aesthetic of the Picturesque, developed by owners of landscape parks in the eighteenth century.

You get the idea. My point is not nationalistic. It would be the same in France, Spain, Russia, Sweden or the United States

– things that are unique to each country have a special savour. Life would be impoverished without them. Our hearts would be heavy if they were gone.

Ancient oaks

They are gouty, dwarfish, shrunken from what they used to be, inordinately fat. Their crowns have thinned, and a once dense canopy of green has been reduced to a scattering of leaves. One should not anthropomorphise ancient trees, but I find it difficult not to. They are Lear-like in their senescence, riven by past lightning strikes, disembowelled – and yet still clinging to a past-sell-by-date vigour, which will result, every so often, in a superabundance of acorns. The indignities of age are borne nobly. They do not complain when limbs drop off, or families of jackdaws set up home about their person. They suffer parasites with patience, fungus with fortitude, rot with a wry smile. No, they do not smile. I am being anthropomorphic again. Let's just say that it is wonderful they should be so very old.

Now, here's the thing. We in this country have far more ancient trees than anywhere else in Northern Europe. Just as the Fellows of Trinity College, Cambridge, are said (by fellows of Trinity College) to include more Nobel Prize winners among their ranks than the whole of France, so Richmond Park supports more five-hundred-year-old trees than France and Germany combined. In excess of twelve hundred. This says something about our history. Hollow trees are very easy to chop up. On the Continent, marauding armies took a toll of them – but fortunately, the English countryside was more settled. A further level of control was provided by the foresters of royal parks and the parks of stately homes, which is where they are nearly always to be found.

How old are these ancient trees, exactly? Impossible to say. Time has taken its toll of their innards; despite the Falstaffian girth, they have been hollowed out, sometimes reduced to a mere membrane of just-about-still-living wood, not much thicker than a blanket. They have been blasted by lightning, or the heartwood has softened and decayed. So it is not possible to count the annual growth rings, and carbon-dating only works on dead matter – whereas these trees still live. But we know that some are more than five hundred years old. Much more. The Queen's Oak in Cowdray Park supposedly sheltered Queen Elizabeth in 1591. The interior of the Bowthorpe Oak was already used as a dining room in the eighteenth century. Are these trees a thousand years old? Oaks live for a long time, although not as long as yews. I once talked to an old, dendrologically minded man who was about to make a pilgrimage to see the Fortingall Yew in Perthshire. It pleased him, as he neared the end of his life, to salute an organism that may have flourished when Jesus Christ was born.

Once the Cowdray Oak and Bowthorpe Oak had to work for their living. Wood was an important resource for the Middle Ages; woods were highly managed. Pollards were cut off short so their crowns would sprout whippy young shoots that could be harvested every couple of years: the trunks of such trees grew outwards rather than up. Squat, wide, grappled to the earth by deep roots, they came to resemble Sumo wrestlers. As they collapse back into the earth, woodpeckers and squirrels take up squatters' rights. More than one thousand three hundred and fifty species of beetle have been recorded in Richmond Park, some of which require the conjunction of decaying and live wood found in ancient trees.

How lucky we are to have these arboreal Methuselahs. But for how long? Thoughtless picnickers throw the embers of disposable barbecues into their hollow trunks, with the inevitable incendiary consequence. Freak storms pull them to pieces. New pests and diseases attack oaks along with other tree species (not that government seems to care much, to judge from Britain's appallingly lax biosecurity). Ancient trees also suffer from the compaction of soil that deprives their roots – four-fifths of which lie near the surface – of water and nutrients. Good news. There is a solution for that. A good layer of mulch suppresses competing grasses and encourages worms.

Chatsworth House, Derbyshire

Consider Chatsworth, the glory of the Peak District, its gilded urns and window frames blazing in the evening sun. This is surely the country house of country houses, and – is it too much to say? – a complete work of art. It is a curious term, perhaps, to use of a building, rather than – as Wagner, who coined the term *Gesamtkunstwerk*, intended – an all-absorbing opera. Even Wagner, though, could only engage the senses of hearing and sight; a country house can better that, adding the scents of the garden (smell) and luxurious fabrics (touch). Taste? There are the fruits of the conservatory. Orchestral sound is less often heard at Chatsworth than at Bayreuth but when the sun shines and a marquee is up, the Chesterfield Brass Band does its best.

A work of art needs a controlling imagination; with its astounding collections – the Leonardo drawings, the Rembrandt paintings, the rare and sumptuously bound books, the antique statues, the Canovas, the Painted Hall, the gardens, the jewels, the contemporary ceramics, the works of virtuoso wood carving – Chatsworth could have become simply an agglomeration of stupendous stuff. Instead, from the moment a visitor enters the grounds, it unfolds as an aesthetic experience whose impact has been carefully coordinated, according to the ideas of a single individual. That individual – without wishing to underplay the achievement of Chatsworth's other owners – was William Cavendish, 6th Duke of Devonshire, who inherited in 1811 at the age of twenty-one. He never married, which saved considerable expense. Instead he lived, principally, for the arts, lavishing money on Chatsworth and his other houses – he had nine altogether – much to the chagrin of the nephew who succeeded him as the 7th Duke.

The present house was built by the 1st Duke of Devonshire, incorporating an Elizabethan building which disappeared from view during the process. (We can console ourselves for the loss of the early Chatsworth with Hardwick Hall, preserved almost as Bess of Hardwick left it: twenty miles away, it was another Cavendish property.) 'It is indeed a palace for a prince,' wrote Daniel Defoe in his *Tour Through the Whole Island of Great Britain*, 'a most magnificent building, and, in spite of all the difficulties or disadvantages of situation, is a perfect beauty.' As well as owning Flying Childers, the top stallion of the 1720s, the 2nd Duke collected Old Masters, gems and coins. The 4th Duke employed Capability Brown to landscape the park. We shall draw a veil over the 5th Duke and his beautiful wife, Georgiana Spencer, remembered for their *ménage à trois* with Lady Elizabeth Foster: no wonder, in view of such complications, the 6th Duke did not marry, although he had long-term relationships with women. Previous dukes, however, had created a superb toy box of collections for the 6th Duke to play with.

We know his thought processes because he described them himself in a *Handbook* that he wrote. It is supposedly addressed to his sister Harriet, whom he imagines arriving on a wet day. Lo! she does not get wet when she descends from the carriage because of the porch that the 6th Duke built for Queen Victoria's visit in 1843. They enter the sub-hall, which had been the kitchen when William and Harriet were growing up:

> The two ancient statues, Domitian and Agrippina, are from the hall at Wanstead. The gilt lead vases, that hinder people from tumbling through the openings from the corridor, were in the Painted Hall here. The stag's head was found at Herculaneum, and was given by the old King of Naples to my mother; and the bust of Jupiter, on the opposite chimney-piece, had its place in the awful room up-stairs, that formerly was called the Den. It frowned from the top of a lofty bookcase . . . The room is greatly improved since the days of cookery: the shafts of the stone columns were in existence then; but the capitals, architrave, frieze and cornice, and the steps are new.

And so it goes on through every room in the house, culminating in the new sculpture gallery. Through his stepmother (the Lady Elizabeth Foster who married the 5th Duke after Georgiana's death), who lived in Rome, the 6th Duke became enamoured of neo-Classicism. He succeeded in buying *The Sleeping Endymion*, a bust of Napoleon, and full-length portraits of Napoleon's mother and sister from the sculptor Antonio Canova. After Canova's death, his sculpting tools were placed in a case on the wall of the sculpture gallery.

Outside Chatsworth, the grounds received equal attention. To welcome the 6th Duke's friend, Tsar Nicholas I of Russia, the Duke had his gardener, the great Sir Joseph Paxton, create an Emperor Fountain that was higher even than the Tsar's fountain at Peterhof. (Sadly, the visit did not take place.) When Chatsworth was *en fête* and the gardens were lit with thousands of glimmering 'Russian lights', the effect must have been magical, thrilling, sublime. What more could you ask of a complete work of art? Except that it should retain those qualities into the present day. Which, even more wonderfully, it does.

Bluebell woods*

No poet in the English language described Nature with such particularity as Gerard Manley Hopkins; ordinary words did not do the job – he had to invent his own. But one flower awed him into a simple declaration: 'I do not think I have ever seen anything more beautiful than the bluebell.' As a Catholic convert and ordained Jesuit, he knew 'the beauty of our Lord by it'. Being Hopkins, he could not leave it there, going on to anatomise the 'cockled petal-ends', the mouth's 'square splay' and the 'square-in-rounding turns of the petals', whose jauntiness reminded him of a jester's cap. That was in 1870. Three years later, he committed another passage to his journal when he saw bluebells:

> all hanging their heads one way. I caught as well as I could . . . the lovely/ what people call/ 'gracious' bidding one to another or all one way, the level or stage or shire of colour they make hanging in the air a foot above the grass, and a notable glare

---

* I know I should choose a single wood for the purposes of this book but that would be impossible. Like the flower itself, it is not the individual bluebell which is so fabulous but the effect en masse.

the eye may abstract and sever from the blue colour/ of light
beating up from so many glassy heads, which like water is good
to float their deeper instress in upon the mind.

Complex stuff. But you do not have to be Hopkins to enjoy bluebells. Their appeal is universal. It is impossible to resist the joy of
their colour, carpeting the floor of a wood as though the world
had been turned upside down and a fragment of sky had ended
up beneath – rather than above – the moist, freshly appearing
leaves of the trees.

The colour changes. Can I compare them to a pair of jeans? On
first appearance – usually in April or early May, depending on the
part of the country – it shows as a deep blue, heading towards
indigo; as the months pass it fades to a paler hue. The honeyed
smell is best caught in the early morning, when it comes in intoxi-
cating wafts – not as powerful as the scent of hyacinth but sweet
and delicate. These are English joys. These islands contain half
the world's population of the flower, whose root sap was used to
glue feathers onto arrows in the Middle Ages and to stiffen Queen
Elizabeth's ruffs.

Once, bluebell gathering was a popular pastime, almost a
seasonal rite. Since they wilt soon after picking, the activity was
somewhat self-defeating. Even *Country Life* could commit this
botanical sin before the Second World War. 'It must be conceded
that bluebells are not really for gathering; they are for worshipping
– and passing by,' wrote a contributor in 1932. 'Not, of course,
that any of us ever follows this counsel of perfection.' In
Wildwood, Roger Deakin remembered 'the trail of trodden,
slippery stalks that used to litter the paths back to suburban

Watford through Cassiobury Park from the wild Whippendell Woods each spring'. Such mass depredations are now rare (although some criminals illegally root up the bulbs for sale).

Today our dainty native bluebells face other dangers, particularly misalliance with the larger, more exuberant Spanish variety, which has escaped from gardens and is cross-pollinating on the leaf litter. Woods, like the rest of the countryside, must be managed if we're to preserve the flowers we love. Neglected woods don't admit enough light. Deer graze everything in reach. We continue to lose plant-rich ancient woodland; in fact woodland species are declining at a faster rate even than meadow flowers. (It is scant consolation to be told that we have much more ancient woodland than hay meadow, for that is simply because hay meadow has become very rare.) What seems to be a gift of Nature that might have been bestowed for the sole purpose of lightening the human load in reality needs a degree of management for the yearly miracle to be repeated.

The Cerne Abbas Giant, Dorset

A club-wielding giant strides across the hillside above Cerne Abbas in Dorset. He is nearly sixty metres tall, his club alone is over thirty-six metres in length and as for his prodigious manhood . . . suffice it to say that he is a figure of formidable vigour in every respect. The Cerne Giant has been intimidating, or titivating, the Cerne Valley for centuries. How many centuries? Nobody knows for certain. He is a mystery, and peculiarly English. Carry on up the giant?

Titter ye not. White figures, scoured into the chalk hillsides of the Downs, are found nowhere else in Europe. The purpose of them is unknown. The White Horse at Uffington is the oldest, its disjointed lines reduced to dots and dashes, in the manner of a

Picasso. Archaeologists think the White Horse could be three millennia old, and is all the more remarkable, from an equine point of view, because horses could not have looked like that when it was made. They were then smaller, stockier animals. Was it intended to evoke a mythical, ideal or divine horse? Did it have magic powers? Again, we cannot say. About thirty hill figures or geoglyphs exist, often horses or, to be more specific, mares.

Giants are few. Two, identified as either the ogrish Gog and Magog, or Gogmagog and the Trojan knight Corineus, brandished clubs on the turf of Plymouth Hoe, until obliterated by the building of the citadel in the reign of Charles II. They are first recorded in the late fifteenth century. In Sussex, Europe's largest representation of the human form is the Long Man of Wilmington; a figure carrying two staffs which may originally have been weapons or tools. A drawing of him exists from 1710: he is similar to a figure on a Roman coin of the fourth century but could have been made long afterwards – or long before. Is the Cerne Giant as old as the Uffington White Horse? His shape, club and erection are reminiscent of the Bronze Age figures painted onto the walls of Swedish caves. Or could he be the Roman Hercules? An outstretched arm appears to have been draped with something – conceivably a lionskin. The Roman Emperor Commodus promoted a Hercules cult at the end of the second century.

But it is only when the Cerne Abbas Churchwardens' Accounts itemise a payment of three shillings 'for repairing of ye Giant' in 1694 that he appears in the written record. Had the dominant, sexually explicit landmark been in existence much before that date, wouldn't somebody have mentioned it? Cerne Abbas grew up around a Benedictine abbey, whose abbots – ruling a community dedicated to prayer, abstinence and celibacy – could hardly have countenanced the presence of such a priapic image on the hill above them. No mention of the Giant is made by Tudor or Stuart travellers, or during the investigation into Sir Walter Raleigh's School of Atheism that took place at Cerne Abbas in 1594. And yet, the making of a naked, sexually exuberant giant during the seventeenth century would itself surely have been a hotly debated, scandalous event in puritan Dorset. Besides, eighteenth-century accounts make it clear that the giant had been in existence a long time, and even very old people from Cerne Abbas had inherited no memory of its creation; they regarded its age as beyond reckoning. In 2020, a study by the National Trust and the University of Gloucestershire, analysing fragments of snail shell among other things, concluded that the Giant is probably not prehistoric but could have been seventeenth-century; however, it was not definitive.

During the prudish Victorian era, the Giant's phallus was erased by filling in the trenches to save the blushes of the impressionable. In 1908, people of Cerne responded to a newspaper campaign to restore the Giant, whose lines had become overgrown, by new-scouring it. In doing so, they inadvertently went to the other extreme by joining the Giant's member to what had been his navel, adding nearly two metres of length. So his most splendid feature is to that extent the result of an Edwardian mistake.

My theory is that the Giant's club is really a cricket bat, for he looks down at one of the loveliest village cricket grounds in the country. Watching a match from the drove way that runs up Giant Hill, with the sun shining, makes one feel part of an immemorial, well-nigh perfect England.

Fountains Abbey, Yorkshire

Ruins, following the Dissolution of the Monasteries under Henry VIII, are part of the English landscape. They are part also of the English aesthetic imagination. Fountains Abbey, near Ripon, stands as a gaunt witness to both the piety and business acumen of the Cistercian Order – while doubling as a feature in an eighteenth-century landscape park.

The monks who founded Fountains Abbey in the twelfth century – dissidents from Benedictine abbeys at York and Whitby who thought the order to which they belonged had gone soft – made a hard life for themselves. When they came to Fountains, they had no shelter other than that of an elm tree; they were reduced to eating its shoots to stay alive. But over time a mighty abbey arose. The rule was austere. No underwear was allowed, only habits of coarse, undyed sheep's wool; food was sparse. Long periods were spent in silence, except for worship and prayer. But the abbey also came to resemble a modern corporation, with the monks as the board of directors supervising a workforce of illiterate lay brothers. The latter provided a pool of unpaid labour, free of feudal obligations. As a result, the order became so rich that – after the Black Death had removed the lay workforce – the original system began to disintegrate under its own weight. Owning more land than they could control, the monks let granges to tenants.

The end for the monks came in 1539. It was not, though, the end for the abbey buildings. Around 1600, stone was quarried from its walls for the building of Fountains Hall; but the abbey was so huge that much was left standing, including the north tower. Eventually they would have collapsed, as old buildings do; but they were saved by the new aesthetic theory that began to take hold of aristocratic minds at the dawn of the next century. In a landscape, buildings could be appreciated as much for the feelings they evoked as for their architectural worth. A ruin was an aid to reflection, inviting the viewer to contemplate transience in all its forms. When John Aislabie began to create a garden around his house of Studley Royal, a mile from Fountains, around 1718, he wanted to incorporate the abbey ruins as part of the scheme.

Aislabie, like other country-house owners in the eighteenth century, was not a paragon of virtue. In modern terms, his fortune came from graft. In 1660 his father George Aislabie, a registrar in the archiepiscopal court at York, had been worth £210. By the time John Aislabie began his garden he was Chancellor of the Exchequer, owning property to the value (very likely underestimated) of £120,000. And that was after he had repaid £45,000 to investors in the South Sea Company in whose notorious Bubble he had been implicated (as Treasurer to the Navy, he had helped negotiate a deal by which the South Sea Company took over the national debt). A House of Commons investigation found him guilty of the 'most notorious, dangerous, and infamous corruption'. So he withdrew to his estates. Like Viscount Cobham, another disappointed politician, at Stowe, Aislabie found consolation in landscaping them. He created a series of canals, lakes, ponds and cascades, framed by the wooded, steeply rising sides of the valley.

By the end of the century, the project had been developed by Aislabie's son William, to become a designed landscape of more than eight hundred acres, enjoyed from over thirty-five miles of walks and rides and culminating in a view of the abbey: William had finally succeeded in buying it in 1768.

The English landscape park has been described as this country's greatest contribution to the visual culture of Europe. Henry VIII, eat my shorts. Fountains Abbey lives on.

The River Thames at Swan Upping

Swan Upping: I commend it to anyone who may be losing faith in the modern world. There is so much that does the heart good. The pageantry of the uniforms, the beauty of the swans, the skill of the oarsmen, the beating of the banners, the peace of the river, the good humour of all concerned – not so much as dented when, on the day I am there, a couple of Swan Uppers dive into the river after a cygnet who is in difficulties. And this charmingly, perhaps eccentrically English activity is not merely a jolly, like a regatta; it helps to conserve the swan population at a time when human behaviour of other kinds is doing it no favours. As so often, the traditional ways of 'upping' swans are the best.

Upping them? The word means removing them from the water. Historically, the reason for doing so, once a year, was to establish who owned the cygnets that had recently hatched; roast swan was a highly prized dish, with ownership of the principal raw ingredient being marked by nicks made in the swans' beaks. Swan keeping declined during the eighteenth century, when turkeys from America became the new luxury bird. These days, swans are no longer eaten and only the Dyers' and Vintners' Companies (on the Thames) and Abbotsbury in Dorset are allowed to own them.

All the other birds can be claimed by H.M. The Queen if she wants them, or are deemed to be wild.

Upping takes place at the time that the adults are moulting, making them easier to catch. Like the better sort of human, swans are, in theory, monogamous, and family comes before all: they seem to be happy to be upped as long as they keep each other in sight.

The man wearing a scarlet coat enjoys the title of Her Majesty's Swan Marker. He sits in a polished mahogany skiff and marshals a couple of other vessels. When a family of swans is spotted, the rowers quickly form a corral. The size of the circle is decreased until a hand reaches out and grabs one of the adults, whose legs are quickly tied behind its back. Once the adults have been immobilised, the cygnets are lifted out. They are then weighed, measured and checked. Discarded fishing lines can snag under a swan's wings. Birds can get other rubbish stuck in their gullets. A swan charity is on hand to deal with any injuries that are discovered.

Swan Upping dates from the twelfth century but has been quietly modernised. Tagging has replaced the nicking of beaks. Science has superseded the management of swans for the table. It tracks the toll taken by the concrete reinforcement of the river-bank and the fall in the quantity of reeds. Not all changes are anti-swan. Many of the pleasure boats that used to use the Thames have gone to Spain; the boatyards are being redeveloped for housing. Altogether, the upper Thames is not as Ratty and Mole would have known it. Another reason to treasure Swan Upping.

King's College Chapel, Cambridge

Cambridge can be a cold city, as winter winds scythe in from the Urals. But as one battles along King's Parade in the teeth of a gale, the heart rises at the sight of King's College Chapel. It is the largest chapel in Cambridge, and with its soaring pinnacles and immense windows, separated by thin buttresses, would be an extraordinary building anywhere. Inside, its famous fan vault is the largest in the country. Which means the largest in the world, since this beautiful, gravity-defying feature of late Gothic – indeed, the whole Perpendicular style of which it is part – was peculiar to England.

As the name suggests, it was the work of kings. Two in particular. The first: pious, weak-minded Henry VI who founded King's College in 1441 at the age of nineteen, clearing a huge site and the church that stood on it to make way for the new work. The chapel was given precedence over all other building activity. From a royal quarry at Tadcaster – a distance of nearly two hundred miles – came the stone, probably by boat. Steady progress was made for fifteen years. The chancel nearly reached the roof.

But Henry VI was overthrown and murdered during the Wars of the Roses and work stopped. Richard III restarted the project, but his brief reign came to an end at the Battle of Bosworth in 1485. His successor was Henry VII: his commitment to finishing it was expressed in the form of a heavily fortified chest of money that he sent to King's College (the chest can still be seen). The chapel now became a Tudor project, its walls smothered in the emblems of the new regime: Tudor roses, portcullises and greyhounds. The vault was completed using £5,000 left for the purpose under Henry's will.

To do this, the new master mason, John Wastell, abandoned the previous design, which had been for a lierne vault, its prominent ribs infilled with smooth masonry; instead, the chapel would have a fan vault. In a lierne vault, the ribs are the structural element, the triangular webs between them being merely infills of stone. Fan vaults are formed of interlocking cones of masonry, made of sheets of stone; the surface pattern of ribs and compartments is only decorative. We architectural nerds believe the idea may have evolved from the distinctive way in which the English made their Gothic vaults, aligning the stones of the infill differently from continental practice, so that their ribs were more integrated with the webs. This may explain why the fan vault is a purely English phenomenon. It originated in the West Country but came to be part of the court style, used, after Henry VII's death, for the Lady Chapel built under his will at Westminster Abbey.

The structure of a fan vault locks together like a puzzle. According to a tradition cited by Horace Walpole, the great Sir Christopher Wren was flummoxed to understand how the roof of King's College Chapel was ever begun. Unlikely. Even so, it conveys something of the wonder of the achievement. Visitors feel as though they are standing not in a building so much as in a forest of stone trees whose branches meet overhead, with light of many colours filtering through the leaves.

Lichen in Wales

I am going off piste here. I am mentioning Wales. (I love Wales and go there often but this is an England-only book and Wales could have a hundred entries on its own.) My reason for doing so? Lichens. Square mile for square mile, there are more types of this fascinating life form recorded in the Principality than anywhere else on earth.

You will know lichens. They are the silver that dusts Cotswold stone, the orange that blotches a boulder, the shaggy grey excrescence that wraps the limbs of old apple trees as though they had been yarn bombed by a deranged knitter. Look at a patch of them through a magnifying lens and a miniature landscape, perhaps in a rainbow of colours, appears, as though you have entered a secret kingdom. They are to be found more or less everywhere in Britain, including such inhospitable habitats as former lead, zinc and copper workings, where little else will grow. Churchyards can be especially rich in them. The number in Wales can be explained by its cleaner air (alas, not so pure as it used to be), diverse geography (including coast, heath, hills, mountains and post-industrial sites) and rain – much rain.

Lichens can be dusty, hairy, bushy or sponge-like, or composed of seaweed-like sheets. Or, to use the correct terminology, leprose (powdery), fruiticose (bushy), foliose (leaf-like) or crustose (crusty). Father Christmas loves them. Cladonia lichens are the main food source for reindeer.

Lichens are not single organisms but a mutualism – a cosy cohabitation between a fungus and a photobiont (a green algae or cyanobacteria), which benefits both parties. This gets quite difficult and I hope I have got the following three sentences right. Fungi are provided with sugar alcohols by the algae, and glucose and nitrogen by the cyanobacteria. The fungi protect the algae from sunlight and drying out, and allow the photobionts to live in areas in which they would never usually survive. In fact, the cohabitation that results from the development of a lichen allows both partners to exist in the world's most extreme environments (from desert to poles). Anyway, the more one discovers about lichens the more complex and remarkable they become. Win, win. A win, too, for the country people and scientists who have harvested lichens, whether to make the red dyes in Harris tweed or exploit the medicinal properties of usnic acid – although faith in the lichen growing on an old skull as a cure for epilepsy was misplaced. These are also indicator species. *Rhizocarpon geographicum* is known as the map lichen because of its cartographical shapes and divisions that resemble field boundaries; easy to spot and relatively quick to grow, it is used to track how fast glaciers are retreating and exposing moraine.

With their large surface area, bushy lichens are exceptionally sensitive to air pollution. Good news: there's now less sulphur in the air and lichens can even be found in city centres. But good news can also be bad news. We do not mine lead any more; there are fewer spoil heaps polluted by heavy metals. So metallophyte lichens which – another astounding fact – require the kind of conditions not seen since the earth first cooled after being a molten mass millions of years ago, are in trouble: some people would like their habitats to be turned into grassland. Fortunately, metal-rich furnace slag was seized upon by Victorian gardeners wanting it for their rockeries; graves were also decorated with gravel from local works. Ecologists now value these extraordinary habitats for the lichen communities they support. What a world of miniaturised wonder to discover, for those who travel with a hand lens or a loupe.

Derbyshire Blue John

Geology is the main factor in shaping the landscape and England's is unusually intricate. On the edge of a continent, this country has been scrunched, pummelled and squeezed by the titanic forces that move the earth's crust over millions of years; and a small-scale, intimate countryside, where the character of landforms, plants and building materials changes every few miles, is the result. There is an embarrassment of good building stone in some counties, none in others. Only Derbyshire, in addition to alabaster and black marble (really a kind of polished limestone: there is no true marble in Britain), can boast that greatest Wonder of the Peak: Blue John.

Blue John is how miners pronounced the French *bleu et jaune* – French because the mineral, a kind of fluorspar, was once famous to connoisseurs throughout Europe; blue and yellow from the colour, although those bald names hardly do justice to it. 'Amethystine violets, bluish-greens and honey yellows' is how one old writer describes the concentric rings that swirl and merge into one another like inks in water. The one place in the world that Blue John can be mined is the village of Castleton.

Blue John's open texture makes it difficult to carve; but the striations of colour proved so irresistible to Georgian taste that the skill was mastered. Kedleston Hall in Derbyshire, the palatial house which Robert Adam built for Lord Scarsdale, has a fine suite of vases carved by the celebrated Richard Brown, as well as some luxurious Blue John inlay. Chatsworth House, also in Derbyshire, where the 5th Duchess had a passion for geology (as well as gambling), went one better. Not only does it possess fine Blue John ornaments but a translucent window made of Blue John squares. It was the idea of the 6th Duke, who devoted his life to his collections and the arrangement of his many houses. As he notes in the *Handbook* that he wrote to explain his aesthetic choices at Chatsworth: 'The stones were intended for a cabinet of minerals, and from their shape could only be arranged in a formal and not graceful pattern'; but his architect, the bluff Sir Jeffry Wyatville, was having none of it, pronouncing the result 'to be the exact resemblance of his grandmother's counterpane'. I'm with His Grace. Blue John is not only a ducally opulent material, but local.

A correspondent to *The Times* explained the geological process by which it was probably made: 'Thermal water charged with hydrofluoric acid, being forced by enormous pressure into the crevices and cavities of the rock, decomposed the limestone, forming crystals of fluoride of lime, often full of the loveliest colours.' It was the Romans who discovered the deposits, while prospecting for lead. Since it is dark blue, almost black, when it comes out of the ground, they must have been delighted when it revealed its latent hues.

Tourists in search of the Picturesque loved the scarily Sublime quality of the landscape around Castleton. 'Here nature presents herself in her rudest forms: down the road the prospect is bounded by the rugged rocks projecting in the most romantic manner, bare and sterile,' wrote J.M. Hedinger in 1824. Then came a transformation, and a land of fine trout streams and productive agriculture appeared. 'Here, traveller, stop and collect thyself! View this fertile valley as one of the greatest gifts of Providence, who has bestowed on the inhabitants of this place all the climate can produce.' See what I mean? Variety of landscape.

Canterbury Cathedral at evensong

Low sunlight is filtering through the stained glass of Canterbury Cathedral; the congregation who have been sitting rather upright in the Gilbert Scott choir stalls stand up, as the choir – a dozen men, a dozen boys – files in. The choristers pick up their music and begin to sing, the vocal lines soaring and weaving around each other like a flight of swallows. Until that moment, the architecture had seemed, despite the gathering dusk, to be made, very solidly, of stone. But as the strains of Anglican chant (harmonised plainsong) resonate around it, pillars and vaults seem to dissolve. Is it the purity of the treble voices, soaring above the earth-bound tenor and bass lines, that's doing it? No, it's my eyes. The beauty of the sound makes them mist over.

This is evensong as it takes place not just at Canterbury but in cathedrals across England every day of the week. The music made by the choirs of cathedrals and great churches is so much a part of our shared aural heritage – think of King's College Chapel at Christmas – that we can forget just how special it is. Cathedral treble choirs do not operate like scout groups, meeting in free time after lessons. Their musical discipline is the result of total immersion, provided by special choir schools. These schools are a survival from the monasteries of the Middle Ages, continuing a tradition that is one thousand four hundred years old. It was a peculiarity of the English Reformation that the boy choirs continued after the Dissolution, along with the schools that exist to supply them. We have Elizabeth I's love of music to thank for it. Nowhere else in the world, except for three Episcopalian churches in the United States and Sydney Cathedral in Australia, which are part of the Anglican Communion, maintains the tradition. It is a daily miracle of singing which worshippers can experience for free.

Carvings on the arch over the entrance to the choir school at Canterbury, fashioned from the fourteenth-century prior's dining hall, show choristers in full-throated song. Around thirty choristers attend it. This makes it smaller than the choir school at St Paul's in London but bigger than Chichester. Westminster Abbey is now the only institution to maintain a school exclusively for its choristers, providing a full academic curriculum alongside the music. Canterbury contracts out the boys' education in subjects other than music to St Edmund's Junior School, which occupies a spacious site outside the city.

Choristers must forgo a normal childhood for the experience. Singing anthems is not on a par with going up chimneys, but insiders can sound a little surprised that more eyebrows are not raised at the workload. They sing or practise for twenty-two hours a week; they record in the evenings; holidays at Christmas and Easter do not start until the last service has been done. Even then, they may be taken up with tours. In a secular age, when excellence as a product of education is notably elusive, it may seem extraordinary that choir schools like Canterbury exist. It is. How lucky we are that they do.

Landscape

England prides itself on its landscape. It is what we do well, in terms of protection. When taken alone, without the other parts of the United Kingdom, England has one of the greatest densities of population of any Western country. The pressures on the countryside are immense. Yet we have been spectacularly successful in preventing the despoliation of rural areas. Other European countries have a better way with towns and cities. We have only recently discovered the joy of urban life – and not in all cities, because some of them will need to be rebuilt before we get pleasure from them. But we have always loved – and, since the late nineteenth century, fiercely protected – the countryside. Countrysides, one should say, because every part of England is different.

Needless to say, we could do better: we have lost 97 per cent of wild-flower meadows since the Second World War (no hay needed for horses). Hedgerows have gone. Bird and insect species have collapsed. Urban sprawl – all those retail sheds surrounded by car parks which are such an extravagant use of land – has eaten into countryside, reducing it bite by bite. But all said, it is still glorious to visit one of the National Parks or an Area of Outstanding Natural Beauty.

If you were blindfolded and dropped by parachute into a randomly chosen rural location (at night, so you couldn't read the road signs), you would, at first light, soon be able to tell where you were, because each small parcel of the country has its own personality. France is, relatively speaking, a big country, with broad landscapes whose character does not change for miles and miles. England is cosy and diverse. Nobody could mistake Cornwall for the Lake District, or Swaledale for the South Downs.

Our love of landscape is the legacy of the eighteenth-century Picturesque movement, a preoccupation for gentlemen landscaping their parks. This informed the vision that John Ruskin, aesthete, watercolourist and seer, had of Nature, as an antidote to the ills of the Industrial Revolution. William Morris took up the baton. The Arts and Crafts movement began the Garden City and the Garden Suburb (and the popularity of the suburb sent the city into its long decline). The Picturesque movement continues to determine the way English people look not only at the countryside but at cities – compare the jumble that is London (Picturesque) to the formality of Paris (Classical).

Enough history. Suffice it to say that England, a small and densely populated country, has managed to preserve the beauty of its many landscapes. What a jewel box. I give you ten pearls beyond price.

Swaledale, Yorkshire

'Swaledale in Yorkshire is a little country in itself,' wrote Ella Pontefract in her charming book *Swaledale*, written in 1934 and illustrated with what, even then, must have seemed old-fashioned wood engravings. All the Yorkshire Dales have this feeling of being self-contained, which is one reason that they appeal so much to visitors and to the imagination. We all need countries of the mind, as a refuge, perhaps, from the surroundings of our workaday lives, which may be less than Arcadian. Pontefract called Swaledale the English Tyrol, because the springy turf with its innumerable wild flowers reminded her of the Swiss Alps. Only, the local people do not wear bright caps and aprons but tweed caps and waterproof clothing the colour of cowpats.

I love Swaledale and only hesitate to make it a Crown Jewel because there are so many other distinctive landscapes in England. The loss of any of them would be mourned. Some of their individuality is already being eroded by the homogenising tendencies of the modern world; but Yorkshire folk are better at resisting these outside pressures than others. Swaledale still magically exemplifies qualities that we especially prize because they are now scarce. Seclusion. The sense of being alone in an unchanging world; a feeling of personal communion with unfettered Nature. Farm animals. The name Swale means 'wild one'. As the seventeenth-century antiquarian William Camden wrote, thinking of the upper reaches of the river, with its exceptionally high fall, the Swale 'rusheth rather than runneth'. It still doth.

And yet it would be an illusion to think that the landscape itself is wild. Like anywhere else, the topography of the valley shaped what people could do with it; the limestone crags that sometimes beetle over the river and high moorlands, deep in peat, do not warm the heart of the farmer. But the feature that gives this landscape much of its character – the many miles of stone wall – shows that it has been tamed and worked for centuries. The nature of the walls gives a clue to the quality of the land. Irregularly shaped fields were won from the hills in the Middle Ages. Less profitable land was enclosed, by removing the previous rights of common from ordinary villagers, in the eighteenth and nineteenth centuries. Here the straight walls seem to tie the hill-sides down like the string on a rolled joint of meat. The purpose of the walls was to create fields in which to keep cattle. Cattle are not nimble beasts and cannot jump much of a wall; for sheep, walls have to be higher – hence, sometimes, a strip of barbed wire.

Over the years, people have used Swaledale for what they could get out of it. Three hundred years ago, that included lead: when the river overflowed, residues from the mine workings poisoned the land. Lead mining has finished, thank goodness. Instead we have grouse. To some people that's also controversial but shooting the king of gamebirds, only to be found in the British Isles, means that its numbers are kept high. And what's good for grouse is good for other wildlife (except vermin) – so the moors teem with species. There's also the income from tourists, whose numbers must be kept high as well. Local identity is cherished, artisanal food rediscovered. The English Tyrol is farmed for its beauty and can be enjoyed in greater comfort than Ella Pontefract would have known. How lucky we are.

Coniston Water, Cumbria

Everyone knows that the Lake District is the most beautiful area of Britain. The secret is so well and truly out that it can become a little crowded for some people's tastes; parts of it, that is. Coniston Water is apt to be overlooked and preserves its beauty much as it was in the nineteenth century. The best view of it is from Brantwood. This is the house that the aesthete, writer, watercolourist and social reformer John Ruskin created, specifically with that view in mind.

Ruskin had grown up in south London, in an atmosphere so claustrophobic that the arrival of the water cart, which he could see being filled from his nursery window, provided one of his few excitements as a small child; the Lake District, which he first visited with his parents, on trips to promote his father's sherry business, was a revelation. Later he valued it as the antidote to all the ugliness that England was inflicting on itself with the Industrial Revolution. He battled for beauty. We have him, as much as anyone, to thank that, while much has been lost, much also survives.

Ruskin's vision of the world grew out of an early love of geology. Rocks took him to landscape. He was a champion of the pre-Raphaelites and the propagandist-in-chief for Turner. A man of strong passions and beliefs, he could live without physical love; when, after a brief disaster of a marriage, his wife ran off with the painter John Everett Millais, Ruskin seemed barely to notice. He turned his energy to fulminations against the industrial city which, in his view, produced not Wealth (money used to improve the human lot) but Illth (the evil that comes from unfettered capitalism). Work was the thing to redeem society. Bookworms ought to be prepared to spend a portion of their day in hard physical work, perhaps mending the roads, while manufacturers should close down their factories and let their workers produce as much as possible by hand. Handwork allowed craftsmen to express their souls.

Ruskin did not need to see Brantwood, then a cottage, before buying it in 1871. He knew the view – and it would not disappoint him. As he wrote to his cousin Joan Severn in December the next year, 'The sun coming down among the thin woods is like enchanted light, and the ivy and walls and waters are all as perfect as ever – so that I never yet had a walk among the lakes so lovely, and few in Italy.' If so much as the tip of an ironworks chimney had appeared over the hills, its value for Ruskin, with his hatred of industrial exploitation, he wrote in *Modern Painters*, would have been completely destroyed. Thankfully none ever has.

The house was only a cottage – and not much of a cottage at that. By the spring of 1872 Ruskin was at work on improvements. But little about this or the many subsequent phases of work was grand or artistically striking. Ruskin favoured local materials and rough finishes – although the builder had to be watched ceaselessly to prevent him from importing Bath stone and from stopping ledges, intended to 'invite stonecrop and swallows, [from being] trimmed away in the advanced style of the railway station at Carnforth'. In about 1878 a new dining room was added. It had a seven-light window. Ruskin planned the roof so that it would shelter bees.

A good oarsman, he began a little harbour in 1873 to shelter his boat the *Jumping Jenny* from stormy weather. His chief assistants in the work were his future biographer, the artist and antiquarian W.G. Collingwood, and Alexander Wedderburn, who had come north to translate Xenophon's *Economist* for an edition for use at Ruskin's utopian Guild of St George. These and the other intellectuals were hopeless at building; walls had to be redone by a local farmer's son to stop them collapsing.

In the early 1880s, Brantwood morphed from being a cottage into 'the new house'. And yet from the outside it remained irregular and jumbled. It was inside that visitors had to look for signs of Ruskin the art critic. Here was his unrivalled collection of Turners. Wallpaper was specially made to a design copied from the priest's embroidered sleeve in Marco Marziale's *The Circumcision of Christ* in the National Gallery. And yet an almost Proust-like reverence for the past made him preserve some of the china and furniture that he remembered from his childhood homes.

The most precise description of the study comes from Ruskin himself. In 1881 he provided a careful inventory to complement a drawing made by Alexander Macdonald. Scattered about on the tables and desks were a medieval lectionary, a missal and various rocks on which Ruskin was working at the time. Propped against the wall were the framed leaves of a psalter; leaning against the desk his own last sketch of porches at St Mark's, Venice – later hung above the shell cabinet in the drawing room. The Luca della

Robbia *Madonna*, which was purchased on Ruskin's behalf in Florence in 1880, had yet to be installed over the fireplace. Two 'bran new globes' had arrived in the 1870s. The globes proved a disappointment. They were too modern; the quantity of information was overwhelming.

The dining room, with its view of the lake, was added in 1878–9. 'Gathered round the pleasantest of tables, the inmates of Brantwood enjoy the freest "flow of soul",' wrote Wedderburn; 'their host directs and sustains, but never monopolises, the talk; nor need any be afraid of being victimised by that spirit of self-conscious dictation or affected silence which has been known to spoil enjoyment in the company of some literary men.' Over the fireplace hung Catena's portrait of Doge Andrea Gritti, then thought to be by Titian. Ruskin's best-loved paintings, however, hung in his bedroom. 'When I die,' he said of the Turners around his bed, 'I hope that they may be the last things my eyes will rest on in this world.'

The greatest beauty, however, was Coniston Water. To see it as Ruskin did is a wonderful thing.

Uskany

I claim the Welsh Marches for England, for the purposes of this book. They are border lands and some of the most beautiful in Britain. The River Wye has been celebrated since the 1700s. People who live around the neighbouring River Usk talk of Uskany. It is a good coinage. The Welsh Marches are lusher than Tuscany, the sun is shier of coming out from behind the clouds, they make – as yet – no wine. But the beauty is of a similar order; in the golden light of a late summer afternoon, it can seem as idyllic as the imagined Italian landscapes painted by Claude Lorrain. We cannot help it, those of us who love these things. We are culturally hard-wired to respond to what eighteenth-century theorists called the Picturesque.

After a tour of Worcestershire, Gloucestershire, Monmouthshire, Herefordshire and Shropshire in 1770, the poet Thomas Gray wrote to his friend Dr Wharton, 'The very principal light, and capital feature of my journey, was the river Wye.' He and his companions had taken a boat from Ross to Chepstow, and would have gone further if the river had not had so little water in it. 'Its banks,' he continued, 'are a succession of nameless beauties.' That same year, the Rev. William Gilpin had made his own trip along the Wye, and Gray encouraged him to publish it. He did so, a dozen years later, as *Observations on the River Wye*, said to be the origin of British tourism: it would become essential reading for British travellers who could not make a Grand Tour on the Continent during the French Revolutionary and Napoleonic Wars of 1792 to 1815.

Wordsworth came, writing his famous 'Lines Composed a Few Miles above Tintern Abbey'. Turner came, painting Tintern and Chepstow Castle. So in 1924 did Eric Gill, sculptor, letter carver and leader of a quasi-monastic community of artists at Capel-y-ffin. Gill was a strange man, with unusual sexual proclivities, but fortunately the Black Mountains were remote.

Hold hard. Arcadia has its limits. It does not extend to the old coal-mining towns of the Welsh valleys which are practically next door. There was industry on the Wye, too, in the Georgian period. Only half a mile from the ruins of Tintern Abbey was the Angidy Ironworks, which, sniffed Gilpin, 'introduce noise and bustle into these regions of tranquility.' A few miles further up was Redbrook's iron and tin works; wire and paper were manufactured at Whitebrook. Llandogo was a centre of boat building, making the flat-bottomed craft known as trows. But these industries withered during the nineteenth century and closed in the twentieth. The Wye was left to make a living from farming, as best it could, and wax prosperous from tourists and retirees.

And we can find more beauties if we have the expert eyes of the chef Chris Harrod. He forages among the Wye's hedgerows, knowing where to find scallop mushrooms beside waterfalls – and knowing what to do with them when he does (which is to serve them at his restaurant Whitebrook). Meadowsweet, mugwort, pennyroyal – names that might have come out of a Shakespearean herbal – appear amid the thick sward of grasses to those who have the eyes to spot them. We of the environmentally challenged twenty-first century enjoy the Wye in new ways.

The South Downs

Close your eyes, picture an English landscape, and what do you see? Many people would say the South Downs. This is a wide open countryside, the sward nibbled close, traditionally, by sheep: ideal conditions for precious chalkland flowers. There may be glimpses of the sea, or the trees of the Weald, and a path stretching into the distance. You feel you can fill your lungs with air, as half a dozen skylarks sing overhead. I picture it through the eyes of the painter Eric Ravilious, a son of Sussex; he would stay at Furlongs, the cottage of the artist Peggy Angus. Ravilious, a war artist, died in 1942, when his plane failed to return to its base in Iceland. His paintings seem to be imbued with an intensely English nostalgia, for summers that are all too soon snatched away.

This should not be an exclusively English landscape because the geological formation continues under the English Channel and pops up in France. Many of the most gruelling battles of the First World War were fought on the same sort of ground as British troops might have known from Sussex and Hampshire. But Picardy is different from our Downs – on a bigger scale, emptier. There are not the pretty villages, with their slightly drunken-looking streets, where the timber-framed houses must seemingly prop each other up to stop themselves falling over; streets that are friendly from the human scale and mix of materials – wood, plaster, tile, brick, plaster – and warmed by the rosy orange hue of the brick.

People love to hike over the South Downs, and their presence is as much a feature of this landscape as the Adonis blue butterfly (indeed, rather more often seen). But these great sweeps of land are not only for striding over. They are also for studying close to. The grassland is rich in more than just grasses; if well maintained, the sheep will have grazed the tall-growing grasses that would have blocked the light from low-growing plants such as autumn lady's tresses, early spider orchid and the horseshoe vetch. With its cheerful yellow flowers, the horseshoe vetch is the only plant on which the caterpillars of the Adonis blue feeds; so the butterfly lays its eggs under its leaves. Watch out for anthills, but they too are important. Ants love the sweet secretion of the Adonis blue's caterpillars and pupae, which they protect jealously – to the extent of burying them overnight. This preserves them from predators. Again, here is another benefit of our friend the sheep. If the grasses were allowed to grow to their full height, they would shade out the anthills, and the ants would go to a sunnier place. The Adonis blue would have to fend for itself.

Incredibly, in this populous part of the country, the South Downs are still loved for their tranquillity. Towns and villages are scattered, lanes sunken into the chalk by what the cleric and naturalist Gilbert White called 'the traffick of ages and the fretting of water'. At his home in Selborne, White could enjoy another feature of the Downs: a steep hillside to which trees are grappled, or beech hanger. White thought its autumn colours, if depicted by 'a masterly land-scape painter', would be too rich to be believed by the outside world. He cut a path through it known as the Zig-Zag and built a hermitage at the top (his brother John was persuaded to dress up as the Old Hermit). The land occupied by the beech hangers of the Downs was too difficult for farmers to cultivate and so they were left; some may contain fragments of the primordial forest that covered much of Britain before humankind cut it down. Some of the ancient yews at Kingley Vale are among the oldest living organisms in Europe. This is truly a landscape of wonders.

Wicken Fen, Cambridgeshire

Immense skies, black earth, a Piet Mondrian-like road pattern of straight lines and right-angles, into which are tucked, in late spring, corners of unharvested daffodils, like party-goers who've forgotten to go home – we are in the Fens. This is not a landscape for everybody. The sunsets can have the ferocity of a Viking burial. Ely Cathedral, whose octagon once served as a lighthouse to guide travellers across the treacherous marshes, still lifts the heart, even of car drivers, with feelings akin to relief: silhouetted again the sky, its great but delicately shaped bulk promises civilisation and tea at the Old Fire Engine House. This can seem a thrillingly foreign land.

Those who have an eye for the Fen landscape think that low horizons, broken, perhaps, by the fretted outline of a wood – or, more likely, by a row of pylons – have an intensity missing from more manicured places. This is a working countryside, from which wilderness has long been banished by geometry. Immense fields are striated with potato rows or striped with the almost luminous colours of salad crops. That's around Gedney, where locals sit on the sea bank and watch the RAF helicopters shoot up the targets on the bombing ranges in the Wash. Do not expect the jolly waterways of the Norfolk Broads with their colourful locks and pleasure boats; the great rectilinear Denver Sluice and other engineering works don't aim to charm. And yet, for all that it's man-made, humankind is strangely absent. Few people live on the Fens. At night, the skies are among the darkest in Britain.

But the Fens have changed. Once this was a truly watery land: the Great Basin into which eight rivers emptied themselves, before their waters trickled into the North Sea. If not under water, then it was prone to flood, and at all times soggy: teeming with eels and other fish, which could be trapped in willow baskets and were so numerous they could be used as currency. Cattle were carried to summer grazing by boat. Fen people pursued a semi-aquatic existence, jumping dykes and streams with the aid of long poles. The seventeenth-century traveller Celia Fiennes, arriving in Ely after heavy rains, called it 'ye dirtyest place I ever saw . . . a perfect quagmire ye whole Citty', objecting strongly to the number of frogs and snails in her bedchamber, although it was twenty steps above ground. In 1663, Samuel Pepys's horse sank up to its belly in water when he visited his Uncle and Aunt Perkins at Parson Drove. But now the Fens have been drained, and as they were made drier, they shrank. In their traditional form, the Fens have all but disappeared.

The evidence exists on Holme Fen. In 1851, a local landowner drove a wooden pile through the peat, embedding it in the underlying clay; the top was cut off level with the ground. The wooden post was soon replaced by an iron column, to which a second was added in the twentieth century. The columns now rise thirteen feet into the air. This is now said to be the lowest place in the UK, being nine feet below sea level. The one exception to the general shrinkage is Wicken Fen, where Charles Darwin collected beetles during the 1820s, when the twinkling of lights for moth-collecting made the fen resemble a small city. It became Britain's first nature reserve in 1899, at first managed and soon owned by the National Trust: a magical oasis of tall reeds, yellow flag irises and dragonflies that remembers what the Fens used to be like.

But around Wicken, a Fen fight-back is taking place. The Great Fen Project, begun in 2001, aims to create 3,700 hectares of wetland. Progress can be measured in the number of lapwings sighted, common cranes to have visited and rare wetland plants and water beetles starting to colonise previously unpromising sites. Re-wetting land is almost as complex as draining it. Whittlesea Mere, famous for its regattas in the nineteenth century, could not now be recreated, since, due to silt deposited on top of the underlying peat having formed a cap, it is now a dome higher than the surrounding land. Nor will it be possible to restore the Fens as they were before drying out. Instead, a new mosaic of habitats will emerge, which will welcome the waters that would otherwise overcharge the rivers and channels in times of flood, rather than adding further strain to the pumps in the effort to send it out into the sea. We shall learn to see the Fens with new eyes. Meanwhile, Wicken Fen survives to remind us of what used to be: the Notre-Dame we have lost.

The Stour Valley, Dorset

Dorset's Stour Valley is typical A1 beautiful England. Why have I promoted a stretch of it (where the river glides between the three villages of West Stour, Stour Provost and Fifehead Magdalen) to Crown Jewel status? Because it represents everything that one would mourn if it were lost, and it is under threat.

Stour Provost rises up the hill on the east side of the river. 'Provost' comes from its association with King's College, Cambridge, which Henry VI founded in the fifteenth century; the land was part of its endowment. In 1828, the College commissioned William Wilkins, who also built the screen on Cambridge's King's Parade, to build a large house on the riverbank for its vice-provost; today it is called the Old Rectory. Otherwise the village is not grand, or full of pretentious architecture, just very well preserved.

That happy state may be a legacy of college ownership, since Stour Provost remained the property of King's until 1925. There are, however, thirty-six listed buildings and a fourteenth-century church. Below the village is an old watermill, on a site recorded in the Domesday Book.

On flows the Stour. We go upstream and find, in West Stour, by ancient stone houses, a red telephone box has been repurposed as a book exchange. If you clamber up to the Church of St Mary Magdalene – a little way out of the village of Fifehead Magdalen – you will be rewarded by the sight of a grand mid-eighteenth-century monument to Sir Richard Newman and his family, carved by the great sculptor Henry Cheere. The old manor house, Fifehead House, no longer exists; but a memory of the people who lived there survives in the ornamental trees that they planted – now a surprising feature among the fields.

But neither monuments nor architecture explain my inclusion of the Stour Valley in this book; its place is won on the landscape. Certainly, the buildings are part of the scene but they would be little without the setting. This is the kind of scene that England does so well: informal, ancient, full of interest, delightful to behold. Generation after generation have lived in this valley, leaving traces of their presence that often seem to be fading slowly into the background of the composition. It is a palimpsest, a thing of fragility and fascination, bearing marks of past activity that are sometimes barely decipherable – but which contribute to an idyll that the most cursory glance would identify as precious.

Recently a snake slithered into this paradise, as snakes do. An application has been made to build a solar farm along one side of the valley: a twenty-first-century intrusion that would destroy the soul-restoring loveliness of this historic and delicate place. 'Farm' is a misnomer. It would be a power station, laid out with serried ranks of reflective panels, raised a metre off the ground and three metres in height. The scale, materials and layout of the panels would have been as alien as a spaceship. Everyone supports green energy and sustainability. But solar power becomes unsustainable when it destroys another essential resource for human life: beautiful countryside. We in Britain have a special gift and feeling for the countryside; generally we've been good at preserving it – just as, conversely, we have been bad at preserving and creating cities.

There are plenty of places where solar panels would not obtrude. Flat landscapes with hedges are better than hills but best of all are built environments. Think of car parks, shopping centres, factories, tower blocks. Put them on roofs of buildings, above railway stations and distribution centres. It would be easy to link them to the national grid. But spare the Stour Valley and everywhere like it, or this country will lose part of its soul.

The Mappa Mundi,
Hereford Cathedral

In a book that is about places and buildings it may seem perverse to include the Mappa Mundi – a two-dimensional object: the Map of the World. But maps are, it might be argued, the platonic ideal of the place – the place stripped of its outward trappings and reduced to an essence, composed of watercourses, contour lines and the all-important presence of a PH (public house). Such are the maps produced by the Ordnance Survey, begun by the Board of Ordnance in the 1780s when the south of England urgently needed mapping in case Britain had to fight off an invasion by France. They enable the map reader to create an image of the area in his head, to walk through it in his imagination. They showed everything that was important to the age in which they were made. Today, the commonest form of map is the satnav, which contains next to no geographical information; topography is dead. Instead it reverts to the medieval tradition of the itinerary, not a map (because geographical maps barely existed, if at all) but a list of points on a route, to enable the traveller to get from his start to his destination by joining the dots. Extraneous information has been sacrificed to speed of travel. For shame.

The Mappa Mundi is a different kind of map, made in the late thirteenth century. Local geography was intensely relevant to the people of the Middle Ages: they could not escape its influence on their lives and had to live with what God had given them in terms of soil fertility, well-managed woods, the hilliness or bogginess of the terrain, the freshness of streams and the minerals in rocks. But to describe this landscape in physical terms would have left out the most momentous thing of all, which was the presence of the Supreme Being – or His opposite, the Evil One. People crossed themselves on waking, began and ended the day with prayers, attended mass daily, more often if anything unusual like going on a journey was at hand, and constantly sought the intercession of their chosen saints with God. The Mappa Mundi reflects this outlook. It was what would now be called a mind map: not so much a record of geographical facts, but an index of things that were known or believed about the world, organised according to importance.

The Mappa Mundi is the most elaborate map of the world to survive from the Middle Ages. To the monk-cartographer it was a Christian world, with Jerusalem at its heart and such biblical landmarks as the Garden of Eden, Noah's Ark and the Tower of Babel nearby. In the quarter of the map depicting Europe (the other continents are Asia and Africa), Rome is shown as the most spectacular city, closely followed by Paris. The kidney-shaped British Isles are squashed onto the edge of the world, with both Scotland and Cornwall severed from England by rivers. The map-maker drew some of the cathedral cities, as well as Conway and a very small Oxford; Ely is represented as completely surrounded by water. Exceptional prominence is given to Lincoln, prompting the thought that this was the map-maker's home city. By contrast, Hereford appears to have been sketched in as an afterthought, presumably after the map arrived here; it was no doubt at this time that the local landmark of Clee Hill was added.

Spaces between the topographical features are enlivened by creatures of natural history and myth. The elephant and camel are surprisingly realistic, the rhinoceros rather less so. There is a pelican, plucking its breast to feed its young, as well as the Golden Fleece, the Minotaur, a salamander and a sphinx. Among the peoples of the world is a Norwegian, complete with bobble hat and skis; less instantly recognisable is (from India) the Sciapod, who shades himself from the scorching sun by raising his one enormous foot. This is not the stuff of Google Maps, whose information reflects the universals of today: coffee bars and motorway congestion.

With all but essential journeys banned by the Coronavirus lockdowns, the Mappa Mundi assumed new relevance. Once again we could travel only in our heads, pondering what and where is precious from the static vantage point of our homes.

Devon lanes

Devon is supposed to have more hedgerows than any other county in England. It is easy to believe it, as you travel round; at times you hardly seem to see the surrounding countryside for the banks that rise on either side of the car. But if you stop for a moment, a different landscape is revealed, spotted with pink, yellow and blue. In early summer, it is a tapestry made up of campions, harebells, primroses, foxgloves, celandines, valerian and ferns. Weaving through it is a tangle of dog roses, honeysuckle and brambles. North-facing banks are shaggy with moss. A survey of a hedgebank at Chudleigh revealed that it contained two hundred and ninety-three types of flowering plant. Looking at such profusion, it is difficult not to feel a sense of wonder at the bounty of Nature, so generous in her ability to invent species of which one has perhaps never heard, with botanical characteristics – and sometimes beauty – that are unique to themselves.

Nature does not do this unaided. The delight of Devon's hedgerows is a by-product of human toil, the legacy of many centuries of animal husbandry, with its need for stock-proof barriers and shelter around fields. At the bottom of the fields are banks of earth faced with stones – although the herbage is so luxuriant that you rarely see this foundation. Hedges were planted on top of the banks; every few years, the hawthorn bushes that give them structure are slashed at their base, bent sideways and interlaced with the neighbouring plants. Any livestock looking for greener pastures found their hopes disappointed: faced with a well-laid, impenetrable hedge, they would have had to stay in the field. What is an obstacle to cattle is a land of opportunity for yellowhammers, blue tits and other farmland birds that nest in hedgerows and sing from them; the berries, nuts, nectar and leaves which the hedgerows produce form a larder for any number of insects, dormice and other small mammals, as well as birds. Trees rise from the hedges, perhaps self-seeded or deliberately planted, sometimes in avenues on two sides of a lane; they rise and intertwine overhead to form green tunnels. Most of Devon's hedgerows are centuries old. Some are prehistoric.

The nemesis of the hedge was barbed wire, invented about 1870 to help American ranchers parcel up the Great Plains, a land too vast for post and rail fences, stone walls and hedges. English farmers soon found that it saved the costly skills and labour of maintaining field boundaries. Surviving hedges have been allowed to grow out, since barbed wire inside them provides the barrier previously formed by carefully laid hawthorn boughs. Straggling, gappy hedges are of far less use to wildlife. Then there is that great twentieth-century institution, the car. We drive around admiring road verges, unaware that the nitrogen from the exhaust is changing the habitat for wild flowers, most of which thrive on poor, unenriched soil; nitrogen acts as a fertiliser that is good for nettles and goosegrass, bad for cowslips and orchids.

(A plea to local authorities: take the cut grass away after it has been mown, to reduce the nitrogen build-up in the soil.)

All this shows that we have to nurture the things we love, even those that appear to be looking after themselves, like Devon's lanes. The good news is that some wild-flower seeds appear to remain viable for a very long time – certainly many decades. When the conditions are right, they come back – to the enchantment of us all.

The Isle of Sheppey

The Isle of Sheppey is not the first place you might think of as a beautiful landscape. At the confluence of the Thames and Medway estuaries, it is hardly manicured. Low-lying and marshy, it was known by the soldiers posted here in the First World War as Mud Island. Remains of Sheppey's twentieth-century defences can still be seen in the remains of concrete structures around the shore.

Prepare, then, to be surprised. In the lee of tall-arcing Sheppey Crossing Bridge lies Elmley, site of the only farmer-run National Nature Reserve in Britain. (It can no longer be called the only privately run NNR in Britain, because the Earl of Leicester now runs the Holkham NNR in Norfolk, having taken Elmley's advice. Not bad company to keep.) Imagine that magical forces had transported you onto the marshes one night; when you opened your eyes at dawn, you might think you were on the West Coast of Scotland.

Those dawns. Storm Dennis had yet to blow itself out when I last visited, scattering the widgeon and other wildfowl to the further lagoons; there were still rafts of them bobbing on the water near the old Kingshill Farmhouse at first light. I had heard them calling shrilly to each other during the night: the French call them *canards souffleurs*, whistling ducks. During the day, they will feed voraciously on the grass of the marsh, as they fatten themselves up for the long flight they will soon be making to Iceland, Scandinavia or Russia. A barn owl laboured past, making slow progress against the wind. In the opposite direction, a flight of pochard, with their chestnut heads, shot past as though they were turbocharged. Wherever I looked, there seemed to be hares, practising for the hundred-metre dash. If I had come a little earlier in the year, in different conditions, I might have seen the sky turn black with waterfowl as they got into the air. This could be called England's Camargue. It has the largest collection of breeding waders in the lowland UK.

This is all the more remarkable because Elmley is also a working farm, with no government help beyond that available to other farmers through agri-environment schemes. But it is in the hands of a remarkable family. Until recently, the chief representative was Philip Merricks, whose involvement began fifty years ago. Elmley was then run on conventional lines, but, as a passionate conservationist, he saw that it had other potential. For the last twenty years, it has been managed for wildlife, with sheep and cattle contributing to the regime.

Let's go out to the marshes. Lapwings are bobbing and wheeling on the wind, apparently for the pleasure of it. A short-eared owl flaps past, then another, making an unhurried patrol of the marshes, since they hunt during the day. From the sea wall you see a couple of factories, one of them making hundreds of millions of cardboard boxes every year to meet the demand from internet retailers. They'll pass eventually. The marshes will remain. They're immemorial.

Good heavens, no, Philip Merricks tells me. Everything you see is the result of human intervention. People have been working and changing this landscape for centuries. 'The sea wall was built in medieval times, using spades – imagine it! The Victorians ploughed the land up for arable, using steam tackle. It fell into grass with the Agricultural Depression that began in the 1880s. During the First World War, it was ploughed up again; then went back to grass between the wars.' The landscape today, with its seemingly natural rills, is entirely artificial. 'In summer, we have very low rainfall. All the water has to be pumped on. The whole idea is to make it look natural but there are probably one hundred and fifty water-control pipes. The height of water can be raised or lowered to the nearest half-inch. The rills are created by bulldozer. If it weren't managed, it would be unpredictable and we'd have far less wildlife.' Foxes are controlled, badgers kept out by means of fences; as a result, hedgehog numbers have boomed. So much for rewilding.

In the evening, the big sky is as luminescent as a Dutch landscape painting and the number of lapwings makes it difficult to leave. Those crested dandies with their peewit call have caused something of a traffic incident, by Elmley standards; three cars have felt compelled to stop and watch them. Ours makes a fourth, until we drive reluctantly away. Little more than an hour from London and we feel we've been on safari.

The Surrey Hills

From the top of the tower on Leith Hill you can see The Shard. London is that close – visible to the naked eye – but the Surrey Hills are a different world. This is a land of hollow lanes, enclosed by banks of knotty tree roots and overhung by pines and beeches; and of intimate villages that may now have BMWs in the driveways but remain delightfully intimate and informal, with an occasional reminder of the ramshackle appearance that they had in the nineteenth century. They are a rhapsody of building materials – brick, timber, flint, weatherboard and marmalade-coloured Bargate stone, so difficult to build with but the only stone that was to hand; of rhododendrons and azaleas; and the occasional big view, like that over the huge natural amphitheatre of the Devil's Punchbowl, near Hindhead. That all this should exist so near the capital, with all its developmental pressures, is an extraordinary and glorious thing.

This landscape was not always viewed so benignly. Reporting to the Board of Agriculture in 1809, William Stevenson wrote, 'it is difficult to conceive a character of soil worse than that of the heaths of Surrey'. Sand lizards and emperor dragonflies were scant compensation for poor fertility; Daniel Defoe had already likened

Bagshot Heath to 'Arabia Deserta'. But the Surrey Hills reinvented themselves when the railways came, reaching Godalming in 1859. The railway brought artists (Birket Foster, Helen Allingham) and this area was rechristened, with some hyperbole, the English Switzerland.

People started to build country houses, and Surrey supplied its own architect of genius to design some of them: Edwin Lutyens, born at Thursley in 1869. It was near Tilford that Lutyens's friend, the playwright J.M. Barrie, had his bolt-hole: Black Lake Pond became the Blue Lagoon in *Peter Pan*. Sir Arthur Conan Doyle, creator of Sherlock Holmes, erected a house at Hindhead – Undershaw, now a charitable foundation – for his wife to recover from tuberculosis (sadly, she did not.) The Poet Laureate Alfred Lord Tennyson rejected Hindhead as being 'very dear at the money' and chose a site near Haslemere instead. The artist George Frederick Watts, a friend of Tennyson, built a house and studio at Compton, to which his wife Mary added, at the bottom of the hill, a cemetery chapel; the terracotta panels in which it is covered had been modelled by local villagers, as part of an effort to revive rural life. A similar spirit pervaded Haslemere, with its weaving guild and Peasant Arts Society, formed in a bid (as the guild's founder Ethel Blount wrote) to 'reconquer the ancient crafts of the home'.

Surrey's hand-wrought houses, built with glorious views and billowing gardens but only a few acres of land, did not turn their back on modernity in all its forms. At Fulbrook House, designed by Lutyens as a Wealden house, with much oak, Mrs Streatfield was an adventurous motorist whose 4.5 hp Locomobile vehicle could cover two miles of the Portsmouth Road in just five and a half minutes. As *The Car Illustrated* described in 1902, she could, with the help of a lad from the village, take out the engine and repair it herself, when required. Fortunately, if paradoxically, the people who built houses in the Surrey Hills were among the most ardent defenders of the traditional landscape. 'When I was a child all this tract of country was undiscovered,' lamented Gertrude Jekyll in *Old West Surrey*, published in 1904; 'now alas! it is over-run'. George Sturt, Ruskinian wheelwright and author, complained about their 'braying' of proliferating motorcars before the First World War. The lights of the villas, impinging on the primordial darkness of the night; the sounds of piano-playing; and 'the affected excitement of a tennis-party' were other signs of decay that undermined 'the home-made civilisation of the rural English'.

But the preservationists fought back; the Surrey Hills are now protected as an Area of Outstanding Natural Beauty. And Surrey has another card up its sleeve. Despite the commuter pressure, it remains – another remarkable thing – the most wooded of English counties. There are lots of big homes but you would hardly know they were there.

Icons of National Identity

There are some places that we could not live without. They are part of us. They help define who we are, as a nation. To lose one would be like losing a limb.

I apologise for the word 'icons': it is overused. And yet I can think of no other noun that quite serves the purpose. We revere the Houses of Parliament as a place, not because of what goes on there but because, in an almost mystical way, it's ours. It is bound up with the way we do things. We may not like that way of doing things. We may not like the architecture of the building. But we cannot deny that it is different from its equivalents elsewhere.

National identity is a tricky subject to some people. Can a country whose population is so mixed have a shared identity? We are proudly cosmopolitan. There was never a British or even an Anglo-Saxon race so much as a hodgepodge of Celtic, Latin, Scandinavian, German, Norman, Huguenot, Jewish and other genes. Waves of immigration from the Commonwealth followed the Second World War. Globalisation has brought people from around the world. How do people from so many different backgrounds share a common identity?

Because, it seems to me, most newcomers want to feel part of their adopted culture. They retain their own traditions – to the enrichment of us all – but still want to fit in. Most families quickly develop a loyalty towards the place they live in. People used to wonder whether a disparate population such as Britain's could form a common purpose; and isn't the nation state in decline? The Coronavirus crisis has shown that a spirit of togetherness does appear when it is most needed. The pandemic was global; but even within the European Union, the response was national. The bunting was out on the seventy-fifth anniversary of VE Day. Even the politically correct BBC managed to feel proud.

Does any of this matter? Even if we did not know the things that are an essential part of what it means to be English, we'd soon learn from foreign visitors. The White Cliffs of Dover, Stonehenge, red telephone boxes – these are the symbols which we know ourselves and by which we are known. Imagine that they disappeared. We would feel denuded.

The White Cliffs of Dover

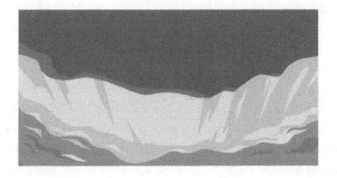

The White Cliffs of Dover stand for England and the English. They are our mental bulwark, the portcullis that stands permanently down against invasion, a natural landmark that overlooks the country's busiest port – which for aeons made them the last thing that people saw as they left British shores and the first thing to be spotted when they returned. It is now possible to quit England, or return to it, by air or the Channel Tunnel; but from the top of the cliffs, cross-Channel ferries, cargo ships, fishing boats and pleasure craft can still be seen performing their endless minuet of manoeuvres around the port of Dover below. To some of the English aboard those ships, the cliffs are so rich in association and cultural meaning that they will still bring a lump of patriotic sentiment to the throat.

When Julius Caesar arrived in 55 BC, he avoided landing beneath the White Cliffs, whose brow was lined with fiercely armed tribesmen (he touched land a few miles to the east). There are no such tribesmen today. But the cliffs retain their imaginative significance. Wars may not be fought in the way that they were a couple of millennia ago, but should Britain ever be invaded in the future, the enemy would probably come via Dover, beneath the towering majesty of the cliffs. Forefend the thought.

Look at the White Cliffs in a different light and they are a compelling natural phenomenon. The chalk of which they are made belongs to a bed that is two hundred and fifty metres deep. Eighty million years ago, the process of forming them began as an infinite number of plankton and other organisms died and floated down to the bottom of the warm sea which then covered Europe. In the course of a million years, the shells of these tiny creatures would combine to make fifteen metres of chalk. The water level dropped and the chalk was exposed. An unimaginably vast torrent of water gouged out the English Channel at the end of the last ice age. The pebbles on the beach are made from the hard flints found embedded in the soft chalk; they were formed from the shells of other sea creatures that contained silica. The cliffs may have shrunk back from the sea, retreating perhaps as much as a hundred metres from the line that greeted Julius Caesar.

The clifftop has its own ecosystem. The plants that grow there thrive on very thin soils; the tracks and abrasions left by man have only encouraged them to flourish. The tapestry of flowery turf represents one of the most diverse plant communities in Britain. Among the orchids, salad burnet, carline thistle, wild thyme, birdsfoot trefoil and horseshoe vetch can be found the wild cabbage brought to Britain by the Romans, from which our own familiar green vegetable descends.

Forget cabbage and think of Shakespeare. 'Come on, Sir,' says Edgar to his newly blinded father, Gloucester, in *King Lear*:

> . . . here's the place: stand still. How fearful
> And dizzy 'tis, to cast one's eyes so low!
> The crows and choughs that wing the midway air
> Show scarce so gross as beetles: half way down
> Hangs one that gathers samphire, dreadful trade!
> Methinks he seems no bigger than his head:
> The fishermen, that walk upon the beach,
> Appear like mice; and yond tall anchoring bark,
> Diminish'd to her cock; her cock, a buoy
> Almost too small for sight: the murmuring surge,
> That on the unnumber'd idle pebbles chafes,
> Cannot be heard so high. I'll look no more;
> Lest my brain turn, and the deficient sight
> Topple down headlong.

Did Shakespeare ever visit the White Cliffs? He did not need to. They exist in the shared imagination of the English, something that unites us all.

The Houses of Parliament

It is the fretted silhouette that does it; that and the sculpture-encrusted walls instantly recognisable from millions of postcards and tourist brochures. The British Houses of Parliament, or Palace of Westminster as they are formally known, are, like the red telephone box, a key ingredient of the national brand. Everyone knows the river façade: long, punctuated with Puginian ornament, almost symmetrical but thrown off balance by the large clock tower containing Big Ben. Strangely, it is not a traditionally British building at all: clock towers are a feature of German and Flemish architecture. England did not have them in the period that the architect, Sir Charles Barry, looked back to: the Elizabethan age. Nobody thinks of that now. Big Ben is us.

When the old Houses of Parliament burnt down in 1834, some of the crowd cheered. A.W.N. Pugin, who would design so much of the detail of the building, from statues to wallpaper, ceiling bosses to ink stands, was among them. Recent work by Sir John Soane had been in the Classical style, which he regarded as ungodly. 'Oh it was a glorious sight,' he wrote to a friend, 'to see his composition mullions and cement pinnacles and battlements flying and cracking while his 2s. 6d. turrets were smoking like so many manufacturing chimneys till the heat shivered them into a thousand pieces.' The fire was caused by the burning of ancient tally sticks, a medieval means of recording payment: it seemed to epitomise the antiquated character of the place. Fortunately, the most historic part of the complex – William II's mighty Westminster Hall, rebuilt by Richard II with a hammer-beam roof – survived the blaze; so did St Stephen's Chapel. Everything else was consumed.

Politicians may not be much more popular today than they were at the time of the Great Reform Act, but the building that they occupy is greatly loved. If today's Houses of Parliament were to be destroyed by another fire, the world would be as shocked as it was by Notre-Dame. The nation would be bereft.

And yet, a disaster may be waiting to happen. Every year, about forty minor fires break out on the premises. Watchful staff put them out, but will they always spot them? It would only take one to catch hold and the result could be catastrophic. Since the building was completed in the Victorian period, it has been abused and over used. The pressure of legislation is such that it has never been given the time off it deserves. The prime object of the authorities has been to keep it in service . . . often at minimum cost to the public purse. Maintenance teams can now do nothing more to modernise the services; they are reduced to patching up what is there. Shades of the Palace of Westminster before 1834.

On 4 April 2019, a sitting of the House of Commons was suspended when what was perhaps euphemistically described as water poured through the ceiling onto the press gallery; it has since been identified by some as raw sewage. MPs were quick to see the possibilities for metaphors about the state of governance. The crisis facing the Palace of Westminster is well understood by Parliament, following official reports and the drawing-up of a refurbishment plan; but the legislators have procrastinated. They do not want the trouble of moving out while the job is done. They cannot decide where to go. This has not been their finest hour.

Nineteenth-century parliamentarians wanted facilities that resembled those of their clubs. Today's priorities are more likely to be new technology and the need to house the ever greater numbers of staff. And yet the symbolism of the building, unlike its wiring, remains fit for purpose. Rich in history painting and medieval ornament, it radiates dignity and national self-confidence, in architecture that combines idealism (what the architects wanted) and practicality (what the first commissioner of works allowed) in a way that mirrors the business of politics itself. Some MPs and peers fear that if Parliament moves out, lock, stock and barrel, for the refurbishment of the Palace of Westminster, it will never return. New premises will be found for it, not necessarily in London. The Houses of Parliament would be sold, probably as a hotel. That would be a disgrace.

Stonehenge, Wiltshire

Of course we must have Stonehenge as a Crown Jewel. It is one of the wonders not just of this country but of the world. The mere sight of it – the great circle of massive stones, alone in the bare landscape – evokes awe. We struggle to imagine the feat of will and organisation necessary to create it in the ancient of days. What an epic achievement. What a mystery. For archaeologists have yet to decode this phenomenon of prehistory. After four thousand years, the key to its meaning has been lost. We ponder it – and ponder again. Part of the hold that Stonehenge has on our imagination is that every age imposes an interpretation that reflects its own values and preoccupations. And so Stonehenge is always fresh, not just as a point of physical continuity with the distant past but as evidence that the humans of that period were not wholly dissimilar from us; they had ambition.

Each age makes its own Stonehenge. To the twelfth-century chronicler Geoffrey of Monmouth it seemed that only the magician Merlin, from the court of King Arthur, could have been responsible for the work. In the seventeenth century, the Classical architect Inigo Jones saw this as a geometrical monument bequeathed to us by the Romans. Antiquarians such as the seventeenth-century John Aubrey (he gave his name to the nearby Aubrey Holes) and the eighteenth-century William Stukeley claimed it as a national monument; the architect John Wood called it part of the Great School of Learning for Druids – a theory that had resonance for hippies in the twentieth century: it conformed to their New Age expectations (albeit ignoring the fact that the Druids worshipped in shady groves, not on open plains). Readers of Edmund Burke's aesthetic theories thrilled at the Sublime qualities of the huge stones. To the great Age of Faith, in the 1800s, the religious purpose of the structure seemed paramount. Children of the Space Age believed that Stonehenge might have been a gigantic prehistoric observatory. And so no doubt the meaning will continue to evolve.

In contrast to the difficulty of interpretation, the form of Stonehenge is relatively easy to describe. It stands in the middle of an earthwork circle made by a six-foot-deep ditch. A little way inside this earthwork is a ring of what used to be fifty-six holes: they were filled in again quite soon after being dug, and nobody knows what they were for. They never held stones or posts. Two stones were set up near the entrance to the circle, of which one survives. It is a type of stone called a sarsen. The word seems to derive from 'Saracen', reflecting the exotic nature of these huge stones, formed out of compressed sand and found in beds of chalk. Originally, sarsens were highly coloured, but centuries of lichen have given them a greyish crust – hence the alternative name that they were given, grey-wethers, meaning old grey sheep. This was the form that the henge took for the first eight hundred years of its existence, from 3100 BC till 2300 BC. In the next phase, the opening to the circle was realigned slightly, and emphasised by further banks; it was oriented towards the point on the horizon where the sun rises at the midsummer solstice. Presumably this was intentional. Presumably, too, the sun played some part in the religion of the builders.

Then came the great ring of standing stones, with lintels, which forms the popular image of Stonehenge. The stones were again sarsens. They are enormous, though not all of the same size. They were also carefully and cleverly shaped. Knobs project from the tops of the uprights, fitting declivities made in the underside of the lintels. The stones' flanks have also been shaped. Given that sarsens are extremely hard, and the men working on them were equipped only with stone tools, such stonemasonry represents quite a feat. Not nearly so much of a feat as transporting them to the site, however. They must have been dragged some distance, probably from the Downs around Marlborough, though possibly from as far as Wales. The sarsen ring dates from around 2000 BC. At some point during the next half-millennium another formation of stones was erected: smaller bluestones (so called from their speckled colour), forming a horseshoe within the enclosure made by the sarsens.

But just as interpretations change, so does the story of the stones itself. During the dry summer of 2014, it was discovered that Stonehenge was a much bigger complex than previously thought. Increasingly, it is regarded not as an isolated monument but as part of a ceremonial landscape that embraced scores of other sites on Salisbury Plain. An inclusive, One World Stonehenge? Could be.

Durham

People see Durham from the train. It is an epic, defiant view: the great central tower of the cathedral rising as though it were its own unconquerable cliff, a symbol of Christian civilisation that has endured centuries of hostile waves to stand triumphant. You see it suddenly, if coming from the south, after the train has passed through a cutting. Wow. The three-towered cathedral, the castle at its feet: both buildings occupying the summit of a great crag, rearing dramatically above a loop in the River Wear. There is nothing to beat it in England. And when you explore the architecture you find that it is just as extraordinary – and excellent – as the setting.

The cathedral contains the bones of St Cuthbert, the ascetic and unworldly abbot of Lindisfarne, who died in 687. Viking raids drove the monks from their island at the end of the ninth century; when they left, they took their most precious possessions, including St Cuthbert's remains, and wandered until the saint himself – by miraculous means – indicated the site of their new home. The saint's coffin, its lid incised with holy images, including the earliest depiction of the Virgin and Child in English art, survives in the cathedral Treasury: a unique example of

Anglo-Saxon wood carving – its preservation, if not quite of the same order of miracles as those performed by the saint himself, showing the importance attached to his cult, which makes Durham Cathedral the longest-lived pilgrimage site in Britain.

The cathedral was completely rebuilt after 1093, the arcade of the nave supported on heroically scaled circular piers, decorated with geometrical designs – chevrons, zigzags and chequers. Two decades earlier, on the orders of William the Conqueror, Waltheof Earl of Northumbria had begun work on the castle. One of the few Anglo-Saxon nobles to survive the regime change of 1066, Waltheof did not last long; he was beheaded after joining a rebellion. His successor as earl was the bishop of the cathedral, Walcher. He would be the first in a succession of prince-bishops. Durham was so important in its position near the Scottish border that William wanted to concentrate his resources there. Alas, the gentle Walcher was not the man for the job: he was murdered in 1080. But the combination of the temporal and the spiritual proved powerful – and Durham's riches increased when an abbey was founded. In the Middle Ages bridges were a sign of wealth, and the city had three, all of which survive. In the Victorian period, Durham was still the richest of all English sees.

Today what survives is extraordinary. Not only is the cathedral intact, and all the more impressive from the stylistic unity that comes from much of it having been built as a piece, but large parts of the abbey are also extant. We have the cloister, a rebuilt chapter house, what was the dormitory and, to one side, the monastic kitchen: an octagonal building whose vaults form a star pattern overhead, and which now serves as the bookshop. The refectory and part of the dormitory house the best monastic library to come down to us. Around an area known as the College are the houses built by the canons of the cathedral: they are on a scale commensurate with Durham's great wealth in the Georgian period. The prince-bishop himself lived in the castle; since he possessed another, Auckland Castle, ten miles to the south of the city, in the 1830s Durham Castle was given to the newly founded university.

By the eighteenth century, Durham's military role had long passed. Instead, its medieval architecture was highly regarded for its Picturesque qualities. When the canons landscaped the gorge in 1753, the poet Thomas Gray pronounced it to be 'one of the most beautiful Vales in England'. In the 1770s, they replaced a bridge that had been washed away by floods, deliberately choosing a spot that would make the most of the view. In the twentieth century, the usually dry architectural historian, Sir Nikolaus Pevsner, considered the Prebends' Bridge the 'most moving' prospect of what he termed 'one of the great experiences of Europe'.

War memorials

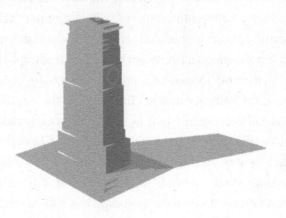

Everybody in England lives near a war memorial. They are part of the ordinary landscape of existence. There were no war memorials, in the sense that we are now familiar with, before the First World War. In previous centuries, individual officers might be remembered in the aisles of cathedrals or parish churches, but not ordinary soldiers – famously characterised by the Duke of Wellington as 'the scum of the earth'. Their bodies were piled into mass graves. A difference in sensibility had emerged by the Boer War, and the immense scale of the First World War unlocked the suppressed emotions of a usually tongue-tied nation that made a cult of self-discipline and sangfroid. The outpouring of grief found spontaneous expression, from 1915, in wayside shrines that were put up at crossroads.

When the Armistice finally came, the floodgates of remembrance burst and every organisation and institution – school, village, town hall, railway company, religious body, workplace, armed services branch – wanted to remember those they had known. There are so many war memorials, indeed, that we pass them by without a second thought. And yet what a gap they would leave if they were not there.

Most were locally commissioned, by ad hoc committees. There were no rules about the form they should take. Crosses are, not surprisingly, the commonest image. They might be Celtic crosses, calvaries with the figure of the Christ crucified, elaborate Gothic crosses adorned with sculpture, or plain crosses in a churchyard or at a crossroads. Most of the war cemeteries in France and Flanders contain a Cross of Sacrifice, designed by Sir Reginald Blomfield. Richer communities and institutions might prefer sculpture. This was the case with regiments such as the Royal Artillery, nearly fifty thousand of whose members had been killed. The R.A. commissioned a memorial that is also a great work of art.

Fortunately, the communities wanting to remember the dead of the First World War could catch the last gasp of the figurative tradition. There were many sculptors equal to meeting the challenge, but it was the monumental realism of the Yorkshireman Charles Sargeant Jagger that best captured the spirit of the undertaking. As a young man, he had won a travelling scholarship to Italy and, in 1914, had just won the Prix de Rome, which would have allowed him to return; instead, he enlisted in the Artists' Rifles. Commissioned with the Worcestershire Regiment, he was shot at Gallipoli, gassed on the Western Front, wounded in

Flanders and, in 1918, awarded the Military Cross. After the war, his style – epic but sombre – was perfectly suited to war memorials that incorporated monumental figures. Those of the artillerymen on the memorial are modelled with an accuracy derived from Jagger's own war experiences. Against a large square pedestal surmounted by a 9.2 inch howitzer in stone stand the more-than-life-sized figures of a battery commander in a greatcoat, and an ammunition carrier; to these were added a cloaked driver and the corpse of a gunner, shrouded in a cloak. The inclusion of the dead figure was controversial; at one point, Jagger offered to pay for its casting himself.

Nearby, the Machine Gun Corps memorial incorporates a figure of the young David, modelled by Francis Derwent Wood, as well as two real Vickers guns. A grimly appropriate biblical quotation was found in the Book of Samuel: 'Saul has slain his thousands, and David his tens of thousands.' There is nothing so histrionic (or in such doubtful taste) on the Royal Artillery Memorial. Like Lutyens's Cenotaph on Whitehall – the national memorial, which relies entirely on geometry for its effect – it is devoid of overt religious imagery. It is only the outstretched arms of the driver that evoke those of Christ on the cross.

When it was unveiled in 1924, contemporaries were shocked by the depiction of the corpse and the absence of religion. Lord Curzon went so far as to declare that 'nothing more hideous could ever be conceived'. Posterity disagrees.

Westminster Abbey

Across the centuries, visitors have thrilled to the history and physical presence of Westminster Abbey, Britain's coronation church. It has the highest Gothic vault in the country. It contains the tomb of its founder Edward the Confessor and the mortal remains, as well as sculpted memorials, of numerous later monarchs. It has become our national Valhalla, monuments encrusting the walls like barnacles on a ship's hull; this is where people of greatness are buried. The greatness is not always so apparent now. As you make your way around the bombastic muddle of old tombs, jumbled together like the contents of Kubla Khan's attics at the end of *Citizen Kane*, you may struggle to remember the identity of some of the figures; wonder what each did to deserve his or her bid for posthumous attention through magnificence of funerary architecture and expense of carving; and conclude that, with a few outstanding exceptions, such as Nollekens's monument to the Royal Navy captains William Bayne, William Blair and Lord Robert Manners, Scheemakers's to Admiral Charles Wager and Roubiliac's to Lady Elizabeth and Joseph Nightingale, sculptors did not always do justice to these lucrative commissions. We are less in awe of officially recognised great men and women than we used to be.

Applause for the actor David Garrick, high up in the transept that is Poets' Corner. He is shown throwing apart a pair of curtains, as though stepping forward to entertain St Peter and the Heavenly Choir – a memorable image. But few people today would emulate the eighteenth-century essayist Joseph Addison by visiting Westminster Abbey to relish the 'gloominess' and 'solemnity' of the place, which, together with the proximity of so many cadavers, were 'apt to fill the mind with a kind of melancholy, or rather thoughtfulness, that is not disagreeable'. Westminster Abbey is now too crowded with tourists, and Poets' Corner, once remarkable for being the place that literary figures were often buried as well as memorialised, is now full up.

But there is another wonderful thing about Westminster Abbey: the sanctuary pavement. You can see it in all its splendour, after the restoration of 2010, both at ground level (so long as you do not walk on it) and from above, thanks to the inspired creation of a museum of cathedral treasures in the triforium. And it is a very rare and precious thing. A Latin inscription in brass letters tells us that it was installed 'in A.D. one thousand two hundred and twelve plus sixty, minus four' – which is to say, 1268. The figures used in the calculation include the date of Henry III's death (1272), his age at death (sixty) and the length of his reign (fifty-six years). Henry had commissioned the luxurious pavement as part of his ambitious campaign to rebuild the eleventh-century abbey – important from its association with Edward the Confessor, who, as both king and saint, formed a counterpoise to the cult of St Thomas à Becket (an archbishop who defied his king) that had, in modern terms, gone viral at Canterbury. Henry wanted his project to express *Romanitas*, aligning his splendid church with the centre of Christianity and symbol of imperial might at Rome. Pavements of the kind he wanted were made only in Rome, by the stone-cutters of the Cosmati family. It is recorded that the Abbot of Westminster, Richard de Ware, was responsible for bringing it back, along with a team of workmen headed by one Odoricus.

Earlier mosaics, such as those found on the floors of Ancient Roman villas or the walls of Byzantine churches, used square stones of equal size. The Cosmatis specialised in a different technique called *opus sectile* – cut work. They created geometrical patterns out of different-coloured stones, shaped as triangles, squares, circles, rectangles and so on. Among them were precious or rare stones, including purple porphyry from antique columns (the whereabouts of the quarry from which the original porphyry had been obtained was no longer known). In a concession to local practice, these stones were set on a bed of Purbeck 'marble' (not really marble but polished limestone), which was being used elsewhere in the Abbey, rather than white marble. There are also pieces of coloured glass, which would not have happened in Rome. They add extra sparkle to this sumptuous and colourful creation.

Nearly twenty-five foot square, the pavement forms a pattern of rectangles and roundels in a border of roundels, which is both symmetrical and, in detail, endlessly multifarious. No two roundels are the same. This expresses a universe of seemingly infinite variety – literally a universe with a roundel of onyx at its centre, representing the *primum mobile*, or earth. Around it are, according to a medieval monk, 'the colours of the four elements, fire, air, water and earth'. Surrounding roundels may represent stars and planets. After the inscription indicating the date of the pavement comes another referring, in coded terms, to the related life expectancies of animals, man and the world itself. The geometry of the pavement thus appears to be a mystical representation of the created universe and its end. Fortunately, the world is still turning and we are alive to enjoy the pavement, a unique work of art (there is no other Cosmati pavement outside Italy) in this most memory-freighted of buildings.

Only one person is allowed to walk across the pavement in high heels, and that is Her Majesty the Queen – and only because the Dean and Chapter have not had the courage to stop her.

The red telephone box

Okay, I accept that the red telephone box is an obvious choice for this list, and yet – even in an age that has moved beyond the landline as a piece of functioning technology – would we not mourn its departure from the scene? Yes, it represents a challenge, now that so many of them are redundant (more of that later). But to me they are also a symbol of an ideal, a time when people in authority respected our shared public spaces and wanted to do things properly, by getting the very best design that they could – as the result of a competition. Contrast that attitude to the one prevailing today. Little thought has been given to the junction boxes required for broadband, which are plonked anywhere on our streets, without regard for their architectural setting. Same goes for the hutch-like structures used to store bicycles. Don't get me started.

Before the mid-1980s, there were so many red kiosks – around sixty-two thousand – that they were simply taken for granted. They were so familiar as to be scarcely noticed. In country villages and by roadsides, that was a desirable quality. No one, surely, would have wanted obtrusive modernity on a village green. And yet the distinctive shape and guardsman-red livery meant that they were easily spotted by anyone who needed to find one in a hurry. They had faults. The phones in them did not always work. A number smelt of urine, because not adequately maintained. But these were – and remain – friendly structures, whose virtues were beyond mere inconspicuousness. They were masterpieces of industrial design, perfectly adapted to the material – cast iron – of which they were made.

They came in two principal versions. The original 1924 design, or K2, was designed by Sir Giles Scott, architect of Liverpool Cathedral and Bankside Power Station (now Tate Modern). Confined exclusively to London – although somebody once said he had spotted a rogue example in Mumbai – the K2 is spacious and dignified. The top is a handkerchief dome derived from the work of the Regency architect Sir John Soane. It not only wears the regal livery of red but carries a crown perforated into the ironwork beneath the dome. In 1935 Scott designed a slightly reduced version: the K6 or 'Jubilee' kiosk (it first made its appearance in the year of George V's Silver Jubilee). Smaller and more economical to produce, it expressed the more streamlined aesthetic of the decade, with widely spaced glazing bars that were derived from early-nineteenth-century sash windows (those of the K2 look distinctly Queen Anne).

Evidently the Classical values of the kiosks were appreciated by the engineers who installed them, or was it just a more civilised age? For it is remarkable how carefully they were sited. In towns they were often placed in pairs, to reflect the symmetry of a street or building. They could actually enhance their surroundings. Certainly there was little public outcry when they were fitted in country locations. Admittedly some fussy people insisted on painting theirs grey, since the red – as the landscape gardener Humphry Repton might have said – added too hot a note to the scene. But the reception was better than it would have been had the design been new-fangled or poorly considered. Very quickly the red telephone box joined the policeman's helmet, the Brigade of Guards, the red postbox and the 1980s punk rocker on the King's Road as an emblem of national identity.

Enter the villain of the piece. When British Telecom was privatised in 1985, it immediately embarked on a change of corporate image. Red was too much associated with the old Post Office. It adopted the new colour of yellow. Attempts to change the colour of London telephone boxes had met with ridicule a few years before. But at privatisation this problem was circumvented by the attempt not to repaint the red boxes, but do away with them altogether. They suggested a leisurely air of dignity, responsibility and tradition. What British Telecom wanted was a zappy new futuristic look. Instead of holding a competition they bought a range of new hoods, off the peg. The results were dire.

Initially, it was decreed that all but a handful of the red telephone boxes would be uprooted and hauled off as scrap. A plucky campaign by what was then the Thirties Society ensured that a good number – thousands upon thousands of them – were kept. But what to do with them now? People don't need public telephones; they have mobile phones. In London and other cities, the police regard the surviving kiosks as a nuisance: whatever they are used for – don't ask – it is not the making of telephone calls. But we must not despair. I have seen some boxes that contain defibrillators for first-aid purposes; others that have been converted into mini information centres, or exchange points for book-lending schemes. If we all think hard enough, we shall be able to come up with a suitable use. If – as the plan had been in the 1980s – the survivors had been simply junked, a little bit of the British soul would have died.

St Paul's Cathedral

Westminster Abbey stands for royal continuity. St Paul's is a symbol of renewal. The first squats on the marsh of what used to be an island – or eyot – of the fraying Thames, as it makes its way sluggishly to the sea; its low profile is reinforced by the absence of a spire. The other rises from the eminence of Ludgate Hill – not a very great eminence, but enough to tower above the streets of the City of London in the paintings of Canaletto; enough to make it a proud symbol of defiance as those streets were set on fire during the Second World War.

It was a conflagration that caused the present structure to be built. In 1666, the Great Fire of London laid waste to an area of one and a half miles by half a mile, containing over thirteen thousand houses, eighty-seven churches and the medieval cathedral of St Paul's. Old St Paul's was begun in the eleventh century on the site of a Roman temple; repairs begun by Inigo Jones were still unfinished when the disaster struck. The fire put an end to any thought of merely patching up the old cathedral; it was so far beyond rescuing that Sir Christopher Wren used none of the old foundations for his new buildings.

Had it not been for the Fire, Wren might not have blossomed

as an architect. He was an astronomer and mathematician. It had been in his rooms, after a lecture, that the 'experimental philosophical clubbe' which became the Royal Society was formed. At the Royal Society, gentlemen amateurs like Samuel Pepys (who in time became its President) mixed with scientists like Isaac Newton and Robert Boyle. Wren had been swept up in the new experimental approach to knowledge when he had gone to Oxford, at the end of the English Civil War. He had a practical cast of mind that delighted in three-dimensional problems: he made pasteboard models to demonstrate the working of muscles. At the age of twenty-five, he became Professor of Astronomy at Gresham College in London; four years later he returned to Oxford as Savilian Professor of Astronomy. Robert Hooke, another scientist turned architect, was to write that there was 'scarce ever met in one man, in so great a perfection, such a Mechanical Hand, and so Philosophical a Mind'. Newton rated him as one of the three greatest geometers of his age.

But before 1666, Wren had built only two significant buildings – one was the splendid Sheldonian Theatre in Oxford, the other being the chapel of Pembroke College, Cambridge. The Sheldonian Theatre is domed, like St Paul's. Domes had been previously unknown in England: Wren derived the idea from France. St Paul's dome was originally intended to rise over the central point of a symmetrical building, planned in the form of a Greek cross. The clergy did not want to innovate; they insisted on a long nave. Wren is supposed to have wept – although this hardly seems to conform with what we know of his personality, which was dry and haughty. But like any Baroque architect, he was also something of a showman; for the tall external profile of the dome bears little relation to the shape within. That is because the internal dome rises little higher than the base of the one outside. This is only one example of Wren's illusionism: another is the parapet wall, giving the façades their rectilinear silhouette which conceals the use of flying buttresses to distribute the thrust of dome and roof. He fooled most people. Rich in detail, bold in mass, his architecture provided an appropriate expression for what was both the first Anglican cathedral built in Britain and a seat of national life.

The events that it has witnessed include Nelson's funeral in 1806 and Wellington's in 1853, Queen Victoria's Diamond Jubilee in 1897, Churchill's funeral in 1965, and the wedding of Charles and Diana in 1981. But there is more to St Paul's than the state occasions that have taken place there. During the aerial bombardments of 1940, when it was still one of the tallest buildings in the City of London, it epitomised the national will to stand firm against German attempts to destroy the capital. Nearly thirty incendiary bombs fell either on St Paul's or near it; one burnt its way through the lead of the roof and landed on the roof of the Stone Gallery, where it could be put out. It would have been another matter if it had got lodged amid the timbers supporting the dome. The attacks suffered by the cathedral only served to strengthen the idea that it was the Blitz spirit that brought Londoners together, determined to outface the enemy.

Today, many buildings around St Paul's are taller than the cathedral; but the need for that sense of common purpose, the togetherness that Londoners discovered at a low point of the war, is just as great.

The Three Graces,
Liverpool waterfront

No, not the *Three Graces* sculpted by Canova for the 6th Duke of Bedford's sculpture gallery at Woburn Abbey, who now commute between the National Galleries of Scotland in Edinburgh and the Victoria and Albert Museum in London – a unique example of marmoreal transhumance. I refer to the Liverpool waterfront, which, at the turn of the twentieth century, was redeveloped with three mighty buildings – known coyly as the Three Graces – whose scale and self-confidence seemed to epitomise Britain's imperial status. They were built on the site of a redundant dock, acquired by the City Corporation. First came the many-domed Mersey Docks and Harbour Board; then, after some years with little interest in the site, the nervous verticality of the Royal Liver Friendly Society; finally, seated between them both, like a man of the world between two overdressed individuals on a bus, the Cunard building, by the soigné Mewès and Davis. Two of the three buildings could not be considered masterpieces, but, like the Empire itself, they all pull together to make considerably more than the sum of their parts: an unforgettable image of commercial bravado. The trio on the Pier Head seem to embody the spirit of Liverpool.

In origin, Liverpool is a medieval city, granted a charter in 1207 by King John. The castle that was built survives in the name of Castle Street but nothing can now be seen of it: the last of its remains were removed in the early eighteenth century, as the port was beginning to boom. Some of the city's Georgian prosperity was borne, alas, on the backs of slaves: at the end of the eighteenth century, Liverpool is said to have controlled over 80 per cent of the British and over 40 per cent of the entire European slave trade. By the Victorian period, slavery had been abolished throughout the British Empire, but Liverpool had found a new source of wealth: cotton. Over one and a half million bales of it, destined for the Lancashire mills, were imported each year from America, Brazil, Egypt and India. With the opening of St George's Hall, a combined concert hall and law court with cells for prisoners in the basement, in 1854, Liverpool put its civic self-pride on display. The city's merchants and bankers outdid each other to commission the most splendid architecture. The Three Graces were a late flowering of this spirit.

By the time they were built, Liverpool had entered on a new life as the glamorous port of embarkation for transatlantic liners like Cunard's *Mauretania* and *Lusitania*, both launched in 1907; called floating palaces, they could cross to New York in less than five days. (Earlier vessels had not seemed so luxurious to the millions of impoverished emigrants who passed through Liverpool on their way to the New World: the diseases rife on the cramped, airless lower decks earned them the name of fever ships.) The tragedy of the *Titanic* is remembered on the promenade in front of the Three Graces by the epic and sober granite *Memorial to the Engine Room Heroes*, designed by

William Goscombe John: by the time of its unveiling in 1916, in the depths of the First World War, it had acquired another resonance. It was the year of the Somme. The same sculptor's statue of a proud Edward VII, the plumes of his hat fluttering, arrived on the same promenade in the same year: a tribute, perhaps, to a heyday that had passed.

For Liverpool had already lost its crown to Southampton, which was closer to London and could take bigger ships; the White Star Line's express vessels were transferred there in 1907. The city began to decline, and then slump; by the third quarter of the twentieth century it had all but abandoned hope.

But Liverpool's famously cocky, irreverent and creative spirit did not die; given voice by the Beatles, it was symbolised by the river to which the city owed its existence. 'So ferry 'cross the Mersey,' sang Gerry and the Pacemakers, ''cause this land's the place I love.' The Three Graces provide the architectural landscape to this song; they are now flag-wavers for the city's renewal.

Windsor Castle

People see Windsor Castle most often from the M4, which runs nearby. There it is, less than ten miles from Heathrow airport, but still bristling with towers and crenellations, its silhouette as fanciful as a medieval romance. It is not simply how Windsor looks, architecturally or decoratively, that is the point of it, though; the Castle is part of our common life: a seat of royalty, a symbol of Norman domination, a magnificent survival of the Middle Ages, romanticised for George IV and upgraded by the Prince Consort, forever associated with the Widow of Windsor, Queen Victoria, who spent much of the last forty years of her reign behind its battlements. Forever associated, too, with our own Queen Elizabeth, the ceremonies of the Garter that take place there, the incomparable Horse Show that is held every summer in its grounds. We have had an intimation of what it would mean if it were to go up in flames, like Notre-Dame, because on 20 November 1992, it did. In the Queen's private chapel that morning, a spotlight had leant against a curtain and set it on fire; by the evening, the State Rooms of the Castle were ablaze, the flames leaping above the walls of the Upper Ward. Nobody who saw the television reports that evening will forget the images. The nation was in shock.

But the lesson of Windsor is that a robust architectural entity can absorb the buffetings of chance. Buildings change; they always have done. They rarely stay exactly as they used to be: if left alone they decay. Palaces and country houses are particularly prone to alteration since, historically, their rich owners wanted to keep abreast of fashion. The process can be seen at Windsor. It was Charles II who awoke Windsor Castle from its medieval sleep. His mistress the Duchess of Portsmouth had an apartment immediately below his own, and Nell Gwynn occupied a house, with the royal bastards, at the bottom of the hill. Charles created the Long Walk, the grandest Baroque avenue in Britain, which stretches for three miles. In the eighteenth century George III, that single-mindedly uxorious monarch, with his string of daughters and quartet of wayward sons, determined to turn the Castle into a centre of domestic life. He built what would be called the Queen's Lodge, a Georgian house such as any of his more prosperous subjects might have inhabited, with the Castle a few yards away. From the onset of his last period of so-called madness in 1811 until his death in 1820, he was confined to his apartment in Windsor Castle, alternately storming about and playing fragments of Handel on the harpsichord.

For the Prince Regent, the future George IV, Windsor was an architectural opportunity. He adored building, decoration and make-believe. Having commissioned works in the Chinese, Hindoo and neo-Classical styles, he could now employ Jeffry Wyatt – whose sense of romance inspired a change of name to Wyatville – to reshape Windsor, making it even more the *beau idéal* of a castle than it had been before. Battlements were crenellated and machicolated, windows were Gothicised; bays and oriel windows made to project and the Norman Round Tower raised by another thirty-five feet. 'It is possible to be less enthusiastic than his contemporaries were about Wyatville's often tame or over-scale detail,' comments Mark Girouard in his book *Windsor, the Most Romantic Castle*, 'but the silhouette is a triumph.' It became a symbol of national pride after Waterloo.

Inside, Wyatville remodelled St George's Hall as a setting for the Garter Feasts that had been reinstituted by George III during the Napoleonic Wars. With tall Gothic windows and a ceiling emblazoned with the shields of Garter Knights, it was broadly medieval. The other reception rooms, opulently gilded, satisfied George IV's taste for costly French decoration and were full of marble and bronze, expensive craftsmanship and fine furniture. Here the King had a suitable setting for the newly fashionable house parties, which he had experienced at Chatsworth, Belvoir and elsewhere.

George IV occupied his new apartments in 1828, leaving little enough time to enjoy them before his death in 1830. Whatever Queen Victoria may have thought of her extravagant, gouty, risible but warmly human uncle, she became the monarch most closely associated with the castle he had remodelled. Like Britain's other female monarchs – Elizabeth I, Elizabeth II – she was frugal in terms of architecture. After her period, Windsor ossified.

The 1992 fire forced an overhaul. The private Chapel, the State Dining Room, the Brunswick Tower and the Crimson Drawing Room had been gutted; St George's Hall and the Grand Reception Rooms were open to the sky. Much was authentically restored but St George's Hall was reimagined, with a roof of new design, made out of green oak in the medieval manner. Arguably it created a better room than its predecessor. By a benign stroke of fate, the contents of the State Apartments had largely been removed for rewiring before the fire, so nearly all the paintings and furniture went back. The Windsor Castle that we see today is different from its condition before 1992, and yet the same. Already the fire has come to seem only an episode in the life of this ancient structure, which has experienced so many vagaries over its many centuries of existence. We must never despair.

Outstanding Beauty

Beauty is back. It is a word that has caused frowns in some quarters. How could people agree on what constitutes beauty? The idea is too normative, too discriminatory against those who do not possess it – assuming that it exists. But before he died in 2019, the aesthetic philosopher Sir Roger Scruton argued that beauty was, in some ways, hard-wired into the human mind. We instinctively agree that some places, some views, some types of arrangement are more appealing than others. These things are not solely cultural, but innate.

Well, let's not argue. You do not have to agree with Sir Roger – I submit the entries in this section as a purely personal choice of places of outstanding, sometimes representative beauty. Representative? There is only one Salisbury Cathedral but there are many West Country villages – Blisland is special, but there are others. Bevis Marks Synagogue is unique but Derek Jarman's Prospect Cottage at Dungeness is one of so many gardens I could have picked. It is an extreme garden because of its position, a garden of consolation because of the circumstances in which it was made. The Heaven Room at Burghley is sublime, superlative. Wormsley Park is not the only country house to have a cricket ground but I defy anyone to go there on a sunny afternoon and not feel it is a bit of heaven – quite different from the Burghley House interpretation.

Forget the eye of the beholder. Beauty is all the better for being shared.

Salisbury Cathedral

Which cathedral is closest to the English heart? Impossible to say, but I will: Salisbury. It approaches architectural perfection more nearly than any of the other cathedrals in England. It is the most harmonious. The tower is the tallest, at four hundred and four feet, although that is not so much when compared to some of the Continent's spires – look at Ulm Minster's. Still, that is close to showing off. Salisbury's spire is seen in conjunction with the watermeadows that still surround the city, themselves a survival of medieval farming practice: and we can hardly help seeing them through the eyes of that singularly English painter, Constable. Henry James, perversely, thought Salisbury was too perfect; what a fussy man.

Whereas other cathedral builders in the Middle Ages had to contend with previously developed sites, Salisbury's Bishop Roger Poore had no such bother. In 1219, he abandoned the previous building where it stood: at Old Sarum, inside the banks of an Iron Age hill fort. Old Sarum had little water and was inconveniently close to a castle full of disputatious knights. 'Let us descend joyfully to the plains, where the valley abounds in corn, where the fields are beautiful and where there is freedom from oppression,'

121

declaimed the papal bull of Honorius III which approved the move. Poore and his unknown architect could lay out the cathedral as they liked; except for the fourteenth-century spire, most of it was built over a period of sixty years – hence it is unified in style. Critics can point with justice to the west front which is relatively banal; it is the distant view and the vaults of the interior that enchant. Although the spire was far taller than the thirteenth-century ideal, it was the 'work of a mason of the highest genius', according to Pevsner in *The Buildings of England*.

Whereas the stone used to build Old Sarum had come from Caen in Normandy, Salisbury was made of English stones; the nave is an unusually disciplined essay in creamy Chilmark limestone from around Tisbury in Wiltshire, and dark-grey Purbeck 'marble' from the Isle of Purbeck in Dorset. Purbeck marble, rich in fossils, was also used for the floor.

Another reason for the unity is less sympathetic. In the 1780s, the cathedral suffered restoration under the hand of James Wyatt – Wyatt the Destroyer as the champion of Gothic architecture, A.W.N. Pugin, furiously called him. Wyatt stripped out the chantry chapels and other features that, to his eyes, cluttered the interior, making it accord better with contemporary taste. In the nineteenth century, Wyatt's work – notably a screen that he had installed, composed of parts of the demolished Gothic work – was itself replaced by Sir George Gilbert Scott. Scott gave Salisbury its present screen of painted ironwork – open and architecturally adventurous: Scott was, in other places, as great a destroyer of old work as Wyatt, but this was one of his better inspirations.

In comparison to other cathedrals and great churches, Salisbury has few monuments to distract the eye; but we cannot leave without noticing the clock to one side of the nave. In 1386, the Dean of Salisbury sold the lease of a shop, the income from which funded the clock, which had been erected in the free-standing bell tower of the cathedral (demolished, of course, by Wyatt). This is the oldest clock in the country; it may be the oldest piece of machinery working anywhere on earth. There are no hands or dial: the hours are marked by the striking of a bell. In a space that speaks so clearly of eternity, does one need more?

Blisland, Cornwall

Many Cornish villages are named after their patron saints, but not Blisland. Just as well; locally the saint in question was known as St Pratt. This was a corruption of St Proteus. In the church's dedication he has been joined by his reputed brother, St Hyacinth, both of them having been martyred during the persecutions of Emperor Valerian in the third century. Instead, Blisland is supposed to have been called after its joyous, blissful situation – which may be fanciful, but suggests how names (as Tristram Shandy's father maintained) can influence personality. Because Blisland is a serene and lovesome place, its friendly green equipped with children's swings and overlooked by houses built of the local moorland granite – but, for once in Cornwall, on a comfortably prosperous scale.

For Sir John Betjeman, the Church of St Proteus and St Hyacinth, carved with such labour out of the adamantine stone, epitomised everything that he felt, throughout his life, a church should be. 'Sir Ninian Comper, that great church architect, says that a church should bring you to your knees when first you enter it. Such a church is Blisland.'

People do not read Betjeman as much as they did in the

second half of the twentieth century; his star has waned, as was perhaps inevitable after to the great popularity of his television programmes. His national position as a celebrity came to overshadow the originality of his verse. But his poetic canvas was distinctive. Few other poets of his generation wrote about faith, change, schooldays, athletic girls for whom he would conceive an unconsummated passion, architecture in the way that he did, often in a metre derived from hymns. Nobody knew more about churches than Betj, as he was known to his admirers; nor anyone with such a love for the England that he had grown up amongst and could see passing. His praise for Blisland is therefore worth noting.

As a boy, Betjeman reached Blisland by bicycle; it was within striking distance of his parents' holiday home by the sea. Straining up hills and careering 'heart-in-mouth' down into the next valley, he slowly left the stunted wind-blown trees of the seaside and emerged into the lusher landscape on the edge of Bodmin moor. On his way to the church he would have passed tombstones lettered like circus posters, in a caprice of different fonts. Did they later inspire the neo-Victorian typography for his *Shell Guides*? Some of the stones in the walls of the church, which crouches low to the ground as though worried about being blown away, are as big as a steamer trunk.

Inside, there are the quirks of age: one of the nave columns leans so rakishly that it had to be propped up by a wooden beam in the fifteenth century, carved with mouldings and roses. The ribs of the roofs recall the upturned hulls of ships. But what Betjeman regarded as the pièce de résistance is – well, I shall let the Poet Laureate himself describe it:

125

Walls white, sun streams in through a clear west window and there – glory of glories! – right across the whole eastern end of the church is a richly-painted screen and rood loft. It is of wood. The panels at its base are red and green. Wooden columns, highly coloured and twisted like barley sugar, burst into gilded tracery and fountain out to hold a panelled loft.

'Incongruous,' sniffs Pevsner, in his *Buildings of England* volume, of this contribution from the 1890s, when the little-known F.C. Eden restored the church. But the colour and the gilding, the saints and the theatre, made a direct appeal to Betjeman's spirituality through his aesthetic sense. Struggling with faith, he wanted architecture to overpower his doubts and open, for the moment that he experienced it, a window onto eternity. Blisland did it for him.

Bevis Marks Synagogue

The Synagogue at Bevis Marks, practically in the shadow of the Gherkin, is not as spatially ingenious as the churches built by Sir Christopher Wren after the Great Fire of London. Wren and his assistant, Robert Hooke, were forced to use the often asymmetrical sites of previous medieval churches, to which – as mathematicians – they gave Classical and geometrical order. Bevis Marks was built on an unencumbered site, some houses that had formerly stood there having been pulled down. It is the work of a Quaker carpenter, Joseph Avis, rather than an architect and scholar. But few other buildings can so effectively teleport the visitor back into the world of 1701, when it was opened on 27 Elul 5461, the Sabbath before Rosh Hashanah. Although Bevis Marks has been in continuous use ever since, the community worshipping in it has been conservative; nothing appears to have changed.

It was Oliver Cromwell, not known for his religious tolerance in other areas, who allowed the Jews openly back into England, for the first time since their expulsion by Edward I. In 1655, Sephardim – Jews from the Iberian peninsula – who had been living covertly in the City of London, often having fled the Inquisition, petitioned him to allow them freedom of worship, as well as the right for others of their faith to join them from overseas. He agreed, largely because of the commercial advantage being gained by the Dutch from the presence of Jewish merchants in Amsterdam. Their first synagogue was in a house, now demolished; by the end of the seventeenth century, they were rich enough to fund a purpose-built structure. Although they were required to choose a secluded location – like Wren's St Mary Abchurch, the synagogue is entered off a quiet yard – the project received high-level support; the future Queen Anne donated one of the main beams.

The general layout of Bevis Marks can be compared to the Great Synagogue in Amsterdam, built in 1675. This is hardly surprising, given the links between the Jewish communities in London and Amsterdam. From the ceiling hang seven brass chandeliers from that city which Pevsner goes so far as to call 'gorgeous'. Other details, however, are strikingly similar to Wren's City churches (in collaboration with Hooke, he built fifty-one, of which a dozen survive in their original form and a further nine have been altered or rebuilt, most after the Blitz). While richly ornamented with swags and garlands, carved by Grinling Gibbons and his contemporaries, these Protestant buildings were more abstract and less demonstrative than the Catholic churches of the Baroque – no emotionally supercharged altarpieces with gesturing saints. The reredos behind the altar may be a Classical composition incorporating the Ten Commandments; this form of design was adopted for the Ark at Bevis Marks, though with opening doors; the Tablets of the Law are of course shown in Hebrew. The twisted balusters in front of the Ark could easily be altar rails. There is a gallery supported on columns, as in contemporary churches.

Again, we should not wonder at the similarities because many of the craftsmen who made Bevis Marks had worked with Wren and his circle. Avis, who signed the contract and probably supplied the design, was a liveryman of the Merchant Taylors' Company: with Hooke, he was responsible for some of the sumptuous carpentry in the old Merchant Taylors' Hall. Not only had he been employed by Wren on several churches, including St James's, Piccadilly, but several of his team – the plumber John Lingar, the bricklayer John Philips, the smith Thomas Robinson and the paviour James Paget – had similar experience. Some were also Dissenters. The result is a work of sober dignity, resonant with the vibrations of three centuries.

Great Chalfield Manor, Wiltshire

Look at a geological atlas and you will see where the limestone occurs. It crosses England diagonally like a sash: slung over her shoulder at Yorkshire, it slants across Lincolnshire, Gloucestershire and Dorset before trailing into the English Channel around Lyme Regis. It dates from around two hundred and fifty million years ago, when England was not what it is now, but tropical, submerged for the most part beneath a shallow sea punctuated with islands and coral reefs. As the tiny creatures swimming in the sea died, their shells drifted down to the ocean floor, which eventually built up to a depth of many feet. What would become south-west England was covered in a vast, calm lagoon whose water was supersaturated with the mineral calcium carbonate. Tiny circular deposits of it formed around grains of sand – each of which is termed an oolith. After millions of years, these dots fused together into butter-smooth oolitic limestone ... and some of Britain's most beautiful manor houses were the result.

One of them is Great Chalfield Manor in Wiltshire. Silvery, lichen-dusted walls rise behind the irises of a moat, while house martins flit around the rooftops: Great Chalfield probably dates from the 1460s. This was a time of civil war, though the builder, Thomas Tropnell, was not a soldier so much as a lawyer, administrator and rapacious deal maker, described as 'a perillous covetouse man'. There was already a moat on the site and Tropnell built up the curtain walls. Within the enclosure, entered by a gatehouse, he created a luxurious mansion out of stone from a local quarry; it's a kind of Bath stone, grey when in shadow but glowing when touched by the sun, and mottled with pinkish and mulberry-coloured lichens. (Originally, though, the stone would not have been visible since it was almost certainly hidden by plaster.)

Architecturally, little good happened at Great Chalfield between the seventeenth century and the end of the nineteenth. These were years of decline. The house was tenanted and part of it was demolished – a common fate for old manor houses with their small, dark rooms and inconvenient plans, in the Georgian and Victorian periods. A 'fine manorial residence . . . but since its partial demolition a farmhouse': such was Wellbridge House in Thomas Hardy's *Tess of the d'Urbervilles*, and houses like it were a familiar sight.

A change of fortune came with the Arts and Crafts movement. William Morris sang the praises of Kelmscott Manor – his domestic ideal – and owners discovered the romance of their previously neglected manor houses. This was to the taste of the infant *Country Life* magazine, begun in 1897, and the fledgling National Trust, which had been founded two years before; it now owns several manor houses that were restored in the early twentieth century.

The Prince Charming who kissed Great Chalfield awake was Robert Fuller. His father George Fuller, an MP, had bought the estate for its farmland in 1878; it seems that George contemplated demolishing more of the house, such was its poor state. Instead, Robert, who had trained as an electrical engineer and was now managing the Avon Rubber works in Melksham, satisfying the craze of the Edwardian age for motoring and golf by making tyres and golf balls, spotted Great Chalfield when he was out fishing. He persuaded his father to let him restore it. The architect chosen for this project was the scholarly Sir Harold Brakspear. They began a detailed correspondence, as the demolished east wing was slowly rebuilt. Rooms were recreated, after old drawings where possible, as they were thought to have been in the Middle Ages. Eight years after the project began, Fuller married; the pace of work picked up, as the Fullers were anxious to move into their home. This was not achieved without friction, and another architect, C.H. Biddulph-Pinchard, was employed to restore the little church in front of the house.

In more recent years, the Arts and Crafts garden, grassed over in the 1960s, has been revived and developed, with romantic plantings. For one of the joys of manor houses is that they are not too big to live in today. Although given to the National Trust in 1943, Great Chalfield is still occupied and gardened *con amore* by members of the donor family.

Cricket at Wormsley Park

Regrets? I would like to have been better at cricket. Whatever the state of the upper echelons, cricket is still – to me at least – hypnotically entrancing at village level, as one drowsy over succeeds another. I would mourn the loss of any beautiful cricket ground, and as I do not even understand the off-side rule (oh no, that may be another game), what is true of me must be so of many others. I am prepared to bet that the loveliest of all grounds is that at Sir Paul Getty's Wormsley Park. Like the music of Mozart, it affords earth-bound humanity a glimpse of heaven.

Sir Paul was, in one respect, like me: he did not actually play cricket. For this he had the excuse of being American by birth; but he loved the game, just as he loved many other things about Britain. Drugs, alcohol, the capture of his then sixteen-year-old son John Paul III by the mafia, who cut off an ear before they released him – Sir Paul's early life had spiralled into chaos. He took refuge in the world of antiquarian books, assembling the great library that is now housed in its own building at Wormsley; listing his occupation in *Who's Who* as philanthropist, he showered generosity onto the parched landscape of the arts, transforming the National Gallery and giving the Lord's Cricket

Ground a new stand; and Wormsley became an Elysium. As the backdrop to a cricket ground it is nothing less than transcendental. A four-acre lake was created – not an easy achievement in the bone-dry Chilterns, and only possible after sinking a bore hole several hundred feet deep. A deer park was stocked with red and fallow deer. Eight miles of private road were remade, entered through a set of splendid gates brought from Ireland. Sarsen stones – those mysterious outcrops that heave themselves out of chalk landscapes – were hauled from the Wiltshire Downs and used to make a bridge, some of the library's footings and markers for roads and paths. Woods of ash, beech, wild cherry and oak were planted. The cricket ground was the crowning glory.

Getty had been introduced to cricket in the 1960s by his neighbour in Cheyne Walk, Mick Jagger; as they drank tea together, Getty became fascinated by his devotion to the Test Matches being shown on television. It was another friend, the cricket commentator Brian Johnston, who persuaded him, when he had bought Wormsley, to make a pitch. No half-measures were taken in doing so: Getty commissioned the groundsman of The Oval, Harry Brind, to lay the square and create Test Match conditions. It is overlooked by a pavilion roofed in thatch. At the opening of the ground in 1992 Bob Wyatt, who with forty caps had been England captain, rang the bell; and Fred Trueman, the legend of sixty-seven England caps, raised the Wormsley flag. H.M. the Queen Mother and the then Prime Minister Sir John Major watched the Sir Paul Getty XI play the MCC.

The tradition continues, with the Sir Paul Getty XI playing host to the Eton Ramblers, the Arabs and I Zingari. In this ideal setting, surrounded by the Chilterns' beechwoods, this national game – whichever teams are playing – aspires to the aesthetic status of ballet.

The Heaven Room,
Burghley House

The Heaven Room at Burghley House is well named; it is in all senses heaven, an impression not diminished by the presence, in the middle of the floor, of what is certainly one of the biggest silver wine coolers in the world, made by a Huguenot silversmith, Philip Rollos, in 1710 – think of the number of bottles to which it has played host over the years. The name, however, derives from the ceiling decoration by Antonio Verrio, and surely his masterpiece. It shows a banquet of the gods on Mount Olympus, attended by the creatures of the Zodiac, all making merry at the sight of Venus (some have suggested she is a portrait of the 5th Countess) being caught by her angry husband Vulcan as she makes love to Mars. They had a cruel sense of humour, those gods.

Verrio was a scallywag. Coming from either Lecce or Naples in southern Italy, he appears to have abandoned his wife and children on going to France, where he became known for good living and lechery. A companion wrote an epigram describing how this painter of grapes and beautiful women liked to satisfy his appetites on both sorts of model (it is pithier but ruder in the original

French). The account of expenses that were paid to him at Burghley includes claret, Canary wine, port, brandy and *'saussissons de boullogne* [sic]'. He seems to have been on excellent terms with his employer, the 5th Earl of Exeter, although the latter called him at one point an 'impudent dogg'. Less cordial, by repute, were his relations with the Burghley housekeeper, who had difficulty keeping her female staff out of his clutches (he immortalised her satirically on the ceiling next door as a Diana of Ephesus with many breasts). If, according to a nineteenth-century guidebook of Burghley, the deities on the ceiling were shown 'disporting themselves as Gods and Goddesses are wont to do', Verrio's behaviour ran equally true to form.

He came to Burghley in 1686 and spent a decade on the ceilings of what came to be known, obscurely, as the George Rooms. There were six of them – the State Dressing Room, Jewel Closet, Drawing Room, Great Drawing Room, State Dining Room and (as the Heaven Room was then known) the Saloon. The work coincided with the abdication of James II in favour of William of Orange, married to James's daughter Mary; this deprived Verrio of the court position to which he had been appointed by Charles II. While working at Burghley he took time out to paint *The Return of the Golden Age* for Exeter's brother-in-law, the 1st Duke of Devonshire, at Chatsworth. Later, he was persuaded to resume royal service and enrich Hampton Court. According to the painter James Thornhill, he was 'paid for the whole Palaces of Windsor and Hampton Court, ceilings, sides, stairs, and back stairs, 8s per foot, which is £3 12-0 per yard, exclusive of gilding'; and 'had wine daily allowed him' – plus, when his eyesight went, a pension of £200 a year and wine for life.

At Burghley, Verrio had a cosmopolitan patron. Exeter and his wife, Anne, had travelled several times to Italy, where they bought works of art. As well as Verrio, they assembled a galaxy of European talent to improve their house – built in the sixteenth century – of whom Grinling Gibbons was one of the few Englishmen. The maidenly and puritanical diarist Celia Fiennes could not approve of the nudity she saw in the Heaven Room; to other visitors, though, this vision of gods and goddesses at their ease must have seemed sumptuous, sophisticated and princely – only, Exeter was not a prince, as one might have expected had this commission been carried out on the Continent, but a great nobleman, at a time when artistic patronage in Britain was passing from the hands of the monarch to those of rich subjects.

For all his wealth, Exeter was unable to finish the scheme he had begun. Verrio could only complete the ceiling of the staircase hall, on the theme of Hell; the murals on the wall below had to wait for the brush of Thomas Stothard, who was at work until 1801. Decoratively, some of the Rooms were altered for visits by Queen Victoria. Fortunately for Verrio's work, his scheme embraced not only the ceiling but the walls of the Heaven Room, meaning that it could hardly be changed. And so it remains, exposed flesh and all. In one corner Verrio painted himself – a wigless, bald-headed man holding a sketchbook – into a scene showing one-eyed Cyclops's forge; he is entitled to his somewhat self-satisfied expression.

Prospect Cottage garden, Dungeness

Dungeness is not a promising locale for a garden. Pylons stride out from the Dungeness B nuclear power plant. Across the shingle, a scattered assortment of tarry black shacks, reminiscent of Peggotty's upturned boat in *David Copperfield*, seems to have been washed up. Some, from the 1920s, are made from old railway carriages, going cheap after a railway disaster in 1915 caused railway companies to renew their wooden carriages. On Denge Marsh, vast concrete dishes known as acoustic mirrors – a defence experiment of the 1930s intended to obtain early warning of approaching enemy planes by means of sound – have been abandoned like gigantic pieces of Lego. Yet Nature does have a toehold. Clumps of cabbage-like seakale and blue-flowering viper's bugloss have colonised the shingle. It is the only place where the Sussex Emerald moth is now found. Larks sing overhead and the charms of greenfinches are caught in the gusting breeze. Watch out for bloodsucking medicinal leeches. In 1986, the film director Derek Jarman actually started a garden here.

Jarman's garden at Prospect Cottage is now famous, and rightly so. It is not only an example of horticultural tenacity but a triumph of the human spirit. He had just been diagnosed as HIV positive when he began. Gardening, though, is about the long term, the joy of seeing plans slowly take shape – or developments you don't expect supersede them. To get going on a garden when your own future is uncertain, probably limited, requires unusual determination and self-belief. Jarman displayed both as a filmmaker, writer and gay rights campaigner. His garden was to be not only highly original but poetic. There are no visible fences or boundaries; it stretches for as long as he wanted it to, towards the horizon. Wild flowers, traditional garden plants and exotics are combined to create an apparently natural effect, which can only be achieved through constant weeding, nurture and hope. Pink foxgloves and valerian coexist with orange California poppies, Mediterranean cistus rubs shoulders with the prostrate broom that colonises new shingle ridges.

The first plants Jarman nurtured were hollies, sunk into the shingle in tubs. They would be eaten by rabbits and blackened by easterly winds. But they were tough little bushes; in Jarman's gardening diary *Modern Nature*, he wrote that he had been encouraged by the sight of hollies growing on the Ness. 'Blasted by the winds into frightful shapes, these ancient trees are first mentioned by Leland in his *Itineraries*; there he says "they bat

fowl and kill manye birds".' What Jarman called 'henges' of
unusually large shingles provide a degree of structure and pattern.
In Spring 2020, the Art Fund raised over £3.7 million to secure
the future of Prospect Cottage, which will be run by Creative
Folkestone.

If you can garden on the shingle of Dungeness, you can garden
anywhere – and the English do. Look at that great national glory,
the 'Yellow Book' of the National Gardens Scheme. Every year it
lists not just hundreds but thousands of private gardens – around
three thousand seven hundred at the last count – which open to
the public for charity, owners often greeting their guests with tea
and cake. That's not to mention show-stoppers like the National
Trust's Stourhead, Sissinghurst and Nymans. Gardens are often
haunted by paradise, said Jarman. Prospect Cottage stands for all
the horticultural Edens in bloom across these fair lands.

The Eleanor Cross, Geddington

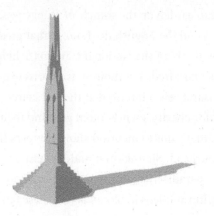

I n the unlikely setting of a Northamptonshire village stands a highly sophisticated Gothic monument, made by the King's own masons in the late thirteenth century. This is a cross to remember Edward I's Queen Eleanor by, and is located, without any further architectural pomp, at a meeting of roads in Geddington. My family and I know it well because we used to have a cottage there; you could see the elegant crown of many crockets rising above the wall of our little garden. I often wondered what the landscape would have been like when the cross was erected: not quite as clod-hopping as one might imagine, because behind the church was a royal 'palace' – in reality a wooden hunting lodge, now represented only by some bumps in the surface of the churchyard. Still, the cross would have soared above the low thatched roofs of the medieval village and astounded the local population. That it survives today seems no less remarkable.

Is it too much to say that this exceptional piece of architecture commemorates a love story? For a royal couple, Queen Eleanor and her husband enjoyed unusually good relations. She often went with him on his travels. On pilgrimage to the Holy Land in 1270, she is supposed to have sucked the venom from a wound that an assassin had made in his arm. And Edward, having hurried back from his campaign against the Scots, was with her when she died at Harby in Nottinghamshire on 28 November 1290. Once her body had been embalmed at Lincoln, it was carried in stages to London; Edward himself led the procession as the chief mourner.

The cortege made slow progress, following a route dictated by the royal houses and monasteries where the King could spend the night. The journey lasted a fortnight. Later, at each stopping place Edward erected an elaborate stone cross. The idea may have been inspired by a French precedent: after the death of Louis IX on crusade in 1270, his bones (the flesh had been boiled off them, the heart and intestines removed) were returned to Paris and carried in procession to the basilica of Saint-Denis. *Flèche*-like crosses called *montjoies* were erected wherever the pall stopped, as part of what would be a successful bid to have the King canonised as St Louis. King Edward erected a dozen Eleanor crosses altogether, the last being at Charing Cross in London (whose name is sometimes incorrectly said to derive from *chère reine*). Only three of the originals now survive, at Hardingstone on the edge of Northampton, at Waltham Cross in Hertfordshire, and at Geddington. Of these, the first two have been heavily restored, but the Geddington cross remains, apart from the weathering of seven centuries, as the King's masons left it.

Actually, Geddington had one of the simplest of the crosses. Tall and slender, it superficially resembles the *montjoies* of Louis IX; but the latter, now destroyed, were more basic structures. The main part of the Eleanor Cross at Geddington is triangular, rising to three niches each of which contains a veiled statue of the Queen behind a column. But it stands on a hexagonal base and rises to a hexagonal upper stage, decorated with crockets and originally surmounted by a cross. Not only is the geometry complex, but the sides of the structure are latticed with ornament in shallow relief, comparable to that on the walls of Westminster Abbey. The effect of such embellishments is to give this substantial stone monument the appearance of a jewel-encrusted reliquary. Unlike Louis IX, Queen Eleanor did not become a saint, but the survival of her cross at Geddington does feel like a species of miracle.

Ranscombe Farm, Kent

The corncockle is all but extinct in the wild. A tall plant whose amethyst-coloured flowers once sparkled like jewels on the golden surface of a wheat field, it has been so reduced in numbers that there is only one place where it can be seen, year after year: Ranscombe Farm, a nature reserve overlooking the River Medway in north Kent.

Why is corncockle so threatened? Because farmers hated it with a passion; its big, heavy seeds were difficult to separate from wheat by winnowing and would spoil the flour. Improvements to herbicides in the twentieth century allowed them to eliminate it. And yet its history is so inextricably linked with the crops amid which it has been growing since humans first began to plough that its seed will only germinate in recently disturbed soil. So it has become the very rarest of all Britain's wild flowers. But Kitchen Field at Ranscombe is ploughed every year by the wild-flower charity Plantlife, founded by a group of botanists in 1989, specially for corncockle.

You find not only corncockle at Ranscombe Farm. In May and June, its fields are speckled with as much colour as an Impressionist painting. There are banks of pink opium poppies (the same species that heroin is made from in warmer climes, they have been growing harmlessly in Britain since the Bronze Age). Other species include maids of Kent and the beguiling 'man' orchid (so-called from clusters of flowers which look like primitive persons). How glorious but how rare the sight is – and a reminder of how far wild flowers have declined. 'When I searched the hungry chalk bank below Wade's Wood for wild strawberries,' the garden writer Tony Venison remembered of his 1930s childhood, 'I knew I would find blue milkwort, wild yellow rockroses, close carpets of thyme, mats of vivid yellow vetch we called miller's thumb, and, here and there, harebells in the chalkiest places.' He was unaware that he was studying an ecological habitat that would soon vanish in the name of agricultural efficiency.

Now even the common wild flowers that used to add colour to lanes and hedgerows are in retreat. Fewer campions, fewer violets, fewer speedwells, fewer orchids. Many wild-flower meadows have been made from seed mixes in recent years, and they are all to the good. They cannot, however, quite replace the particularly British joy of seeing blooms appearing spontaneously: as Rupert Brooke put it when comparing the charm of Grantchester to the regimentation of the German countryside: 'Unkempt about those hedges blows/ An English unofficial rose.'

The blame is not all down to farming. Whole swathes of Britain have been put under concrete in recent decades; woodlands have been sacrificed to development, or poorly managed. Exhaust fumes from road vehicles contribute to the nitrogen already present in the atmosphere from other sources; it makes the soil of verges too rich for delicate wild flowers, which generally thrive on starved land. Ranscombe's chalky, flint-ridden soil – it would strike misery into the heart of an East Anglian barley baron – is low on nutrients. This is exactly the sort of habitat which thrifty wild-flower species need.

Consequently, botanising clergymen were able to identify previously known species here in the seventeenth and eighteenth centuries: meadow clary, with its spike of blue flowers (1699), and the rough or hairy mallow, a charming, low-growing plant with large pink flowers (1792). This history makes Ranscombe doubly exceptional . . . and yet it is with a shade of reluctance that I award it Crown Jewel status. It's not that readers have probably never heard of it: they would still mourn its passing if it disappeared. But wild flowers ought not to be confined to the equivalent of zoos. They should be everywhere in the countryside. Is Ranscombe a last redoubt – or the first bridgehead in a campaign of recolonisation? Let us hope it is the latter. The fight-back starts here.*

---

* Full disclosure: I'm a trustee of Plantlife.

The Fitzwilliam Museum, Cambridge

Is the Fitzwilliam Museum the most beautiful art gallery and museum in Britain? I think so. It stands as a reminder that cultural life need not, as is so often the case with bigger institutions, depend on the state. The Fitzwilliam was born out of the exceptional collecting passions of its founder Richard, 7th Viscount Fitzwilliam, and grew, under the benign eye of Cambridge University, as other collections were given to it in the course of the nineteenth and twentieth centuries. The story is not so different, except in the variety and quality of the objects, from that of other provincial museums that reflect the enlightened interests of local industrialists and other benefactors. Many of them, alas, have struggled to maintain their services, due to the parsimony of their funding authorities – often local councils. With its different funding structure and genius for attracting support from many quarters, the Fitzwilliam is in good heart. Recently the polychromatic decoration of the entrance hall was restored; the pineapples on the flamboyantly spiked railings outside the museum have been regilded. The Friends of the Fitzwilliam, founded in 1909, is the oldest society of its kind.

The Fitzwilliam may not be as old as the Ashmolean Museum in Oxford: opened in 1683, the Ashmolean is the oldest museum in the country, incorporating the Ark that the gardener John Tradescant had created in Lambeth in the early 1600s – armour, stuffed animals, shells, cups made of rhinoceros horn, Henry VIII's stirrups, the costume worn by Henrietta Maria's dwarf during court masks, what was reputed to be a phoenix's wing, were among the curiosities to be found there. Fitzwilliam's tastes were more aristocratic and his founding bequest to the university comprised printed books, illuminated manuscripts, pictures, drawings and engravings: in fact, ten thousand printed books, one hundred and forty-four paintings – including works by Titian, Veronese and Palma Vecchio – and one hundred and thirty medieval manuscripts and many music manuscripts. Some of these works were inherited.

Fitzwilliam's own focus was musical antiquarianism. Having attended Cambridge in the 1760s, he had left his harpsichord with the poet Thomas Gray, then a professor, and set off to study composition in Paris. From there he travelled widely, collecting scores by Domenico Scarlatti and other seventeenth- and eighteenth-century composers. But he would return to Paris, where one clue as to his otherwise mysterious personal life can be found in an inscription in an almanac for 1784: 'Lord Fitzwilliam aime Zacharie.' Which was answered by: 'Zacharie aime Lord Fitzwilliam plus qu'elle Même.' Mlle Zacharie (Anne Bernard) was a dancer at the Opéra, who bore him three children. Among the treasures that Fitzwilliam left to the university were autographed music by Purcell and Handel and the Fitzwilliam Virginal Book, which constitutes the most important contemporary collection of sixteenth- and seventeenth-century keyboard music in existence.

Fitzwilliam died in 1816. Twenty years later, dividends from investments he had left accrued to the point that the syndics of the Museum could contemplate a new building, on a site carved out of the Peterhouse deer park. George Basevi won the competition and produced a rich but relatively chaste design. After his death from falling off scaffolding at Ely Cathedral, his work was completed, in a richer vein of neo-Classicism, by C.R. Cockerell: he designed the railings, and an oculus over the entrance hall surrounded by caryatids. Although the building opened in 1848, the decoration of the entrance hall was not completed until the 1870s, in a scheme of opulent colour and gilding by E.M. Barry. Thus the museum presents in its own building a history of neo-Classical taste in the early Victorian period.

Other benefactors followed Fitzwilliam, of whom the greatest was Charles Brinsley Marlay at the start of the twentieth century. This was the beginning of a golden age for the museum, which saw its superb paintings displayed sumptuously above furniture, rugs and other objects. 'I found [the museum] a pigsty,' declared its director of twenty-nine years, Sidney Cockerell; 'I turned it into a palace.' His legacy is still felt in the supremely civilised character of the galleries today, which display paintings amid furniture, rugs and objects of decorative art.

As this book has been inspired by a catastrophe in Paris, it is worth reflecting on another disaster inflicted on the patrimony of the French: the French Revolution. Fitzwilliam was alive at the time and able to benefit from the sale of paintings by the Duke of Orléans (Philippe Égalité) in 1791. Fitzwilliam did not succeed in buying the whole collection but Palma Vecchio's *Venus and Cupid*, Titian's *Venus, Cupid and the Lute-Player* and Veronese's *Hermes, Herse and Aglauros* are now among the greatest masterpieces in the museum. The Orléans sale is said to have strengthened his resolution to found a gallery whose works would never suffer dispersal. Even today The Founder's Collection, as Lord F's bequest is called, may never be lent. This was a stipulation in his will and means you cannot enjoy this glorious museum without going there. Which is no hardship.

History

History is told in places as well as in books. We do not know exactly what happened during the centuries that Maiden Castle was an active settlement: the structure is the only document we have – but it is a compelling one, which excites the imagination even of people who do not know or care much about archaeology. St Michael's Mount, Roman Bath and Hexham Abbey similarly allow us to reach out and touch the past, feeling, perhaps, an electric spark that we may not be able entirely to explain. I have avoided battlefields because they are a minority taste – but come on, fellas, allow me 1066; Battle Abbey is William the Conqueror's thanks offering for having got away with it – you can feel the relief, nearly a millennium later.

There must be a castle, and there is none better than Kenilworth – Simon de Montfort, John of Gaunt and Queen Elizabeth I are a heady mix. The Great Fire of London, remembered in The Monument, dramatically ended the City of London as a medieval entity; and yet the medieval street plan lived on. It brought out both the best and the worst of the seventeenth century. Apsley House still breathes the spirit of Old Nosey, the victor of Waterloo: a man who despised his own troops but husbanded them as a resource (Napoleon was more profligate with human life). The Napoleonic Wars shaped Britain's destiny in the nineteenth century: there would have been no far-flung Empire if she had lost. The Second World War was the defining episode of the twentieth century, the second act of the tragedy that began in 1914. Coventry Cathedral is a symbol of resurrection in more than the religious sense: a nation rekindled the flame of civilisation that had so nearly been extinguished on the battlefields, in the concentration camps and beneath the thousand bomber raids. St Pancras Station and its associated hotel are another story of revival: the great redbrick cliff of Victorian Gothic that rises above the Euston Road was empty for many years. The Eurostar Terminal provides an umbilical connection with continental Europe, with which British history is inextricably linked.

Maiden Castle, Dorset

Maiden Castle, outside Dorchester, is a vast monument covering forty-seven acres: very difficult to fit into a grab-bag or onto a crown. But we have to find room for it. This is the biggest hill fort in the country, if not Europe. Low in silhouette, it has a warty, knobbly profile, resembling, thought Thomas Hardy, 'an enormous many-limbed organism of antediluvian time ... lying lifeless and covered with a thin green cloth'. On a sunny day, Maiden Castle is not quite such a brooding presence as Hardy describes but it is certainly a spectacular landform, which captures the imagination and provokes our sense of mystery. Was that what the original builders intended, thousands of years ago? That is part of the mystery. We do not know.

Around 4000 BC, Neolithic people marked out the site. They

cleared trees from the hilltop and dug two concentric ditches: not, it would seem, as a defensive feature, since the ditches are not continuous, but simply to enclose a space and separate it from the surrounding forest. This space appears to have served as an important focus for a wide area; a large mound called Bank Barrow – which scholars say is unique within the British Isles – was constructed. The enclosure was inhabited for several centuries. This can be seen from the number of flint tools, pottery fragments and skeletons that have been found. Most of the archaeological evidence from this period, however, was grubbed up by farming during the late Middle Ages. Nothing can now be seen of the ditches, which disappeared beneath later earthworks. It seems that Neolithic man deserted the site, only returning, perhaps centuries later, to use it for burials. And so Hardy's giant went to sleep.

It was rudely woken up again during the Iron Age, when what had been an enclosure, defined by ditches, was turned into a hill fort surrounded by ramparts. The transformation began around 450 BC. Bronze Age society had been dominated by powerful individuals, living among small groups; the Iron Age was organised into bigger communities, one of which lived within the bounds of Maiden Castle. A variety of artisans – such as potters, blacksmiths, jewellers – lived among the tribesmen responsible for maintaining the defences. Complex ramparts were developed to bamboozle the enemy. From there, defenders had a superb view of the plain to all sides, on part of which modern Dorchester would be built.

To anyone attacking Maiden Castle, the gently sloping ridge on which the great earthworks were constructed would have been evident enough – although he might have found that the gradient was steeper and went on for longer than he'd anticipated. But he would have had no idea what lay in store on the further side of the ridge, which was artificial and followed by others, separated by deep ditches. The entrance to the site, where the slope of the land was shallowest, was protected by a kind of maze, at any twist of which defenders, hurling pebbles from their slings, could spring out; the attackers could only guess what obstacle was coming next.

When the complex reached its zenith, towards the beginning of the first century BC, Dorset was home to the Durries tribe; judging from its size, Maiden Castle may have been the stronghold of their chieftain. Beyond that, the cloak of mystery descends. It was up to the Roman legionaries who bravely attacked the earthworks in AD 43 or 44 to pierce through it. Under the efficient generalship of the future Emperor Vespasian, they probably attacked the end opposite the main entrance, fought their way over the banks, set fire to some newly built huts and, under the ensuing smoke screen, stormed the ramparts, killing indiscriminately. Once the castle had been subdued, the traumatised survivors were left to bury their dead, along with the food and trinkets that would help them in the next life.

The Romans destroyed some of the earth banks and built Dorchester. In about AD 70 Maiden Castle was abandoned. The giant pulled the cloak of mystery around his shoulders and returned to his slumbers.

St Michael's Mount, Cornwall

Off the coast of Cornwall, a castle straddles the top of a granite rock. You can walk to it across the sands when the sea is out but at high tide the island is cut off from the mainland, accessible only by boat. Obviously, a good defensive position, as well as the sort of place that would have appealed to holy men, wanting to shun the world. And there was indeed a monastery here, to which pilgrims came, paying reverence to St Michael the Archangel, the patron saint of fishermen, who was said to have appeared on the west side of the island to keep some of them from deadly peril. Other miracles were supposed to have taken place in the thirteenth century. This is England's answer to the Mont Saint-Michel, off the Normandy coast – also dedicated to St

Michael. You cannot see it without feeling stirrings of romantic, if not religious, emotion.

More prosaically, the Mount, as locals call it, seems to have entered history for straightforwardly commercial reasons, before either Christianity or castles reached Britain: it was a prehistoric trading centre to which skilfully worked tin was brought from Cornish mines to be sold to foreign merchants. It has been suggested that it was the island of Ictis mentioned by the Greek traveller Posidonius in the first century BC, whose account survives in a later copy by Diodorus: 'during the recess of the tide, the intervening space is left dry, and they carry over abundance of tin to this place in their carts'. By the eighteenth century, the monastery and fort had long been abandoned. Despite the freakish waves that battered violently for more than four hours during the tsunami following the second Lisbon earthquake in 1761, the buildings had been transformed, according to a local antiquary writing the next year, into 'a neat comfortable and secure dwelling house'.

Neat, comfortable and secure? These seem odd words to choose, but contemporary illustrations show that the castle had been rebuilt with Gothic windows, improved towers and fresh battlements – a toy castle, or a get-away in castle dress. The man responsible for this work, Sir John St Aubyn, 3rd Baronet, was a proto-Romantic, who responded to the spirit of the place without abandoning his sense of proportion.

It was another Sir John St Aubyn, the 2nd Baronet of the new creation (his father had been one of the fifteen illegitimate children of the 5th Baronet), who turned the house into something more permanent – and massive. Good on him for employing his cousin, James Piers St Aubyn. Though a cheerless church architect, this St Aubyn created a dwelling fit for a Wagnerian hero – not delicate, somewhat grim, but somewhat thrilling seen from a distance. As so often, what we first interpret as natural, immemorial romance has been amplified by the Victorians. Which only makes places like St Michael's Mount (not that there is anywhere *exactly* like it) all the more precious: they embody layer upon layer of human activity, each of which yields place to the next but without wholly obliterating it; each of them washed by the timeless sea.

Bath

In 1871, the city architect of Bath, Major Charles Edward Davis, was worried about a leak from the King's Bath. Adjacent to the Pump Room, this was the largest of the four public baths in the city, and visitors had been soaking themselves in its hot, malodorous waters since the early Middle Ages. With semicircular recesses in which they could rest, and overlooked by a statue of Bath's mythical founder King Bladud, the architecture was now a mix of periods from the twelfth to the eighteenth century; a drawing of 1675 shows a fanciful pavilion in the centre and a strapwork balcony on which spectators could lean while surveying the men and women below – bathing was still mixed and naked. Victorian Bath was more demure, but failing. While it continued to advertise the curative properties of its waters, good for rheumatism, gout, palsy and general debility, the Georgian heyday was long over. Seaside resorts had captured the summer market, and Bath's winter season was eclipsed by that of newcomers such as Harrogate. The escape of water from the King's Bath, lowering its level, symbolised a wider decline.

To investigate the leak, Davis brought powerful pumps to the site. A mixture of mud, Roman tiles and old building materials was removed to a depth of twenty feet. This revealed the bottom of a Roman bath lined with lead. Work had to stop when the owner of the nearby eighteenth-century Duke of Kingston Bath objected to the loss of water. But Davis returned to the task later in the decade, when Bath Corporation obtained the rights to the water. A builder and his team were employed to tunnel along an ancient drain. Six feet below ground, the drain, partially collapsed, was little more than a yard in height; there was no light down there, and steam from the hot spring got ever more intense as the tunnellers worked their way along it. But they persevered.

Eventually they found that they were progressing in parallel to a large Roman wall. Davis drained the King's Bath, and when he dug through the bottom he found that it was directly above the source of the hot spring, still gushing into the lead-lined reservoir into which Romans had thrown precious offerings to the goddess Sulis Minerva, the native deity – Sulis – having been fused with the Romans' Minerva. The sacred steaming waters that, orange from their burden of minerals, poured from a fissure in the rock came from the only hot spring in Britain. How welcome they must have been to men and women used to warmer climes. Davis had rediscovered the Roman bath that had been lost since its roof collapsed over it in Saxon times.

By the end of the first century AD, the Romans had built the first phase of a large bathing complex, the main part of which being a pool, big enough to swim in, covered by a prodigious vault. Next to the baths was a temple to Sulis Minerva, the podium of which had been identified by an archaeologically minded clerk of works when an old inn that had stood on Stall Street was demolished in the late 1860s. Otherwise, the baths and the temple, which lay far beneath the nineteenth-century streets, had disappeared.

One may wonder how such a total eclipse of these large buildings could have occurred, and the answer partly lies in two destructive events. In 577, the Battle of Dyrham was fought a few miles outside the city: the surviving Romano-Britons who had previously held Bath were driven west and it was seized by some West Saxons. Then, in 1088, Bath suffered again when it was burnt by the Norman bishop Geoffrey of Coutances in a rebellion against King William Rufus. When the antiquary John Leland visited Bath after the Dissolution of the Monasteries, he found that statues and funerary monuments were among the 'divers notable antiquitees' that medieval builders had used instead of stones for the town wall. The magnificent buildings from which these carvings had come had to wait another four centuries before Davis dug out the drain.

Hurray for Davis (although not for his own buildings, which are banausic, or for his attempt to rig the competition to build an extension to the Pump Room in his own favour – naughty). Hurray for Bath! It was a Classical city under the Romans. It became a triumph of Classical town planning during the Georgian period, and yet provides a harmonious setting for the Abbey, built shortly before the Dissolution. It is now a UNESCO World Heritage site. Generally, the last century has not been kind to Britain's towns and cities; those on the Continent so often have a greater sense of self-respect than those in the UK. Hurray again for Bath!

Hexham Abbey,
Northumberland

There are places where only the word numinous will do. Little Gidding in Cambridgeshire is one, but I have saved this big word for another space: Hexham Abbey – more specifically, the crypt. St Wilfrid made it back in the mists of the seventh century AD. The son of a nobleman who lived between monasteries and courts, Wilfrid travelled to Rome several times in the course of his life; on his first pilgrimage, as a young man, he had been hugely impressed by the Holy See – its buildings, its rituals and its relics. He vowed on the spot to become an evangelist. Parts of England remained pagan and when his ship ran aground in the hostile territory of Sussex, he and his companions were forced to fight off the local priesthood, slaying their leader before escaping on the high tide. Made Abbot of Ripon as well as (disputed) Bishop of Northumbria, he began building new churches. In 672, a Saxon queen granted him a large estate at Hexham, where he founded a monastery cum cathedral; it was for this that he constructed the crypt.

This was a time of religious controversy within the Christian Church in England. Hexham Abbey sought to rise above it by evoking the splendours that Wilfrid had seen in Rome. While there, he had acquired – we do not know how – a number of relics. These would be the focus of an intense veneration, heightened by drama. Pilgrims appear to have progressed, via a dark, tortuous corridor, towards the crypt, conceived as a replica of the Holy Sepulchre where Christ had been entombed for three days. When they arrived at the reliquaries, they found a scene of intense colour and decoration, lit by four smoking oil lamps. (Monks would collect the soot to make ink.)

Above all, this was a building of stone. Generally, the Saxons preferred to use wood, particularly in the wild, remote landscapes chosen for abbeys; skilled masons were few. Fortunately for Wilfrid, a supply of cut stone existed close at hand, at Coria, now Corbridge, one of the forts along Hadrian's Wall. Even moving the stones must have been a job; but he and his followers managed it, depositing them in a deep pit they had dug prior to the construction of the Abbey's walls. The origin of the stones is clear: some of them bear carved friezes suggesting that they originally came from high-status buildings, such as the praetorium of the fort's commander. These details were of no interest to Wilfrid, who had them used without regard for their original purpose, sometimes upside down. Two stones in the roof have carved inscriptions, one of them referring to the building of a granary during the rule of Septimius Severus and his sons. At some point during the Saxon period or the Middle Ages, a memorial to the Roman standard-bearer Flavinius, who died sometime in the first century at the age of twenty-five, was used in the foundations to the south transept; young Flavinius is shown on his horse, trampling a crouching barbarian. The stone was discovered and liberated from this indignity in 1881.

The relics have gone from the crypt; it is no longer painted, or lit by oil lamps. But St Wilfrid's spirit is still present. In the choir of the Abbey, it is possible to imagine him sitting on the carved sandstone Frith Stool (Saxon, and conceivably commissioned by Wilfrid); this was the bishop's *cathedra*, or official seat. *Frith* is a Saxon word meaning peace or safety from molestation: from its location near the high altar, it was regarded as a safe place for those seeking sanctuary in the church. An image of Wilfrid, as the fifteenth century imagined him, appears in the paintings of the chancel choir stalls, which constitute another extraordinary survival.

Battle Abbey, Sussex

The Battle of Hastings is the English foundation myth. The Normans came, overthrew the Saxon establishment and imposed their own way of doing things, with a new legal system, a centralised monarchy and a structure of feudal obligations. Generations of schoolchildren were brought up to believe, proudly, that 1066 was the last time England had been success-fully invaded. This ignored other regime changes backed by foreign powers: Henry Tudor, soon to be Henry VII, came with a French mercenary army in 1485 and William of Orange, a Dutchman married to Princess Mary, defeated his father-in-law James II in 1688. It was 1066 that got seared into the public consciousness as the key date of English history: everybody knew what it meant.

The significance of 1066 was not confined to the battle itself. Evidence of the previous Saxon hierarchy, with its wooden buildings, was obliterated. The Normans were skilled stonemasons. They constructed castles from which they could dominate the local population; many of their castles, in well-chosen locations, became the nucleus of later, more splendid structures; Windsor Castle, Warwick Castle and the Tower of London were all begun soon after the Conquest. Although the Normans, descended from Vikings, were ferocious in war, they were also pious. They built cathedrals and churches on a more imposing scale than their predecessors, and no activity could be undertaken without prayers being offered in church – the architecture reinforced their authority. Stone being more durable than wood, many Norman churches are extant, in whole or part, whereas Saxon ones have nearly all disappeared.

There was also a new official language which would eventually, helped by Latin, seep into the vernacular. Baron, beef, chancellor, cloister, conceive, government, matron, mutton, parish, patron, peasant, pork, procession, vicar – these are among the many common words derived from Norman French. This linguistic legacy reflects a new relationship with continental Europe: for the first time since the Roman legions had left in the fifth century, England found itself part of an Empire, centred on what is now part of France; this would have enormous consequences for both trade and warfare over the coming centuries.

Typically, William not only fought a battle near Hastings: he also raised a monument in the shape of Battle Abbey. It was built on the most important feature of the battlefield: the ridge along which the Saxon King Harold had formed his daunting shield wall, defended by axemen wielding two-handed axes. Harold had arrived after a lightning march from Yorkshire, where he had destroyed the army of the Norwegian king, Harold Hardrada, and his own half-brother Tostig, at the Battle of Stamford Bridge. Surprisingly, William had allowed him to occupy a strong position which required his own men to attack uphill. The Normans, however, had the advantage both of more bowmen and of cavalry, their horses brought over in longboats with the rest of the army from France. Harold's men used horses for travel but fought on foot. The battle was a close-run thing. After a good opening for the Saxons, the discipline of Harold's shield wall broke when it seemed that the Normans were in retreat. The Saxons ran downhill after them, but when the Normans turned, the scattered Saxons were cut to pieces. The high altar of Battle Abbey was sited on the spot that Harold died – perhaps, as the Bayeux Tapestry appears to suggest, from an arrow in the eye.

William claimed that the Abbey was built in fulfilment of a vow that he had made to God before the battle. It may also have been a way of populating a relatively empty corner of England which had recently shown itself vulnerable to attack. The location was hardly convenient, lacking an abundant supply of water and so narrow that massive buttresses were needed to prevent the eastern walls slipping down the hill. Since the Dissolution of the Monasteries, all but the west range, now used as a school, has been ruined. But as William the Conqueror intended, it remains one of the Crown Jewels of England.

Kenilworth Castle, Warwickshire

'Though I have kind invitations enough to visit America,' wrote John Ruskin in *Praeterita*, 'I could not, even for a couple of months, live in a country so miserable as to possess no castles.' Visit Kenilworth, and you can see what he meant. It is a castle for aficionados of the genre. There are many, many other English castles, of course – I salute Dr John Goodall for writing a majestic tome on them. I cannot think of another which is so steeped in architecture and story, having been a stronghold of individuals who, in two different eras, challenged the Crown.

At its core, Kenilworth has a Norman keep, its impregnably thick walls splaying out towards the ground as a defence against undermining. Around it, King John had not only thrown a curtain wall, protected by towers, but a big lake – the Great Mere – created by means of a fortified dam. In the thirteenth century, the French knight Simon de Montfort – not content with having married the King's sister – made Kenilworth the centre of his state-within-a-state, from which he led England's other magnates in opposition to Henry III.

Rivalry led to disaster. Although de Montfort defeated Henry at the Battle of Lewes in 1264, he was not savvy enough to prevent the King from forming a new coalition with his barons, who now had no use for a leader who was in danger of eclipsing them. His end came at Evesham, with a small army hemmed into a loop of the river and royalist soldiers in command of the only bridge. To begin with it seemed that the army marching towards de Montfort from the east belonged to his son; then the horror of the predicament dawned when his barber climbed the abbey tower. 'We are all dead men!' he is supposed to have shouted down. Henry had achieved the deception by carrying the banners that he had captured from de Montfort's son, Simon the Younger, who had foolishly allowed his army – a large one – to enjoy the comforts that lay in Kenilworth town rather than bringing his men within the castle walls. They had been surprised as they slept. Simon de Montfort the Elder was killed and his body dismembered. Simon the Younger arrived to see his father's head on a pike. Afterwards, the garrison at Kenilworth Castle was besieged; they replied to the King's messenger, sent to negotiate, by cutting off his hand. The king responded in equally symbolic terms. The sword of state was brought to his tent and the Archbishop of Canterbury arrived to excommunicate the rebels. The latter dressed up a barber in robes to perform a mock excommunication of the besiegers from the battlements. Eventually, however, the defenders fell victim to plague, and surrendered, on the promise of fair treatment, as their food ran out. The siege had lasted nearly nine months. Robert Dudley, Earl of Leicester, did not make de Montfort's mistake; he sought to charm rather than bludgeon Queen Elizabeth – and largely succeeded. Kenilworth was one of the many rewards granted to him, along with his title, in 1564. By now, the castle had been remodelled as a palace by John of Gaunt, the powerful third surviving son of Edward III. When Elizabeth visited Kenilworth for nineteen days in 1575, Dudley repaid his royal patron by transforming the castle into a fairy-tale palace, where no extravagance was too lavish, no ingenuity too contrived, no symbolism too flagrant to enchant her eye.

You do not have to be Sir Walter Scott, who wrote a novel, *Kenilworth*, about it, to be swept up into the romance.

The Monument

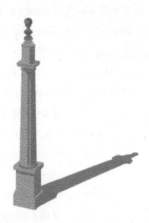

Since this book was inspired by a fire, I could hardly omit The Monument. The name itself is portentous: *The* Monument – as though there were no other. So it must have seemed to inhabitants of the City of London after the Great Fire of 1666, which had been in every way a searing experience; everyone would have known what the gigantic column, envisaged in the Rebuilding Act of 1667 and begun four years later, was meant to commemorate. Its height, two hundred and two feet, was the distance it stands from the outbreak of the Fire in Pudding Lane; when built, it towered above the surrounding streets. Capped with a golden ball of flame, it is now glimpsed between the commercial slabs that surround and overtop it. But it remains an inspiration.

There was a time, The Monument seems to be telling us, when kings and city aldermen cared about the dignity of their city; when they were ready, too, to learn the lessons of history. Who knows when the next catastrophe – financial, environmental, social – will strike, or what form it will take? The sobriety of The Monument's Doric style reminds us of the behaviour best calculated to avert it. This glorious, stately conception belongs to a tradition that stretches back for more than two millennia, to the temples of the Ancient Greeks and the town planning of the Romans. Who can see it, crowded but not subdued by the towers of Mammon, without feeling it gives us something noble to live up to? Who can see the city skyline today and wonder how far we've been equal to the challenge?

When the Great Fire broke out in the early hours of a September morning, London was the biggest metropolis in the world. In the narrow streets, flames leapt from one timber-framed house, roofed in thatch, to another. The ubiquitous Samuel Pepys took a boat to the Palace of Westminster to warn the King, Charles II. The Lord Mayor was overwhelmed. At one point, the King himself, stripped to his shirtsleeves, took personal control of the effort to create firebreaks: householders whose property had stood in the path of the fire had until then been too concerned to preserve their possessions to allow their dwellings to be pulled down. It was too late to save large swathes of the City, two-thirds of which – including eighty-five churches and the old St Paul's Cathedral – were destroyed.

The previous year, the hugger-mugger still-medieval City had been visited by the Plague. It killed nearly a fifth of the population. The Great Fire by contrast may have claimed as few as half a dozen lives (one of the dead being the maid in the house of the King's baker, Thomas Farynor, where it is thought the fire started – she was too frightened to climb to safety over the roof). But the destruction caused to dwelling places as well as to livelihoods – people often lived and worked in the same building – was immense: tents and shacks for those made homeless stretched as far as Highgate.

The Monument, erected to commemorate the disaster, is also a memory of what might have been. Even before the ashes of the Fire had stopped smouldering, the Royal Surveyor Christopher Wren had come forward with a plan for a new city, complete with broad streets, unencumbered access to London Bridge and an open quay along the river. How forward-looking, but how foreign. Not one of the old streets would have been kept under his plan. It was rejected: the King and his advisers wanted the City to be rebuilt quickly, which meant keeping the legal disputes over land-ownership to a minimum. The way to do that was to retain the old crooked and illogical street plan.

The Monument seems to have been principally designed by Robert Hooke, as City Surveyor, whose plans were approved by his friend Wren. Both men were scientists. So this great com-memorative column doubled as a laboratory. Taking advantage of its height, Hooke installed an astronomical telescope and a long pendulum.

The experiments that took place may not have been very successful – but, hey, that's science.

Apsley House, Hyde Park Corner

Apsley House, on Hyde Park Corner in London, is a rare example of an aristocratic town palace, furnished as it was in its heyday during the first half of the nineteenth century. We now have a rather skewed view of architectural history; we have a vivid idea of country-house life, thanks to the National Trust, but it can be a surprise to discover that, until the watershed of the First World War, the place that great families wanted to show off their richest possessions and decoration was in London. When it became impossible to sustain the old way of life, they always chose – unlike their counterparts in France, who would never have surrendered their *hôtels particuliers* in Paris instead of their chateaux – to dispose of their great London houses and regroup in their country houses. Many were demolished. Devonshire

House on Piccadilly was replaced with offices, Dorchester House on Park Lane with the Dorchester Hotel; and so on. Only Spencer House (sumptuously restored as a house museum and event venue in the 1980s), Lancaster House (owned by the government), Home House (opened as a private members' club in 1998) and Apsley House survive as evidence of past splendour. While Spencer House and Lancaster House are grander, Apsley House has greater historical *réclame*, having been the home of the 1st Duke of Wellington.

Wellington bought it in 1817. The victor of Waterloo, he had spent the previous two years as Ambassador in Paris and was now intent on following his military victories with glories on the political stage. He needed a power base and was not shy in advertising the triumphs of his army career. Built originally by Robert Adam for the 2nd Earl of Bathurst (previously Baron Apsley) in 1771–8, Apsley House was enlarged for Wellington by Benjamin Dean Wyatt, who added the giant portico and encased it in Bath stone. Visitors to the palace that emerged could hardly fail to regard the Duke as a natural leader of the country.

Wyatt's new staircase swirls around a giant statue of Napoleon, in the style of a god or athlete, sculpted by Antonio Canova in 1802–6. When Napoleon saw it, he understandably disapproved (the nude figure would take a lot of living up to), and it remained packed away in the Louvre until the British government bought it for Wellington in 1816. Canova sent detailed instructions as to how it should be put up. On the first floor, Wyatt created the Waterloo Gallery, royally decorated in white and gold, to display the Duke's Old Masters. (The yellow damask with which it is hung distressed the Duke's close friend Mrs Arbuthnot who thought it would 'kill the effect of the gilding'.) Many of the paintings came from a collection captured at the Battle of Vitoria in 1813, which was presented to Wellington in gratitude by the King of Spain. Among them are four works by Velázquez, including *The Waterseller of Seville*.

From 1820, Wellington had been holding annual Waterloo Banquets for the surviving officers of the battle; these originally took place in the dining room, which could seat thirty-five people, necessarily restricting the guests to the officers who had actually been there. The Waterloo Gallery, completed in 1830, allowed more space for the banquets, and they became larger and grander. The table was decorated with a Portuguese silver-gilt service, comprising a thousand pieces designed by the court painter in Lisbon, Domingos António de Sequeira. With sphinxes, figures of the continents and military fasces, all in an austerely opulent neo-Classical style, it was presented to Wellington by the Portuguese nation. The side tables groaned with plate, including the sumptuous shield and candelabra designed by Thomas Stothard and made by Benjamin Smith, which were given by the City of London. These pieces are still in the house, along with the Sèvres Egyptian service, designed as a present to Josephine from Napoleon on their divorce; understandably, she rejected it.

In 1828, Wellington succeeded in his ambition of becoming Prime Minister. It was a turbulent time and he became a hate figure for the mob, who broke the windows of Apsley House on two occasions. The iron shutters that were put up to reinforce them are still there.

Coventry Cathedral

Coventry Cathedral is a national symbol of hope. In it, the seeds of civilisation were rescued from the ashes of a man-wrought calamity, and replanted, to bloom in a way that some people at the time may have thought weird and artistically challenging, but which even critics recognised as expressing continuity. Out of the ruins of the medieval arose a new and different building, possessed of its own poetry and redolent of meaning. What was it all about?

On the night of 14 November 1940, the medieval city of Coventry had been hit by a German bombing raid that killed five hundred and sixty-eight people. Incendiary bombs set fire to the cathedral, one of the wonders of Perpendicular Gothic architecture. By the next morning the nave had been reduced to a husk, its burnt-out shell contrasting with the beautiful spire that, as though by a miracle, remained upright. While the Luftwaffe's primary target may have been the industry for which Coventry was famous, the desecration of the cathedral seemed deeply shocking. The local clergy immediately declared their intention to rebuild. When work began fifteen years later, it seemed to encapsulate the national desire for rebirth.

Basil Spence, chosen as architect after a competition and later knighted for his achievement, saw the ruins as an emblem of sacrifice. It was his vision that they should be kept, as a prelude to the light and transparent new structure that he designed to stand next to them. Visitors were invited to follow a spiritual journey, akin to a pilgrimage route or the Stations of the Cross. It took them through the open-air monument that was the ruins – unadorned except for a Charred Cross made of burnt timbers – through an opening made in the old ambulatory wall and into the radiance of the new building, whose liturgically west wall (facing the ruins) is made entirely of glass etched with figures of angels and saints. The openness and light – the very newness – evoke the Resurrection of Easter that follows the Good Friday of suffering.

Even today, when the use of concrete for walls no longer seems fresh, the new cathedral seems bold and modern. There are no columns, no screens, to interrupt the great plain space. And yet, as in any great work of architecture, your experience is controlled by the space and the carefully positioned works of art. There is quite clearly a nave and quite clearly a chancel – none of the worship 'in the round' of Frederick Gibberd's Metropolitan Cathedral of Christ in Liverpool (irreverently christened Paddy's Wigwam), begun in 1962, the year Coventry was finished. The liturgically east end is dominated by Graham Sutherland's gigantic tapestry, descending the full height of the nave, of Christ in Glory, against a background of vivid green. Looking back from the altar, stained glass shines in a series of tall strips shaped like the gills of a fish. These effects are dramatic.

All the most talented artists of their generation were asked to contribute. Jacob Epstein sculpted the bronze figure of St Michael and the Devil on the flank of the building (good stands triumphant, evil languishes in chains); the Baptistry window was designed by John Piper, the bronze eagle on the lectern is by Elizabeth Frink. Often, the small scale of the artworks contrasts with Spence's vast, unadorned envelope, creating a sense of intimacy and humanity. Ralph Beyer, a German-born pupil of Eric Gill, cut or designed most of the lettering in the cathedral, treating each letter individually so as to 'maintain', as he put it, 'a feeling of the *human hand* at work, rather than to aim at the precision of a printing press'; Spence described the effect as having 'the sensitive irregularity of the letter panels in the catacombs' in Rome.

Unusually in post-Second World War Britain, Coventry Cathedral was a building in which even otherwise rather conventional people felt a sense of national pride. Even today, opposite a new university whose students have no memory of the Second World War, its power to move is intense.

St Pancras Station

Walk into St Pancras Station and the spirits lift. In part, this is because of the raw self-confidence of the nineteenth-century complex – the Midland Grand Hotel (now St Pancras Renaissance) rising cliff-like above the ever-moving sea of the Euston Road, the train shed sheltering Midland Mainline passengers beneath its giant canopy of iron and glass. Glorious. But those with long memories know that it was not always like this. For decades, the hotel, latterly offices, had been locked, the station underused, the whole place shabby. But wait! Cinderella did go to the ball. This once doleful train shed shelters the glamour of Eurostar; the hotel was restored as, yes, a hotel, by the groovy Manhattan Loft Corporation. High-speed Javelin trains scythe a path through north London before racing to Stratford International, Ebbsfleet International, Ashford International and Britain's umbilical link to the Continent, the Channel Tunnel (or trundling towards Canterbury and the Isle of Thanet). In the 1970s, train travel was a misery. Today, if you choose your line carefully, it can be bliss. The twenty-first century does get some things right.

Sir Giles Gilbert Scott, the architect of the Midland Grand Hotel – as the front part of St Pancras was originally called – was a Goth, committed to a revival of the best stylistic period (as he saw it) of the Middle Ages. There was something in romantic medievalism for everyone. To opponents of the French Revolution, it meant anti-Enlightenment patriotism. To John Keats, writing 'The Eve of St Agnes', it meant sex. To the promoters of the Midland Railway, who were late in elbowing their way into the capital, it meant a chance to wipe the eye of King's Cross, Euston, and the other grand stations that had got there first. To Scott, it meant work. And he was ubiquitous. You can hardly move a mile through England without encountering him. He built and restored churches by the score; he raised the Albert Memorial, in Hyde Park – to the chagrin of prisoner C.C.3, Reading Gaol, aka Oscar Wilde, who hated it; he fought a battle of the styles over the Foreign Office building on Whitehall (swallowing his pride when he lost). Never a man to warm to, he took on far more work than he could supervise in detail but genuinely loved Gothic architecture: his quest for the natural origins of a certain kind of carved detail literally haunted his dreams. But he loved success in the world even more.

It could hardly be said that no expense was spared on Scott's triumph at St Pancras; shareholders, concerned by rocketing interest rates, wanted to spare expense wherever possible. But however little it may have conformed to modern ideas of luxury – only nine baths, albeit cans of hot water brought, at a price, to bedrooms – the Midland Grand certainly lived up to its name. It was grand.

Behind this lay the engineering marvel of the train shed. With its slightly pointed (Gothic) profile, which has structural advantages over a segmental one, it is the tallest, widest single-span train shed in the country, very nearly in the world. Because the sides are locked into place by girders under the platform, only the superstructure is affected by thermal expansion, the effect being likened by the architectural historian Simon Bradley to 'the shallow breathing of a mighty creature in its sleep'. Respect to the engineer who designed it, William Henry Barlow.

Modernists loved the train shed, deplored Scott's historicism – but that is another battle of the styles which has passed. In the early twenty-first century, both station and hotel were restored – reimagined might be a better word – as the London terminus for Eurostar. A brand-new train shed was created for the super-long trains. With it came shops, eating places, even a champagne bar. A similar transformation has been wrought upon all the London termini except Victoria. It would not have happened under British Rail.

The English Eye

The English have a particular way of seeing. It originates in the eighteenth-century aesthetic of the Picturesque, which produced Stourhead, and morphed, via Ruskin, into another home-grown phenomenon: the Arts and Crafts movement (a child of which was F.L. Griggs at Chipping Campden). We put a high value on Nature, wild or tamed. We create Arcadias, be they around country houses like The Grange in Hampshire or in London square gardens. The cities of the Industrial Revolution were so polluted that we created suburbs – all of which follow an ideal of leafiness whose ineffable expression is Hampstead Garden Suburb. Significant, there, that Garden was part of the name. We are a nation of gardeners, whatever the space available – a balcony or a window box are enough of a canvas to paint some flower picture on. (I once worked with an editor who grew tomato plants in his office, oblivious to the effect of the grow bag on the walnut veneer of the early-eighteenth-century bureau beneath it.) Late Victorian England developed a style of gardening – painterly, bosomy, uncorseted – that remained the image of terrestrial perfection for more than a century. This was our thing.

Allotments are gardening democratised; they have an ethic

and an aesthetic of their own. And it is not only spaces specifically reserved for plants and vegetables that are gardened in England, but whole landscapes; the lace of damson blossom that decorates the Lyth Valley in Westmorland every spring is the result of the conscious actions of farmers, over the generations, in planting and looking after the trees. Do they do this purely for the value of the damson crop? I doubt it.

Where would we be without animals? Zoos are now controversial but London Zoo contains happy memories of childhood visits, or visits with children, for many of us. Note that it is a zoological *garden*. The Arts and Crafts movement originated in England, and if it can be found in a pub like the Black Friar near Blackfriars Bridge in London – that is surely a double whammy.

Chipping Campden, Gloucestershire

For at least the last century, Chipping Campden, in the Cotswolds, has been widely regarded as a paradise on earth. This was certainly the view of the etcher and topographical artist Frederick Landseer Griggs, who came to live there in 1904; he knew, however, that paradise must be defended if it is to remain free of snakes. He sympathetically restored some of the houses on the beautiful High Street; he battled against the ugliness that was plaguing other towns and villages in the early twentieth century; and he used money that he could ill afford to safeguard the surroundings. He also strove to demonstrate the continuing viability of the domestic architecture that he admired from the past by building his own house, out of the scant income he received from his artistic projects. It was a heroic struggle against the world – perhaps an unequal one as regards his own domestic aspirations, but triumphant in respect of the continuing loveliness of Chipping Campden.

The best of Campden – locals drop the Chipping – dates from the seventeenth and eighteenth centuries; in the Jacobean period, the London mercer and moneylender Sir Baptist Hicks built a splendid house of which the banqueting houses survive (the house itself was destroyed in the Civil War). But the charm of the town derives from its streets of less pretentious houses, built of the local stone, from which sundials and hood moulds have occasionally been carved. Griggs first roared into Chipping on his Rex motor tricycle in 1903: an unlikely advent for a man who forever deplored the influence of the internal combustion engine. He was researching subjects for the *Oxford and the Cotswolds* volume of Macmillan's Highways and Byways series, for which he worked for forty years.

Campden was not entirely the sleepy backwater it may have seemed. The year before, C.R. Ashbee had arrived at the head of fifty or so craftsmen belonging to the Guild of Handicraft, previously located in Whitechapel. In Campden, they occupied some of the cottages that the collapse of agriculture had left empty, and took enthusiastically to the joys of rural life, surprising the inhabitants of Campden with Swedish exercises and swimming expeditions, amateur dramatics and marching bands. Griggs had friends among the Guildsmen and made Campden his home. Sometimes gloomy, always dogged, he refused to compromise with the forces that threatened to spoil his adopted town. He insisted that telephone and electricity cables were run underground; that the council would not encroach on Campden's prominent grass verges; and that the horror of red brick, intended for a group of new council houses, was rejected in favour of roughcast and stone quoins. No Art Deco cinema was built. Griggs designed the lanterns by which the streets were lit and the wrought-iron that hung outside shops. Other telephone kiosks might be red: Chipping Campden's was painted grey.

In 1926, he bought Dover's Hill – the glorious natural amphitheatre that, in the seventeenth century, had been the site of the

'Olympicks' organised by the lawyer Robert Dover – when it came up for auction; he had feared it would be developed. This was a matter of acute financial anxiety until a benefactor saved the day. Griggs later raised the money to buy a field called the Coneygree, to prevent despoliation. Both Dover's Hill and the Coneygree were given to the National Trust.

Lucky Campden – but Griggs's neighbours may not have thought so. That refusal to compromise did not always endear him. A squall of controversy was caused by the war memorial, conceived by Griggs as a cross in an architectural setting, next to the famous market hall. Griggs had not fought in the war, having been declared unfit; he was also a Catholic convert. His cross was considered 'Papistical'. As usual, he got his own way. He also got married, a step that prompted the building of New Dover's House, begun in 1927, to serve as both family home and studio. It was an ambitious project and at the time of Griggs's death in 1938, he was hopelessly in debt. This had not spoiled the fun. There were tennis parties, Twelfth Night parties, the painful sewing of tough laurel leaves, threaded with scarlet ribbon, to make wreaths for Christmas; a house always full of people; hearty luncheons, prepared using vegetables from the garden and fruit from the orchard, during which everyone – including the children and the governess – was expected to contribute to the conversational buzz; clouds of tobacco smoke, laughter, pencil-and-paper games, singing, and walks through the fields around the town.

'Could Eden have been lovelier than we *know* England once was?' Griggs once sighed in a letter to a poet friend. Fortunately, thanks to Griggs and people like him, Chipping Campden remains in a largely prelapsarian state.

The Grange, Hampshire

The Grange, about ten miles from Winchester, is a vision of Arcadia. From its plinth, a great Greek Doric portico looks out over golden fields of corn; the scene is all the more evocative for the semi-ruined condition of the house. As the seventeenth-century French master Nicolas Poussin suggested in his painting *Et in Arcadia Ego*, death finds its way even into the serenest landscapes.

This extraordinary house was the creation, principally, of a banker and a Cambridge mathematics don. The banker was Henry Drummond, who inherited the estate at the age of eighteen. A mercurial, many-talented man, he was described by Thomas Carlyle as a combination of 'the saint, the wit, the philosopher' and the dandy (to which he added, in his *Reminiscences*, 'haughty', conceited and possessed by a 'restless inconsistency'). In 1804, having returned from a Grand Tour of Greece and the Mediterranean, he turned to William Wilkins to rebuild the substantial Restoration house on the site. Wilkins was a fellow of Caius College, who had completed his education, like Drummond, with Mediterranean travel. The Greek Revival was now in full bloom and Wilkins was an enthusiast for it – as well as, such was the eclecticism of the time, for Gothic.

Wilkins could sometimes be dry; his National Gallery is too refined to command Trafalgar Square. But The Grange achieved poetry. Here he had the inspiration to add a baseless Greek Doric portico to a building so that it really looked like a temple front; which he did by placing it, not in the middle of a long façade, but occupying the whole width of a short one. The idea may not have been entirely original; Wilkins probably borrowed it from a design made by Robert Mitchell a few years earlier. But Wilkins was the only architect in Europe to make it a reality. It was a sham, made of brick covered in cement, rather than marble as would have been the case in a genuine Greek temple – but it was four storeys tall and in the best spirit of the Picturesque movement: it looked the part, in the landscape. The *Gardeners' Magazine* got the point: 'Situated on a gentle declivity, and sloping towards a fine piece of water . . . embosomed in wood . . . and approached by magnificent avenues, [The Grange] has the effect in the landscape of those ideal scenes which, indulged only in the painters' imagination, are hardly expected to be realised in nature.'

By the date those words were written, 1826, the house was not Wilkins's alone. Drummond had got bored before the house was even finished. In 1817, he rejected the fripperies of the world, sold

The Grange, broke up his hunting establishment and set off for Palestine, becoming a religious crank. The Grange was bought by Alexander, son of Sir Francis Baring, who found Wilkins's building inconvenient and old-fashioned; he turned first to Sir Robert Smirke and then to the great Greek Revivalist C.R. Cockerell to extend the house, to form an L. For the new dining room, Cockerell used the Ionic order from the Temple Apollo Epikourios at Bassae, which he had helped excavate himself.

Since then another phase of Picturesque existence has overtaken the house. Following an attempt by John Baring, 7th Baron Ashburnham, to demolish it – he was stopped by a newspaper campaign – it was reduced to a shell. It now stands as a ruin, like the monuments that Wilkins and Henry Baring had seen on their travels; not, however, a forlorn one. The Grange Park Opera company have converted it into an opera house, staging its first summer festival there in 1998. And so this great building has been reimagined, in the spirit of a stage production – faithful to the original work of art but given a new twist for the twenty-first century.

The London squares

Look down on London from an aeroplane and you will see dense blocks of green between the cityscape of roofs and roads. These are the famous London squares. The proportion of tree cover in London is so high that, although a world city, it meets the definition of a forest.

In 1931, the London Squares Preservation Act identified 461 squares in the British capital. Usually enclosed by tall terraces of houses, they are a particularly English building type, not so much for the shape – other countries have *places*, *piazze* or *Stadtplätze* – as for the centrepiece, which is generally a garden.

Britain's first square was the Duke of Bedford's Covent Garden in London, designed by no less an architect than Inigo Jones in 1631. While this provided a 'Piazza', by the end of the same decade Lincoln's Inn Fields had set a greener course: in the centre was a large garden. Old engravings of Bloomsbury Square, another early one, whose width was determined by the Earl of Southampton's pre-existing house, suggest that the garden element was, in this case, restricted to lawn. But other ideas came with the Picturesque movement. 'Capability' Brown designed some of the square gardens on the Cadogan Estate, in collaboration with his son-in-law, Henry Holland.

By the early nineteenth century, the commentator on French life, Alexander Cavalié Mercer, who had won fame as the commander of G Troop Royal Horse Artillery at the Battle of Waterloo, found that London trounced the French capital in its squares:

> The costly iron railings, the masterly statues that decorate some, and the pleasant shrubberies, smooth, well-kept turf, and well-rolled walks which characterise most of them, are nowhere to be seen in Paris. The Place Louis Quinze is not what we should call a square in London; it is a sort of esplanade.

Ah, the railings. Only keyholders could enter. It has always been a vexed point. To my mind the ne plus ultra of the square was reached with the development of the Ladbroke Estate, first envisaged by Thomas Allasadon in 1821. Before that, this part of Notting Hill was open country, partly colonised by brickmakers, potters and a racecourse. Initially Allason envisaged a huge circus, 500 metres across, at the centre of the estate. As so often happens, a building recession caused the scheme to be redesigned. By the 1840s the circus had been replaced by the Ladbroke Estate's singular idea: sixteen enclosed – or semi-enclosed – garden squares, little more than half a hectare each in most cases. These turned the idea of the conventional square inside out; instead of the square being overlooked by the fronts of the surrounding houses, which were separated from it by a street, the enclosure was formed by the backs of the houses. The green space was directly accessible. Rough sleepers, who have been known to climb over the railings of a conventional square and doss down, with consequent issues of hygiene, cannot get access. Children can run directly from their back doors into the square garden – no need to be helped across roads.

Or as Anne Scott-James, married to the cartoonist Osbert Lancaster who had grown up on the Ladbroke Estate's Elgin Crescent, remarked in her book *The Pleasure Garden*, the arrangement was particularly suitable for children: 'here a mother who had sacked or been given notice by her nursery-maid could deposit her children and continue her own life in the house'. That was written in the 1970s when nursery-maids were fewer on the ground than in the Victorian period, when the squares were built. Already the pace of modern life was taking its toll of communal life, reducing the square to 'little more than a dog walk, where owners with trousers pulled over pyjamas or a tweed coat pulled over a nightdress, led their dogs for five minutes before breakfast.' The image still has a sort of charm.

Not all enclosed garden squares are the preserve of the affluent middle classes. Penrhyn Street, near King's Cross Station in London, has a communal garden running along the back of its houses, probably created after the Second World War: Camden council, which owned Penrhyn Street and the parallel Charrington Street, knocked all the small gardens into one shared space; the resulting squares have proved very popular with residents. Time for a revival?

Port Sunlight, Cheshire

Victorian industrialism had a conscience. Often it was Nonconformist in religion and posed itself the question of how industrial methods of production could co-exist with a decent standard of life for the workforce. In 1851, the mill owner Titus Salt had moved his operation from Bradford to the countryside, building a model factory and village to which he gave a Congregational church, a Sunday school, club, infirmary, park and other amenities. In the same spirit, the Quaker chocolate-making Cadbury brothers moved their business from Birmingham to rural Bournville, with a recreation ground, swimming pool, dining rooms and semi-detached houses; Bournville flourished, and the Cadburys bought farmland around it to protect it from encroachment by Birmingham. So when in 1890, William Hesketh Lever, the future Lord Leverhulme, created a new soap works and model village beside the Mersey, Port Sunlight, he was not the first to put into practice the belief that happy workers were productive workers; but he added a new ingredient to the mix, in the form of art.

With his bottomless energy, reforming conscience, profound civic sense and commitment to fresh air and exercise, Leverhulme, born in 1851, was a great Victorian. His guiding lights were the

Congregational church and Samuel Smiles's manual for pulling yourself up by your bootstraps, *Self-Help* (1859). He could also look forward. He had a genius for marketing; having identified a new way of making soap, from vegetable oil rather than tallow, he called it Sunlight, wrapped it in eye-catching packaging and advertised hard. His Sunlight soap would, it was claimed, wash clothes by itself, and keep housewives looking young at the same time. Art was conscripted in aid of the cause. Sir John Millais was not unduly put out when his painting *Bubbles* was used to promote Pears' soap, but W.P. Frith caused a controversy by objecting to his Royal Academy painting *The New Frock*, in which a girl holds up a white pinafore, appearing under the title *So Clean* in another Lever advertisement.

The Lady Lever Art Gallery at Port Sunlight was begun in 1914 and opened in 1922. Ever since buying a pair of Derby porcelain figures as a young man, Leverhulme had been an unstoppable collector, amassing an ever burgeoning quantity of paintings, furniture and porcelain, and his country house at the village of Thornton Hough, despite existing in an almost permanent state of remodelling, was full to bursting; most of it was put on public display for the benefit of his workers. The profits of industry could, Leverhulme believed, build a better world.

The collection contains Wedgwood jasperware, superb French furniture and late-nineteenth-century paintings – many pre-Raphaelites, a bravura Sargent of a boy fishing, and a few less familiar masterpieces like *Salem*, a picture of a Welsh chapel painted by Sydney Curnow Vosper in 1908. An outlier is Élisabeth Vigée-Lebrun's portrait of Nelson's mistress Emma Hamilton as a *bacchante*: its inclusion can be explained by the fact that Emma was born nearby at Ness.

Although Lever Brothers exported its products to a hundred and thirty-four countries and built its success on soap made with palm oil, to obtain which Lever acquired plantations in Sierra Leone and Nigeria, the architecture of Port Sunlight was solidly, almost programmatically English in style. This was equally, if not more, true of Thornton Hough. Leverhulme's son William, the 2nd Viscount, remembered it as having been picturesque in its pre-Leverhulme incarnation. But the thatched roofs and whitewashed walls hid damp, dark and unhealthy interiors. 'In fact, the more picturesque the exterior of the cottage, the more impossible did the internal arrangements appear to be, and Lever saw that complete demolition was the only remedy,' William wrote in 1927. Not all the villagers were happy about this – even unwholesome houses can contain memories – but he persuaded them (did they have an option?) that rebuilding was necessary.

Cottages sprang up, each with three to five bedrooms. Then came blocks of houses in a solid, tough, serviceable style, mixing red brick and curly gables and black-and-white and sandstone – not quite pretty but, as you might say, full of Vim (another Lever Brothers brand). The land in front of the parish church was left as a green for football, cricket, tennis, bowling and quoits. Lever's old friend Jonathan Simpson designed a school, his son J.L. Simpson a new Congregational church. The old smithy that was demolished to make way for the church was replaced with one next to – as any smithy should be – a spreading chestnut tree. A Liberal Club, reflecting Lever's own politics, was provided for social events. After the First World War, 'with the altered spirit of the times', its name was changed to the Village Club: the benevolent despot felt he had to back off.

Stourhead, Wiltshire

Stourhead is surely the most beautiful of all landscape parks. The estate was bought by Henry Hoare – Good Henry, as he is known, for his philanthropy – in 1717; it was his son, another Henry in this banking dynasty, many of whom shared the same name, who made the garden. As a young man, this Henry had lived a fashionably dissolute existence but acquired the sobriquet of The Magnificent on account of his art collecting and patronage. Well travelled and well read, he became devoted to his family. In 1743 his second wife died, leaving him with a thirteen-year-old son and two younger daughters. Hoare never remarried; the year after, he began the landscape garden which occupied him for the remainder of his life, becoming a tour de force of the Picturesque movement.

In the eighteenth century, Picturesque meant literally 'like a picture'. Hitherto, the object of gardening had been to create a sense of order based on geometry: man demonstrated his power over Nature by taming it. But a number of English architects and writers began to formulate a different approach. Vanbrugh argued that the Duchess of Marlborough should preserve Old Woodstock Manor because it stirred the imagination. The essayist Joseph

Addison objected to trees being clipped into artificial topiary shapes, wanting them to grow freely. The poet Alexander Pope extolled the *genius loci*, or spirit of the place, which 'Paints as you plant, and as you work, Designs'. His choice of words prefigures the desire of gentlemen returning from a Grand Tour wishing to recreate the landscapes they had seen around Rome – or to be more exact, that they had acquired in the form of paintings by, for instance, Claude Lorrain and Gaspard Dughet. Hoare was in this camp. He owned two large paintings by Dughet, and took them as the yardstick for his own landscape-making. 'The view of the bridge, village and church altogether will be a charming Gaspard picture at that end of the water,' he wrote. The course that visitors took around his lake, formed by damming the local river, was strictly controlled to provide a series of views of buildings that Hoare had constructed to make the landscape more suggestive. Prodigious amounts of digging and earth-moving were necessary to achieve his ideal.

Like paintings, Hoare's views were intended to inspire uplifting thoughts, whether about the natural qualities of the spot (a grotto invokes water deities), about the Classical world (the Temple of Flora, the Temple of Apollo, the Pantheon), about British patriotism (Alfred's Tower celebrates the king who saved England from invasion); or about the nation's mercantile prosperity (Bristol's medieval High Cross was brought here in 1764). Thoughts of the ascetic life were aroused by the presence of a hermit, employed to haunt if not actually inhabit the Grotto or Hermit's Cave (he had another dwelling nearby); like other hermits employed by gentlemen, the burden of solitude proved too much for him and he was dismissed for drinking. There was another theme. It seems that after the death of his son at the age of twenty-one – 'a grief I ne'er expected nor wished to have survived' – Hoare turned to Virgil's *Aeneid*, a poem of loss, grief and fortitude.

Before beginning his garden, he had known several leaders of Picturesque taste through their accounts at his bank: their borrowings, which mounted as their works evolved, contributed to his profits. Hoare, by contrast, never neglected the source of the family business that was the source of his wealth. It has been suggested that the inclusion of native icons, such as Alfred's Tower and the Bristol High Cross, reflected his fears for the welfare of the nation as a whole, which proved all too justified when the American colonies were lost. He set up an endowment for Stourhead, which was inherited by his grandson Richard Colt Hoare.

What's this? Alterations. Richard planted some of the first species of rhododendron to come into the country. They make a spectacular show but it is hardly Virgil. Virgil might have reflected that, like all earthly things, gardens change. They have to.

Hampstead Garden Suburb

Buds are opening. The sun is finding its way down hedge-lined alleyways (or 'twittens', as they call them around here) and through wooden garden gates. Children play on village greens, while dormer windows are thrown open to the soft air. Spring has come to London NW11. Hampstead Garden Suburb opens an eye and realises it's time to get up. It is a child of the Heath, located on the rim of the North Circular Road, yet belongs to an older, village England, half-remembering the fields out of which it was created, where Queen Anne joins hands, architecturally, with the Arts and Crafts movement, a place of high ideals, now reserved for higher incomes. Where did development go wrong? Hampstead Garden Suburb showed how it should be done over a century ago, but the volume housebuilders have yet to learn the lesson.

HGS knows it is special. Special people live here. Showbiz rubs shoulders with the King of Greece. Although almost pluto-cratically comfortable (businessmen and financiers flock like starlings), the Suburb lists to the Left, freighted with more liberal-minded intellectuals than you could shake a Hampstead Heath stick at. The fact that over a third of the electoral ward is Jewish may have something to do with it.

The Garden Suburb stands in a tradition of model housing projects that goes back to Titus Salt, who built Saltaire in Yorkshire in the 1850s. Working in the slums of the East End, Canon Samuel Barnett and his wife Henrietta had been evolving similar ideas; probably talking them over in the house they had acquired above Hampstead Heath – a refuge both for themselves and for many of their parishioners. They imagined a community based on the neighbourliness of the English village or market town. The impetus to take it forward came in 1896, when a Northern Line Tube station was proposed for Golders Green. The Barnetts foresaw that the Underground would trail bricks and mortar in its wake, despoiling what was then still farmland, north of the Heath. Henrietta, having previously worked with the social reformer Octavia Hill, co-founder of the National Trust and a champion of the Commons Registration movement, set about preserving a northward extension of the heath. These eight acres of open ground would become the lung of a 'garden suburb for all classes', to be built on the surrounding land. If north Hampstead had to be developed, she would see that it was developed properly.

Part of the land in question was owned by Eton College. But Eton would not deal with a woman, and so Henrietta put together a syndicate which included two earls and a bishop. Raymond Unwin, one of the architects of Ebenezer Howard's Letchworth Garden City, was commissioned to draw plans. 'We desire to do something to meet the housing problem, by putting within the reach of working people the opportunity of taking a cottage with a garden within a 2d fare of Central London, and at a moderate rent,' announced the Hampstead Garden Suburb Committee in 1905. Since philanthropy has to be paid for, room was also found for 'wealthy persons' who could pay good money for their homes. 'We have met together to make a bit of God's earth beautiful for generations ahead,' Barnett told a rapturous audience when the first sod was turned in 1907.

A picture gallery, a bandstand, refreshment rooms, ponds for paddling and sailing, barns for tools, and tenements for the old – such facilities, marked on the map that Unwin drew for the new settlement, show the utopianism of the enterprise. Houses were placed so that none could spoil the outlook of any other. Plots were divided by hedges and trellis, rather than walls. Old trees were preserved, along with the whole of two woods – Big Wood and Little Wood. Waterlow Court, a quadrangle designed by M.H. Baillie Scott in 1909, demonstrates the progressive spirit of the project. It was conceived as an answer to the problem of single working women who were too hard up to keep house – which in the Edwardian age meant employing servants – for themselves; they could enjoy a communal dining room and lounges, as well as a lawn enclosed by a cloister.

One of Henrietta's associates was the brilliant sportsman, lawyer and politician Alfred Lyttelton, a patron of Edwin Lutyens. In 1909 Barnett commissioned Lutyens to build two churches on Hampstead Garden Suburb's Central Square. St Jude's, for Church of England congregations, was named after Canon Barnett's church in the East End. The Free Church provided a shared spiritual home for other denominations. Flushed with his rediscovery of the formal values of the Wrenaissance (as Lutyens referred to the English Renaissance of Sir Christopher Wren), the architect proposed two monumental designs, one with an immense, though not wholly Gothic spire, the other domed. Barnett wanted something more homely. 'A nice woman', was how Lutyens described her to his wife, 'but proud of being a philistine – has no idea much beyond a window box full of geraniums, calceolarias and lobelias, over which you can see a goose on a green.'

HGS has changed socially from what the Barnetts planned for it. As with other desirable villages and neighbourhoods across Britain, rising property prices mean that homes intended for Edwardian artisans are occupied by twenty-first-century professionals. Children still play on greens and in the woods, and go to schools; but the Institute, intended to provide self-improvement for adults – 'to help the poor out of poverty by education', as Henrietta put it; Canon Barnett had previously founded Toynbee Hall – has left the Lutyens building, which is now a grammar school to which children come from all over the borough, not just from the Suburb.

But the private realm continues to nourish its inhabitants, and to be nourished by them in return – under the strict eye of the Hampstead Garden Suburb Trust. To a unique degree, the Garden Suburb's identity has survived the banality of the twentieth century and the gigantism of the present age. You cannot alter or enlarge the original houses; as a consequence, some very rich individuals must be content to live in spaces designed for a less expansive age. And they are content, willing to forgo their own potential house extensions in the knowledge that all must abide by the same rules: thus the charm of HGS survives as a common good. Nowhere else in Britain, in planning terms, is so strictly policed. Many places could learn from it.

Allotments

I am going against the rules with this one. Nearly all the other entries in this book are about specific places; this is a generic. How could it be otherwise? Allotments are a glorious and specially British thing; but you could not choose one over others. That is not the point of them. They are a delightful expression of some deep-seated British attitudes. Of self-reliance. Of idiosyncrasy. Of the desire to grow things. There they are, seen from the train window perhaps, on the edge of towns and villages, distinguished from neighbouring, horticulturally more prissy gardens by their makeshift quality, polytunnels patched with old plastic sacks, an ex-living-room sofa that now spends its days in the open air; strings threaded with shiny CDs to scare the birds away. Each plot, in the mind of the person gardening it, is an island. Here a neat wigwam of runner beans, next to it a bosomy bed of big-blooming dahlias. There is no design rationale, just (in some cases) a competitive urge to grow the biggest marrow, or escape the wife. One friend with a glut of carrots from his allotment juiced so many that he turned orange.

Allotment-keeping suits England. Always has. Although Sweden, for example, has a similar system – plots of kitchen garden that can be rented at a modest price – the English were at it first. It was the French Revolution that sparked the idea. With farm labourers in a sorry plight, landowners, noticing the fate meted out to their kind on the other side of the Channel, wanted to support social order. Yet they had no desire to increase the cost of poor relief, which they had to pay for. One solution that was eagerly canvassed in some quarters was the allotment. The agriculturalist Arthur Young, secretary to the Board of Agriculture, believed that the government should turn the wastes, or commons – scrub and open land on which villagers had previously grazed animals – into smallholdings. As a temporary measure, farmers allowed their workers to grow potatoes on fallow land, which relieved some of the worst distress. Evangelicals thought allotments would help keep labourers out of the pub.

Step forward the Rev. George Henry Law. He gave Willingham, in Cambridge, the village of which he was rector, allotments in 1806. When he became Bishop of Bath and Wells eighteen years later, he took the allotment idea to the West Country. The result, according to one description, was 'a terrestrial paradise'. Hundreds of families 'would be almost in a state of starvation without the land'. These days, allotments still put food on the table, although it may take the shape of yacon, Inca berries or achocha. For allotments are not only the preserve of old-school Northerners but of London trendies, wanting to create something of Hugh Fearnley-Whittingstall's self-sufficient River Cottage lifestyle on Denmark Hill.

Some allotments are thrown open to the public, for a small charity offering, through the incomparable National Gardens Scheme. 'Delightfully located on the edge of the village', Satin

Lane allotments, Banbury, were established in 1925 and some of the allotment holders work the same land as their grandparents did. 'A charismatic array of homespun fences have [sic] sprouted, adorned with climbing vegetables and flowers.' That's the spirit. The Pebworth allotments at Stratford-upon-Avon have only been in existence for a few years but already 'some of the allotmentiers are real characters'. In Islington, the Rt Hon. Jeremy Corbyn MP is one of them. Would he mind his patch being a Crown Jewel? I wonder.

The Lyth Valley, Westmorland

The damsons of the Lyth Valley in Westmorland were so famous that Lord Haw-Haw, the Nazi propagandist, mentioned them in one of his Germany Calling broadcasts during the Second World War. That was the era when charabancs of visitors and crocodiles of hikers would come during mid-April to see the blossom, which turned the fellsides white. Lorries would come from jam-makers around the country to carry away hundreds of tons of fruit at the end of summer. But as the twentieth century wore on, the damson – a small, inkily dark-skinned plum, with (unsweetened) a sour but intense flavour – fell out of fashion. It cost too much to pick the fruit, and they were left to rot on the trees. Orchards went unpruned. But in 1996, a rearguard action was mounted by Peter Cartmell, scion of a local landowning family, who remembered the sea of blossom that he had seen as a boy. He wrote to the *Westmorland Gazette*, asking whether anyone would join him in a campaign to revive the orchards. The Crosthwaite village hall was booked in the expectation that a few people would turn up; in the event, it was packed, one grower even reciting a poem that he had written. The Westmorland Damson Association was born.

Damsons are not, strictly speaking, native to Britain. Their exotic origin is reflected in their name: they came from the countryside around Damascus. They may have been popularised by the Crusades, but were known in Britain before that. From the number that grew around Roman camps it has been suggested that the Romans introduced them. Damson stones have been excavated from the Viking settlement at York. The Victorians ate damsons in many forms – damson fool, compote, vol-au-vent and soufflé; venison with damsons, mallard with damson and onion sauce, grouse with damson-gin gravy; damson cheese, a kind of fruit mould, similar to the membrillo which the Spanish make out of quince. These delicacies are all described in Victoria Barratt's *A Taste of Damsons*, published by the Westmorland Damson Association in 1997. She sells the book as well as damson gin from Cowmire Hall, a seventeenth-century house incorporating a pele tower, at Crosthwaite. There is a holiday flat over the cellar that stores the damson gin.

Valerie and John Harrison used to run Crosthwaite's village shop and post office, until they retired in 2005. In 1999, Valerie published a little book of walks called *Damson Country*; now out of print, but the community website www.crosthwaiteandlyth. co.uk has put the whole of it online. Change has not been wholly arrested: walks no longer start from the village shop, but only because it has become The Old Post Office. But this is an area that has clung to many of the old ways. Walk 11 leaves from the Church of St Anthony, Cartmel Fell, a simple embodiment of plain faith which seems hardly to have been touched since it was built in 1504 – the whole of the interior lurches downhill towards the altar, between walls that have long given up the effort to stand straight; behind the three-decker pulpit, dated 1698, are ancient family box pews, and the Ten Commandments have been inscribed beneath paintings of bare-breasted female torsos with wings, which one might take to be either angels or griffins.

From Cartmel Fell, you can look down on the Lyth and Winster Valleys during blossom time, and if they do not froth with white as they would have done at one time, at least you will know that the number of orchards and individual trees decked in the delicate white lace of damson blossom is increasing, as are the opportunities to enjoy damson products.

London Zoo

Does the world still love zoos? They are out of favour in some quarters – hence the intense discussion as to the location of London Zoo. Should it be moved from Regent's Park to somewhere outside London, where it would have more room and the animals could roam in greater freedom? It has not moved as yet and if it did, its departure would be mourned by many people for whom it was a childhood destination – and remembered as a distinctive experience: fun, weird and slightly frightening – as well as a seemingly immemorial landmark on the metropolitan scene. Animals are, famously, a British thing. We dote on them; we form societies to promote their welfare, whether in this country or overseas. We have been collecting and studying them for ages.

Zoos have a precursor in the menageries of exotic beasts that were formed in the Middle Ages. It was a courtly taste; how thrilled Henry III must have been to see heraldry come to life in the shape of two 'leopards' (probably lions), when they came as a present from his brother-in-law Frederick II, the Holy Roman Emperor, in 1235. Henry's great-great-grandfather, Henry I, had already kept a menagerie at his manor of Woodstock in Oxfordshire; one was now started at the Tower of London, where it remained until 1834. In the eighteenth century, what had been a courtly taste became popular, with the exhibition of animals to the paying public in travelling beast shows. Wombwell's Menagerie comprised elephants, freak shows, the Intelligent Pig and Wallace, the first lion to be born in captivity in Britain (born in Edinburgh, it was named after William Wallace, the Scottish patriot). 'No one probably has done so much to forward practically the study of natural history amongst the masses,' pronounced *The Times* in the obituary that followed George Wombwell's death in 1850.

Science was on the march. The Zoological Society of London (which now likes to be known by its initials, ZSL) was formed in 1826; two years later it opened the first zoological garden, in which foreign animals collected for study were displayed in agreeable park-like grounds, laid out by Decimus Burton. In the 1830s, the versifier and artist Edward Lear was often to be seen there, drawing parrots for his sumptuous *Illustrations of the Family of Psittacidae, or Parrots.*

The Zoological Society of London was for members only. There had been thoughts of admitting the public to the zoo, but the doors opened to them only when it was necessary to raise money, in 1847. Their presence seems not to have impeded development

– if anything the reverse, to judge by the innovations made in the second half of the century: the world's first reptile house (1849), the first public aquarium (1853) and the first insect house (1881). In the twentieth century, the zoo put itself in the architectural avant-garde: houses for animals seemed an appropriate platform for Modern Movement experiment, at a time when humans had yet to warm to the style. Berthold Lubetkin and the Tecton Group's Penguin Pool, constructed in 1934, celebrated the new material of reinforced concrete, with white ribbon-like walkways intertwined above an elliptical blue pool. (Alas, renovation of the concrete and other surfaces proved unsatisfactory and the penguins developed a bacterial infection called bumblefoot; the pool was replaced by a new one and Lubetkin's creation is empty.)

Today, London Zoo continues to house six hundred and fifty species – reptiles, fish, invertebrates, birds and small mammals, as well as lions and tigers. Many of them are endangered in the wild. One modern purpose of the zoo – or rather, of its owner, ZSL – is to support wild populations through breeding schemes, whether corncrakes in England or sand gazelles in the Empty Quarter of Saudi Arabia. Conservation translocation techniques are used to relocate threatened species that exist in one area of the wild but have become locally extinct in another. Such work may not be very visible to visitors to the Zoo, but everyone must be pleased to know they exist.

The Black Friar pub, Blackfriars

Reader, I am sure you are with me: there has to be a pub in this book. In towns and villages, beside railway stations and village greens, they are an essential part of the English scene. I have thought long and hard, dredging my personal experience, as to which one pub it should be. Despite closures, England still has countless numbers of them, and most will be held very dear by their regulars. Even pubs that people do not visit so often, but remember from earlier days or holidays, may wear a golden aura; they are all the better for occupying a place in the imagination, as a touchstone of the best. All of them, if consumed in some appalling beer-generated conflagration, or – not so impossible – closed at some future date by puritanical edict on supposed grounds of public health, would be mourned*. It is therefore with some hesitancy that I commit myself to a choice of only one, but . . . yes, I must do it. My Crown Jewel of pubs is the Black Friar on Queen Victoria Street in London.

---

* They were closed on grounds of public health during the time of Coronavirus. One of our locals has already gone bust.

Explain yourself, Aslet! I admit I have selected an oddity. The Black Friar, occupying a wedged-shaped site on what used to be land belonging to the Blackfriars Monastery, hence the name, dates from 1905; but the style of decoration is quite unlike that of the dazzling gin palaces of the day. Instead of plate-glass windows and bright lighting are leaded lights and richly coloured marble, mosaics and copper reliefs showing jolly monks. The monks pursue a range of cheery activities with a gusto not usually associated with monastic life; they sing carols, collect fish and eels for Fish Fridays – one is about to boil an egg. The decoration extends to the fire basket, with ends in the form of goblins. Several sculptors and craftsmen were involved – Nathaniel Hitch, Frederick T. Callcott, Henry Poole, and Farmer & Brindley – and continued to be, until the 1920s. (Note to geeks: the figure of the Black Friar over the entrance door is even later, having probably been added in the 1980s.)

It is nothing if not exuberant – some would say kitsch. But not as kitsch as Friar Park outside Henley, owned by the lawyer Sir Frank Crisp. As part of a whole programme of friar-themed decoration, the electric light was switched on by pushing a friar's nose. Forgive my name drop, but the house used to be owned – and beautifully cared for – by the Beatle George Harrison.

The architectural critic Ian Nairn likened the Black Friar to the Soane Museum, 'with mirrors and deception everywhere. It reaches a climax in the Snack Bar at the back of the Saloon with a barrel-vaulted alcove in which real views through to the bar are expertly balanced against multiple reflections.' It would only be fair to say that Nairn also made some derogatory remarks – but who cares? Architecture is not the point. I like the Black Friar because it refuses to change. In recent decades we have seen pubs close, unable to contend with the twin challenges of the smoking ban and the availability of cheap booze from supermarkets. In the 1970s, when I worked briefly behind a bar of a pub in Surrey, old codgers would come in every evening, because the smoke-fuddled warmth of the bar was better than their unmodernised homes, where, in any case, their wives ruled the roost. People are now more comfortably housed and own home entertainment systems. Successful pubs now rely on food sales to make money – but the gastro pub is, while a step up in some ways, a different thing. The Black Friar remains what it always has been: dark, cosy and individual. Cheers.

Architecture

Architecture is the inescapable art. It is not hidden away in art galleries, which you must make a conscious decision to visit. It provides the background to daily life. We see it, move through it, live amongst it. Nothing so much sets the character of our towns and cities. Old buildings put the past before our eyes. They speak of the great communal effort needed to make them, or of the powerful individuals who had them built. History joins hands with the present, because how we use and care for old buildings reflects on us. Are we rooted in our collective past, or a species of tumbleweed that does not know where it will be taken by the wind? We find the answer in our treatment of the built heritage. Architecture defines who we are.

Hadrian's Wall is a tour de force, architect unknown. See it and you think, as is often the case before epic monuments: here great people have been, capable of great works. York Minster is the only medieval building where you can enjoy the overpowering effect of colour intended by its creators, through the glass. Thank you, Lord Fairfax, Parliamentary commander during the English Civil War, who came from nearby, for saving it. Winchester College is a place of great antiquity whose resonance has grown with each generation of boys that has passed through it: the stones, in the way of old stones, are hallowed.

With the Banqueting House, we enter into the era of named architects. My list pays tribute to some of the greatest of them (Sir Christopher Wren having already made his appearance at St Paul's.) The Banqueting House survived the fire of 1698 that destroyed the rest of Whitehall Palace: William III had the southern window bricked up to prevent the flames reaching the interior. It is a testament to the genius of Inigo Jones, whose settings for the court of Charles I – many ephemeral – equal the international importance of the King's art collection. The Radcliffe Camera (James Gibbs) is Oxford's most handsome building – which is saying something. In Sir William Chambers's Somerset House we have a magnificent space, created for civil servants but equally if not more happy in its new use as a public space and arts hub.

Holkham Hall is a supreme example of English Palladianism – albeit nothing much like the work of Andrea Palladio. The partnership of the 1st Earl of Leicester and William Kent is beguiling. Sir John Soane's obsessions made him a genius. In Sir Edwin Lutyens we have an architect who defined his age through the romance of his country houses, the universal reach of his monuments and the epic buildings created for the Empire at its last gasp.

Hadrian's Wall

Hadrian's Wall does not obviously strike one as fragile; it has stood there, a stone necklace across the throat of Britain, since the Emperor Hadrian commanded it to be built in the early second century AD. Defining the northernmost border of the Roman Empire, the wall is an extravagant, almost theatrical construction, far stronger, taller and more elaborate than needed for its purported aim of separating conquered England from the wild tribes north of the Border. The troops, drilled to fight in the open, did not have the sort of weapons needed to defend a wall. It is now interpreted as much as a statement about Rome as a fortification. When it was built, the Roman Empire covered most of the known world, stretching from the North of England to what is today Iraq. The imperial challenge, now, was to organise and consolidate within its borders. Hadrian's Wall was an emphatic full stop; on one side lay the organisation and prosperity of the Empire, on the other side (to Roman eyes) Barbarian chaos. As a feat of construction, it was – and remains – awesome.

It has decayed, of course; there are now only a couple of hundred yards, at Housesteads in Northumberland, that you can actually walk along. When the Stanegate was replaced by a new military road to rush troops from one side of the country to the other after the Jacobite rebellion of 1745, the wall provided a ready source of building materials, which reduced its height. The forts along its length can be seen only as foundations and stumps of walls. They would not be visible at all if it had not been for the archaeologists who have been investigating them, with ever greater levels of precision, for the last two hundred years. But the impression remains one of awe-inspiring permanence. The Roman cohorts may have gone, but it is difficult not to look out over the windswept landscape of Northumberland and Cumbria and picture what life on the wall must have been like for one of those soldiers. Admittedly he was likely to have come from Northern Europe rather than the Mediterranean. Even so, the word that most often comes to mind is 'bleak'.

But the appearance of imperturbable massiveness masks a complex, delicate hidden life. Evidence of this could so easily have been destroyed – and it is dismal to imagine how much has been, over the years, sometimes during the course of historic but unintentionally clumsy excavation. That anything at all has been recovered is a kind of miracle. The most astonishing finds are a few dozen little slivers of smooth wood, used in the manner of papyrus. They still bear traces of the original ink. Infrared photography renders the writing more or less legible to expert eyes accustomed to script dashed off by a busy scribe, using a shorthand-like series of abbreviations, and able to translate Latin slang. Elsewhere in the Empire, wax tablets were used for everyday written communications; at Vindolanda, a little way south of the wall, the chosen medium was pen and ink, the latter being applied with a dip pen of the kind familiar from old-fashioned schoolrooms and still to be seen in gentlemen's clubs. They include the first example known to history of a woman – the wife of Aelius Brocchus, commander of a fort near Vindolanda – writing in her own hand. This lady had dictated a birthday invitation, addressed to Sulpicia Lepidina, wife of Flavius Cerialis, Prefect of the ninth cohort of Batavians, to a scribe, adding at the end of it a few words in her own less fluent script: in translation they read, ' I shall expect you, sister. Farewell, sister, my dearest soul, as I hope to prosper, and hail.'

Some tablets were found amid the bracken and heather that were used as carpets at Vindolanda, others at the bottom of some old files that Flavius Cerialis had ordered to be destroyed when the Batavians were leaving the fort around AD 100. They were preserved because Vindolanda, a fort originally used during the conquest of Britain and whose earliest phases pre-date Hadrian's Wall, was originally built of wood and thereafter often rebuilt. At each rebuilding, the previous ground level was simply covered in a thick layer of clay and turf to create a flat surface to build on; this had the effect of creating an anaerobic seal that preserved everything beneath it. Although fragmentary, the fragile tablets, first excavated in the early 1970s, reveal many details of ordinary life, including the previously unknown fact that the soldiers, bless them, wore underpants. Difficult to spot amid the detritus, the tablets had, when first discovered, what has been described as the consistency of damp blotting paper. How many, many other records must have been accidentally destroyed over the years – sometimes by well-intentioned archaeologists?

And what more secrets does the Wall have to reveal?

York Minster's stained glass

Medieval life was short on colour. The materials to produce it were expensive, and most people dressed and lived in a palette of dun-grey. There was one exception to the universal monochrome: when they entered a great church, their eyes would be regaled with a blaze of colour: paintings on the walls, the priests' rich vestments and, most glorious of all, the glowing reds, greens, blues and yellows of the stained glass. The effect, so different from anything they experienced elsewhere, must have seemed a foretaste of heaven.

Alas, it is difficult for us to share their wonder. Most medieval glass that was within reach of anyone wanting to smash it was destroyed during the Dissolution of the Monasteries and the Civil War. (The Victorians tried to replace some of it, as well as to adorn their own churches, but the result is not the same; it is apt to look too regular.) By the end of the Middle Ages, after several centuries of glass-making, the colours, the stories represented in the windows – telling of the kings of Juda, the local saints and the great clerics, the donors of recent years – all this must have overwhelmed worshippers with a sense of splendid profusion. Occasional stylistic infelicities, when

Norman glass was reused at a later period, did not matter. All contributed to the glory of God.

There is only one great church in England where it is possible to feel the joy of so much colour, as a medieval person might have done. This is York Minster, where the one hundred and twenty-eight windows still contain glass most of which was made in the Middle Ages. You see it and marvel – mournfully – at the thought that all the great churches of England built before the sixteenth century must have resembled this one. This is not merely of antiquarian interest, as a curiosity from the past: the glass, created over a period of several centuries, is of a high technical and artistic calibre. As the Minster changed and grew, earlier parts being demolished and rebuilt, generations of patrons – rich noblemen and merchants – as well as churchmen, kept faith with the original programme: to saturate the building with colour.

The York glass plunges us into the faith and mindset of the Middle Ages. Some of it speaks of the importance of this northern province of the English Church, which could jostle for position with Canterbury. We can follow the stories of St Cuthbert, a northern saint, and of twelfth-century St William, who belonged to York, having been archbishop of that city – significant for the Minster authorities who, until his canonisation in 1227, had lacked a special focus for veneration. Pilgrims came, assembling in the south transept: directly facing them were the Five Sisters, tall, narrow windows filled with glass decorated with abstract, linear patterns; this grisaille created a shimmer of silver that would have evoked St John the Divine's description of the New Jerusalem, whose walls were 'pure gold, like unto clear glass'. The chapter house brings together the saints most important to the devotional life of the Minster in the thirteenth century. Heraldry identifies kings and magnates; the widow of the goldsmith and bellfounder Richard Tunnoc commissioned scenes of bellfounding, as well as an image of St William.

Stained glass needs windows to put it in. As the Middle Ages progressed, so did building technology; by the 1370s, when the lady chapel was built, stonemasons could create walls that were practically all window. The lady chapel's east window is a *Wunderwerk*. Made during the years 1390–1410, it depicts the beginning and end of things, as told in Genesis and Revelation.

We have Fernando Fairfax and his son Sir Thomas, the Parliamentary general, to thank for the preservation of the York Minster glass. After the Battle of Marston Moor and the relief of the Royalist siege of York at the end of the Civil War, Fernando, the city's governor, aided by Sir Thomas, prevented the Parliamentarian troops from smashing up York's churches. Although Calvinists, they came from Yorkshire and felt pride in their county town. Not that the Minster has been proof against other disasters. Fire struck in 1829 and 1840, lightning in 1984. Fortunately, since 1967, the York Glaziers' Trust has been on hand to care for its medieval glass as well as that of other churches. Restoration of the east window finished in 2017.

Winchester College

With its ancient buildings, its spreading lawns, its Arcadian surroundings, its traditions, its impenetrable tribal language, its studious calm and erudite ivory tower-ishness, Winchester College is apt to arouse memories of a nostalgic and finely privileged youth, even in people who never went there. Forgive me, egalitarian reader: it is a public – which is to say, a private – school, with a knack of producing young men who famously feel superior to other mortals; and it costs a lot to go there (as does any boarding school, for that matter). But whatever objections may be harboured on grounds of class, educational privilege or by the general unfairness of life, should be swallowed on account of the architecture. You could not find Winchester College anywhere else. It is English to its ancient bones.

In the late fourteenth century, the College was conceived as part of a grand scheme by the man who effectively ran England, William of Wykeham, Bishop of Winchester and Chancellor under Edward III and Richard II. It was intended as what would now be called a feeder school for New College, Oxford, founded by Wykeham on ground that had been abandoned since the Black Death; the object was to maintain an adequate supply of pupils who knew Latin (as well as say prayers for his soul). The school was opened in 1394. As the headmaster James Sabben-Clare wrote in his book *Winchester College*, published in 1981: 'it is a quite remarkable thing that nearly six hundred years later most of the original buildings should still be standing, and within and around them the process of education should still be carried on by the same people as are named in the original statutes – albeit in different ways and in company with many others: a Warden and ten Fellows, two masters, seventy scholars, three chaplains, three lay-clerks, and sixteen quiristers or choirboys'.

By tact, diplomacy and guile, successive wardens managed to dodge the blows aimed at them during the Dissolution of the Monasteries and the turbulence of the Civil War (during which the rest of Winchester was sacked). Indeed, the College emerged from the Dissolution with its landholdings enhanced by the addition of the College of St Elizabeth which stood next door – though Henry VIII's reforms also removed the original purpose of educating future priests to speak Latin. Similarly, a new Sick House was built in the Cromwellian period. Over the next century and a half, the school even survived the greed of the fellows, who applied the income originally intended for the support of the pupils to themselves.

The College does not give much away from College Street, but once you have passed through the late-fourteenth-century entrance gate you feel you might be in an Oxford or Cambridge college. This is not to be wondered at: the master mason William Wynford was responsible for both Winchester and New College, and his plan set the style for later colleges. There are two courts, the main one being Chamber Court, still paved with ancient flints. On one side is the chapel, with a lierne vault on the way to becoming a fan vault, probably by Richard II's master carpenter Hugh Herland; Wykeham wanted the College to preach Christ 'frequently and fervently'. Next to the chapel is the hall, where the school community of over a hundred in the Middle Ages would have dined. There are over ninety listed buildings on the site, including two chantry chapels, erected so that prayers could be said for the souls of dead masters.

All wonderful, and in conjunction with the ancient water meadows, the playing fields, Herbert Baker's war memorial cloister listing the names of the five hundred Wykehamists who gave their lives in the First World War, and the Areas of Outstanding Natural Beauty on Twyford Down and St Catherine's Hill, it is enough to bring tears to your eyes.

The Banqueting House

The Banqueting House on Whitehall is the greatest surviving work of Inigo Jones, drenched in memories of the early-seventeenth-century Stuart court. The Stuarts were not distinguished for their administrative competence but Charles I – and to a lesser extent his father James I – loved the arts, particularly the esoteric theatrical genre known as the masque. The Banqueting House, replacing another that had burnt down in 1619, was constructed for the staging of masques, which were usually designed by the building's architect. Jones created a festive structure, with swags of garlands in the frieze of the principal façade – which would originally have been composed of honey-coloured and pinkish-brown stone – the pale-grey, pollution-resisting Portland stone with which it is faced today came in the nineteenth century. Charles I commissioned a ceiling for the main space from no less an artist than Rubens; the subject was the apotheosis – or ascent into heaven – of James I. Admittedly the King's hopes of rebuilding Whitehall Palace completely were dashed by the chaotic finances of his regime; but the fragment of his vision that we have in the Banqueting House is a marvel.

Inigo Jones, painter, connoisseur and antiquarian, as well as architect and man of the theatre, must have dazzled and astounded contemporaries; as one might expect, this did not always make them love him, and the accounts that have come down – notably lampoons by Ben Jonson after the pair had fallen out – suggest that he was mightily full of himself. '*Huomo vanissimo e molto vantatore*,' concluded an Italian, having watched him pronounce on some of Charles I's newly arrived Italian paintings. An impression of vanity is not entirely excluded from Van Dyck's memorable portrait drawing of him, though this suggests many other qualities too, such as intelligence, refinement and spirit. He is shown with his eyes straining to discern some distant vision. Contemporaries seem to have thought him arrogant, and it would hardly be surprising if he was: to achieve anything new in architecture requires self-confidence. A double dose must have been needed to get anything done, given the state of the Stuart exchequer. Perhaps the most surprising thing is that so little was written about Jones during his lifetime. He was prominent at the highest levels of the court, friendly with kings and queens – a striking figure with an unusual name. Yet diarists and letter writers seem to have been blind to him.

Jones was the son of a London cloth worker. In his twenties he travelled in Italy for several years. In 1606 a friend wrote a Latin inscription on the fly-leaf of a book he was giving him, expressing the hope that through Jones 'sculpture, modelling, architecture, painting, acting and all that is praiseworthy in the elegant arts of the ancients, may one day find their way across the Alps into our England'. By some means he entered the service of King Christian IV of Denmark, not yet twenty, and brother of the English Queen. It is difficult to imagine the refined Jones being happy at that notoriously boozy court. Before long, he was back in his native land, having transferred from the service of the brother to that of the sister. His first work for Anne of Denmark was to stage a masque.

What was a masque? There was something of the pantomime about it, with an emphasis on outlandish costumes and seemingly magical transformations of scene. But the best masques must also have been very beautiful. Certainly, they were lavishly expensive: for the price of some productions it would have been possible to build a country house. And they could be erudite too. A number were written by Ben Jonson, in classicising vein. Words, however, took second place to dance. The object of the masque was to demonstrate the virtues of the monarch, in an entertainment in which the court itself participated through dancing. At one point the masquers would dance and take partners from the court, dissolving the barrier between the ideal, as represented on stage, and the real, as embodied in the audience. Of course, there were realities beyond the court, but the masque took no cognisance of them. With its arcane symbolism, it reflected the court's growing insularity.

Symbolism of another kind would lie heavy over the Banqueting House in January 1649. One sharp morning Charles I, wearing a long black cloak, his order of St George, a rich red-striped waistcoat and two linen shirts, was marched there from St James's Palace. Soon afterwards he walked out of a side window onto scaffolding, gave a short speech and knelt before the executioner's block. He was a small man. It took only one blow for the axe to do its job.

The Radcliffe Camera, Oxford

Oxford is – well, it is Oxford. Seat of learning, boom town in today's knowledge-based economy, seat of Charles I's court during the English Civil War, focus of intellectual and religious debate during the Victorian period, home of Lewis Carroll, magnet for tourist groups and Asian honeymoon couples with photographers: place of dreaming spires so freighted with fictional depictions (*Jude the Obscure*, *Brideshead Revisited*, Colin Dexter's Inspector Morse) which sometimes threaten to overtake the real thing. Cambridge is quieter; for some unfathomable reason, given that both universities are about the same distance away, Oxford has closer links to the capital. It is more worldly; always has been. But then it has always been a proper city, given its own bishop in 1542 and acquiring its own industry in Morris

Motors in the twentieth century; Cambridge remained, until the Science Park took off in the late twentieth century, a rather backward fenland town with a good university attached. With its Backs along the river Cam, Cambridge is laid out on Picturesque lines in which landscape is paramount; Oxford is more an architectural capriccio, densely crowded, and many of the buildings first-rate.

Primus inter pares – if I may be permitted a donnish expression – is the Radcliffe Camera. This grand building is primarily a dome on a circular base of coupled columns: a reinterpretation on a bigger scale and with lusher ornament of Donato Bramante's Tempietto in Rome. And you can see the dome from practically everywhere in the city; whatever the view, the Radcliffe Camera seems to be part of it. Fortunately, the rotunda deserves the prominence it commands, for it is a masterpiece. Not only that, but it is entirely suited to its location, a library that is both magisterial and magnificent.

Dr John Radcliffe, who left money for the building in his will, had a chequered relationship with the university. Refusing to take holy orders, he was expelled from his fellowship. Instead, he became a physician and rose to the post of doctor to the Royal Family – although he never seems to have acquired the tact of manner such a position usually requires: 'I would not have your Majesty's legs for three kingdoms!' he told William III. By 1714 he had decided to leave his fortune to Oxford to build a library (although he would not die until 1736). Consideration of what form it would take began in 1721. The planning committee bought up the old streets that would be demolished to form a square. Nicholas Hawksmoor, then at work on a number of

Oxford projects including All Souls College, was approached for a design: he proposed a rotunda. This may have been inspired by two unrealised designs by Sir Christopher Wren, a mausoleum for Charles I and a scheme for the Wren Library at Trinity College, Cambridge.

But the building is not Hawksmoor's. He was old and ill by the time it was built; the architect whose name it bears is James Gibbs, well known to the university in Cambridge and probably introduced to this scheme by the son of his old patron, Edward Harley, 2nd Earl of Oxford. The 3rd Earl, also Edward, was a trustee. Gibbs took Hawksmoor's idea and ran with it. He raised the profile of the dome, coupled the columns around the outside of the building and gave it a sense of drama that had previously been lacking. The great room on the first floor is sumptuous; the drum of the dome is supported on giant arches which evoke the splendour of Rome – and the tradition of classical learning, at a time when many of the books read would have been in Latin. Gibbs's friend Mr Handel wrote music for the opening in 1749.

Radcliffe used to be described as the last great secular donor to the university. In this age of billionaires, there have been others; let us hope there will be more to come.

Somerset House

There is a prehistory to Somerset House. It is named after the Duke of Somerset, Lord Protector of England, who ran the country (1547–9) for the boy king Edward VI until he was beheaded after a coup by other noblemen. His house on the Thames was one of a string of palaces, built – originally by bishops – for great persons of state needing to be near the monarch at Whitehall. The York Watergate is the sole surviving fragment of this era, built as part of the Duke of Buckingham's fabulous palace soon after Charles I came to the throne. Somerset House became, traditionally, a property of the English queens, the last who lived there being Charles I's widow, Henrietta-Maria. After her husband's execution, she returned at the Restoration with an entourage of twenty-four menservants: being French, she dressed them in long black velvet cassocks emblazoned with nothing but a golden sun. *Quel chic.*

By the mid-eighteenth century, when the court had moved to Kensington and Buckingham Palace and fashion had long deserted the riverbank, Somerset House had become a place of ghosts, so Sir William Chambers was commissioned to convert the site into a different kind of palace, this time for civil servants.

He began in 1776 and the job took twenty years. Among the occupants were the Royal Society, the Society of Antiquaries and the Royal Academy; they were given pride of place in the Strand block. Vaults beneath them were intended as a repository for the public records. The Navy Office was accommodated in the west half of the range overlooking the river; it was here, to the Seamen's Hall, that the officers of Nelson's Navy came to discover which ships had been assigned to them. Near the Navy Office, in the west range, were the Sick and Hurt, Navy Pay and Victualling Offices, while the east half of the riverfront was occupied by the Stamp Office. All these offices were disposed around a grand classical courtyard.

On the Strand, the narrow façade was inspired by the Hôtel des Monnaies in Paris; people entered – as they still do – beneath a supremely elegant vestibule of paired columns and vaults. By contrast, the riverfront was of prodigious length: although the river was losing ground to road as a means of transport around London, old habits died hard. Rising out of the water, the bottom level was composed of bold rustication, with river entrances flanked by pairs of columns banded with vermiculation; the vermiculation – a way of treating stone to make it look as though it is covered with worm casts – had something in common with the riverbed. Above was a terrace and a suavely urbane façade. What a masterpiece.

Oh, how it sank during the twentieth century. Chambers's dome, columns and rusticated façades looked down on a courtyard reduced to the status of a car park for the bean counters of the Inland Revenue. Eventually a time came when the civil servants were expelled. In place of cars came cafés, fountains, a winter skating rink . . . For Somerset House is now run as a trust for artists, craftsmen and exhibitions. The architecture has been restored, the spaces it surrounds brought to life. Somerset House is home not only to the Courtauld Institute of Art and its Gallery but to one hundred artists, three hundred and fifty makers, one hundred and twenty creative businesses and organisations, such as dance companies and the British Fashion Council. We must not entirely forget the ghosts, but they have been displaced by the life injected by workers, tourists and the general public. The best of the old has met the best of the new, and the result is a triumph for the twenty-first century.

Holkham Hall, Norfolk

Holkham Hall, on the north Norfolk coast, is less country house than palace. It is in what is generally known as the English Palladian style, with its emphasis on ideal proportions; the splendour is far beyond that of the country houses on the Veneto built by the sixteenth-century architect Andrea Palladio for Venetian aristocrats, which were originally quite simple and doubled as farmhouses. Holkham has a hall built out of marble (or to be exact, alabaster). I used to think of it as a rather cold production but that was before I read the letters of the 1st Earl of Leicester, who did as much as anyone to design it; some are written to or about William Kent, another person I would love to have got to a dinner party. Kent was an architect, a furniture designer, a garden designer, but fortunately he gave up his first art, which was painting. He was not very good; but the charm of his personality was such that, during the ten years he spent in Italy, he managed to persuade the English *milordi* whom he met there to overlook the fact and employ him on their projects at home. One of them was Leicester, who would thereafter refer to Kent as Il Signor or Kentino.

Leicester was at that stage plain Thomas Coke. His parents had died when he was a child, leaving guardians to manage the estates he inherited; there was land in Suffolk, Buckinghamshire, Oxfordshire, Staffordshire, Dorset, Kent, Somerset and London. They did so conscientiously. There were no debts when Coke came of age and he had an income of £10,000 a year: this made him one of the richest commoners in the country. From an early age he saw himself as a *virtuoso*. On his Grand Tour, begun at the age of fifteen, he bought sculpture, paintings, drawings, books and manuscripts. He also fell under Kent's spell. They were – despite the gulf in social position – soulmates.

For all the glory of his inheritance and the pomposity of his full-bottomed wig, Coke was a naturally boisterous man, irrepressibly witty and not at all inclined to stand on ceremony when dealing with people sharing his passion for the arts. He was irrepressible in other ways too. Despite the rosy condition of his estate when he came into it, he soon got into debt; this he compounded by investing heavily in the South Sea Company, losing over £35,000 when the Bubble burst. Despite marriage, he continued to live like a bachelor, leaving his wife in Norfolk while he enjoyed the pleasures of London. Even so, he was determined to build a great country house. Architecture was his 'Amusement'.

Several hands were involved at Holkham. Essentially, Matthew Brettingham the Elder, a local man, was the executive architect. The designs came from Kent under Coke's close supervision, and were vetted by the arbiter of taste Lord Burlington. The project began in 1734 but did not finish until 1765; by then Kent had been dead for twenty-four years and Coke himself for six. Coke's uncertain finances had held up the works.

Faced in yellow brick, Holkham takes the form of a central block, surrounded at each of the corners by pavilions. It is not an entirely happy composition. But there are wonders inside. The Marble Hall is a recreation of a type described by the Roman architect Vitruvius. At Holkham, a rising site gave the opportunity to add a degree of theatre to this grand space: it is entered at a level lower than the colonnade, which soars above the visitor's head. Overhead curves a coffered ceiling of the type Kent and Leicester would have seen in the Baths of Diocletian and Caracalla in Rome. Even today – and however often you see it – the effect is sensational. This is an imperial space, immense and imposing – but also flamboyant and festive. It is easy to imagine the fun that the *virtuosi* had in making it.

In 1784, fifteen years after Coke's death, by which time taste in country-house architecture had moved on, a foreign visitor considered Holkham one of the 'most elegant' of English houses, being also 'above all, one of the best provided with every kind of comfort and convenience'. A well was sunk and a horse walking around a circular track operated the pump that drew water. Much water was needed for the exceptional number of water closets and, incredibly, bathrooms. The family wing alone contained three water closets. There were double-seaters elsewhere for the upper servants. The bathroom in the family wing contained a 'mahogany bathing tub', presumably cold; a hot bath, and a 'biddeau'. This really was the country house that had everything.

Sir John Soane's Museum

The architect Sir John Soane turned his house into a museum, to be preserved, under the trust he created, exactly as it was after his death in 1837. Some of the paintings, sculptures and antiquities are certainly of museum quality – but the house is not merely a showcase for them but for Soane's mind and imagination. Cross the threshold and you are plunged into a world of architectural drama, where the relatively confined space provided by two adjacent London houses was fretted over and obsessively altered by Soane to create extraordinary spatial effects: grand, astounding, even vertiginous, despite their small scale. It is like the sonatas of Beethoven in three dimensions.

The son of a bricklayer, Soane was something of an autodidact, intensely interested in the latest architectural thinking in France. Despite a prickly temperament, he was friends with Turner, Coleridge and other leading figures of the arts. His taste was that of the Regency, refracted and heightened through the lens of his own genius. His home displays his highly personal architectural language, derived from the neo-Classicism of the day but without much use of columns; he favoured shallow domes, segmental arches and pilasters incised with geometrical patterns.

Light might penetrate from a concealed window or through coloured class.

Other collectors had, like Soane, visited Rome and bought ancient sculptures, casts and architectural fragments – but they did not display them as they are shown at 12–13 Lincoln's Inn Fields. Soane placed huge pieces of carved marble in tight spaces, the effect of which, claustrophobic and overwhelming, would have delighted the Roman engraver Piranesi, whom Soane knew from his travels. Throughout the house can be seen drawings and casts by the austere neo-Classical sculptor John Flaxman who, like Soane, was a professor at the Royal Academy. And yet Soane also enjoyed the pleasurable frissons afforded by the Gothic Revival at its most gloomy. Hence the Monk's Parlour that he created – the monk who inhabited it being conceived as Padre Giovanni, his own alter ego.

Among the works of art that Soane bought were Hogarth's series 'The Rake's Progress' and 'The Election'. There were so many paintings to fit into the Picture Room that he fixed them onto 'moveable planes' by means of which a 'space of 13ft 8in. in length, 12ft 4in. in breadth, and 19ft 6in. in height, which are the actual dimensions of this room, is rendered capable of containing as many pictures as a gallery of the same height, 20ft broad and 45ft long'. Perhaps Soane's greatest coup as a collector was the acquisition of the newly discovered sarcophagus of Seti I, offered to the British Museum but rejected because the price of £2,000 was too high. To bring the sarcophagus into the Sepulchral Chamber required the demolition of a wall, and he showed off the result with a party at which the sarcophagus was spookily lit from within.

One of the most remarkable of all the spaces that Soane created was his own Little Study, a narrow room that is little more than a corridor, decorated in deep cherry red and hung with fragments of classical architecture. Here, from 1788, without any heating other than that supplied by the underfloor system (which did not work), Soane would pull out a little desk and draw the first sketches for such masterpieces as the Bank of England. Next door was a dressing room, in which he could wash his hands and put on his coat, ready to meet either the grand guests who arrived by the front door or the builders and craftsmen who came by the back.

Soane was not easy to live with. Cruelly disappointed in his wastrel sons, neither of whom followed him into architecture, he disinherited one (the other had died) after a disastrous row which he blamed for hastening his wife's death. The rupture was a tragedy for those concerned; but had Soane's home been inherited in the usual way, it would doubtless have been altered and broken up. There would have been no Sir John Soane's Museum.

Ludlow

There are times when England gets it almost completely right. One of them is Ludlow, a town that grew up around its hilltop castle, above the serenity of the River Teme. To Christopher Hussey, a writer as steeped in the traditions of the Picturesque as anyone before or since, Ludlow was so beautiful he could hardly believe he was in England at all – not in Burgundy or Bavaria. Mug of beer in hand, he gazed from the garden of an inn beside Ludford Bridge

> across the green swirling water below, up the steep streets opposite at the fantastic silhouette of town and castle. So strange is it in England now to be able to do so without also seeing hoardings, a gas works, a goods yard, and the mean back parts of garages and cinemas at the same time. Yet all is wholly English, the great trees, the soft warm colouring, the snug Georgian domesticity infusing the feudal shell. And if you climb the Whitcliff beyond the river – the alp-like slopes and hanging woods that have been Ludlow's own park for seven centuries – all foreign analogies are forgotten. The famous view of Ludlow across Dinham Bridge to the Clee

Hill is an epitome of England at its loveliest, not to be surpassed anywhere.

This appeared in *Country Life* in the portentous year of 1945, when the Second World War had made the English acutely aware of their own identity and of what could be lost. Incredibly, since then, the idyll has not been marred: if anything, in line with the general increase in England's material prosperity, it has gained. Ludlow is not stuck in a time warp. It has internet cafés as well as antique shops, Tesco (reluctantly) as well as market stalls. But Ludlow's essential character has not changed and it has infinitely better food now.

At one point in the late 1990s, no fewer than three Michelin stars shone down on this Shropshire burgh of eight thousand souls. This level of gastronomic recognition could not be sustained, but there is still the famous Food Festival, started in 1995, still the market. Ludlow feels buoyant. Other towns not far away are manifestly struggling: built to service the needs of farmers at a time when agriculture meant everything in this part of the world, they have not discovered a new raison d'être now that the industry has shrunk.

What is the reason for Ludlow's better fortune?

In the words I quoted from Hussey: the beauty of the place. It had been important in the Middle Ages as the administrative capital of Wales (not that it is in Wales now); that role ceased in 1689 but it continued to function as a fashionable centre for gentry and nobility, who spent the winter there. Some of the Georgian houses are exceptionally fine. By the Victorian period, Ludlow had become a rural backwater and the twentieth century largely passed it by ... until the last quarter when it experienced an influx of writers and publishers, some retired: people who did not need to be in London all the time and were early adopters of new technology. They restored houses; they invited their friends; they fulfilled their mission as members of the chattering classes, and chatttered. Word got out. Today, people can increasingly live where they want to and choose a high quality of life. I said England can get some things almost completely right. Delete the 'almost'.

Goddards, Surrey

S ir Edwin Landseer Lutyens was one of the greatest of all
British architects. His Liverpool Cathedral, which never got
higher than the undercroft, would have stood comparison with
Sir Christopher Wren's St Paul's. This towering figure built
country houses, offices, war memorials, the Cenotaph itself, as
well as a shimmering palace for the Viceroy of India at New
Delhi, the city which he helped to plan: the Viceroy's House is
bigger than Versailles. Having opened his first office at nineteen,
he was practically a child prodigy (most architects get going late).
He was also highly successful. As a result, he produced an
amazing volume of work of all kinds; no British architect can
boast such variety. A monumental cathedral on the one hand,
nursery furniture on the other.

Out of the immensity of this oeuvre I put before you Goddards,
at Abinger Common in Surrey. It is one of the country houses
from the first phase of his career, at the turn of the twentieth
century. These days, Lutyens's houses are not so easy to see: most
are private. Goddards, however, is owned by the Lutyens Trust;
from whom it is leased by the Landmark Trust, meaning that
people can stay there. Everything that Lutyens and his mentor,

the garden designer and nurserywoman Gertrude Jekyll, loved can be seen there: the local vernacular motifs that he had absorbed as a boy, confined to his Surrey home because of illness but able to ramble the lanes round about with a sketchbook; the local material, Bargate stone, used with contrasting – and beautifully laid – brick. Lutyens rejoiced in such materials: the roof is half Horsham stone slabs, half red-clay tile.

The spirit of Lutyens's houses in these years was summed up by Jekyll, in writing about Munstead Wood, the home he designed for her near Godalming:

> It does not stare with newness; it is not new in any way that is disquieting to the eye; it is neither raw nor callow. On the contrary, it almost gives the impression of a comfortable maturity of something like a couple of hundred years. And yet there is nothing sham-old about it; it is not trumped-up with any specious or fashionable devices of spurious antiquity; there is no pretending to be anything that it is not – no affectation whatever ... the house is not in any way a copy of an old building, though it embodies the general characteristics of the older structures of its own district.

Rather than an electric doorbell, visitors rang a 'belfry' that would once have stood above the shoulders of horses going to market – the sort of object from a dying rural tradition that Jekyll described in her book *Old West Surrey*.

Goddards did not begin life as a country house. Lutyens was originally approached in 1898 to build a holiday home for a charity. The client, Sir Frederick Mirrielees, was a man of his age, having been a partner in Muir and Mirrielees which opened Russia's first department store, from which he retired on marrying a shipping heiress; he became chairman of the Union Castle line. The charity provided holidays (as *Country Life* described in 1904) for 'nurses from hospitals, ladies of small means who could not otherwise afford a holiday, East End workers exhausted by care for others' who for two or three weeks had 'a bright social life there, readings, games and, perhaps best of all, a lovely garden'. There was also a skittles alley. According to Lutyens, 'the inmates love it and invariably weep when they leave'. Goddards was enlarged when it became a weekend home for Sir Frederick's son, Donald, and his American wife; the ladies of small means were provided with a converted barn.

Lutyens's country houses, Goddards among them, bear witness to the Edwardian ideal, part dream and part technical and social innovation. The dream lay in the aesthetic loveliness of silvery oak and softly coloured hand-made bricks and tiles, or locally quarried stone, set amid yew topiaries and billowing flower borders. It helped that he was, by temperament, a romantic himself: a man who moved in a self-created world of delight, entranced by geometry, steeped in extravagant notions of chivalry, particularly towards women, whom he did not perhaps understand. Novelty came in the way of life: lit by electric light (denied the ladies of small means but installed for Donald and his wife), convenient for the metropolis and served by that wonder of the times – the motor car. The way of life for which Lutyens provided the domestic setting was not backward-looking but new. Although, I fear, Sir Frederick Mirrielees was not a progressive: he chaired the Dorking Branch of the National League for Opposing Women's Suffrage.

Works of Skill,
Ingenuity and Art

Human beings are by nature ingenious. Progress came through the application of the cleverness of the brain to the agility of the hand in making things. These days, few people in England rely on craft skills for their existence. Thumbs, developed by repeated use of mobile devices, are set to become more important digits than fingers. But we are hard-wired to admire ingenuity in others. This can be the ingenuity of the past, displayed, con brio, in the collections of Waddesdon Manor. We are awed by the feats of our remote ancestors, wondering how they could possibly have raised Silbury Hill with only antlers to use as spades. The building of the London sewers was a similar order of achievement, involving armies of people and depths of engineering knowledge and vision.

The vision continues, the knowledge changes. Today the greatest wonder is science. Sometimes it is called upon to prevent the great extinction that doomsayers predict as a result of the dominance of *Homo sapiens* as top species on the planet. Engineers may be able to stop London flooding. They have worked a small miracle (although not so small, possibly) in making Tube trains run so frequently. Let us marvel. Let us take hope that other of the world's problems will find answers. What are the odds?

Waddesdon Manor, Buckinghamshire

In the entrance hall of Waddesdon Manor in Buckinghamshire stands an automaton, made in 1774. Over four feet tall, it takes the form of a bronze elephant, decorated with paint, paste, mother-of-pearl and glass. A clockwork mechanism plays tinkling tunes, wiggles the elephant's trunk and tail, makes its ears flap and its eyes swivel, sets in motion the stars and serpents on its sides and rotates a cast of oriental figures; the effect so delighted the Shah of Persia when he visited that he called for it to be played again and again. Ingenious, intricately made *objets de luxe* appealed to the taste of Baron Ferdinand de Rothschild, who built the house. They appealed to all his family, who had what can only be described as a genetic impulse to collect such pieces, as well as beautiful, usually French works of art; sometimes different family members would bid against each other for the same thing. The result is astounding, no less so today under the present Lord Rothschild – who acts as Waddesdon's impresario, having secured an agreement with the National Trust to run the place – than it was in the nineteenth century. Everything is of the best: one fascinating bibelot follows another. Even Waddesdon's collection of eighteenth-century buttons is memorable and exquisite.

There were once forty Rothschild houses across Europe, furnished in a style which gave rise to the term, *le goût Rothschild*. Waddesdon, begun in 1877, is one of the very few that remain intact. Eighteenth-century masterpieces are seen against a background of French *boiseries*, Buhl cabinets, Meissen ornaments and Gobelins tapestries. A writing desk, enriched with marquetry scenes of Rome, had originally been made for the playwright Beaumarchais.

Waddesdon was created for Baron Ferdinand and his small circle of friends to enjoy. It was extremely comfortable, and the people who visited were very grand. But the host who gave these Saturday-to-Mondays was, underneath, a lonely and far from merry individual. He had no interest in the family bank. Though he employed a superb French cook, he himself would only eat toast; he never touched wine. What he liked to call self-deprecatingly his gimcracks – the precious objects that had been made for princes and kings – probably gave him more pleasure than anything else. His most precious objects were contained in a 'Renaissance museum' whose contents were left to the British Museum, in the shape of the Waddesdon Bequest.

Today Waddesdon is enjoyed by the visiting public, and the loss of the Renaissance museum has been made good by the present Lord Rothschild in a Treasury that displays a hoard of fabulous objects: Baroque pearls, Limoges enamel mirror backs, Roman coins, a jasper so-called sewing box (which has recently been revealed as an opium-smoking set), silver gilt by the great Paul Storr, and a temple by Luigi Valadier made in about 1780 from marble, lapis lazuli, crystal, mother-of-pearl and ormolu; inside the nine muses are dancing.

When Baron Ferdinand parted with his large painting by

François Boucher of Madame de Pompadour, now in the Alte Pinakothek in Munich, he kept the frame. Lord Rothschild commissioned a 3-D printed copy from the Factum Foundation to fill the gap, as well as a copy of the small Boucher version of the same painting: they are now displayed side by side and the public is challenged to identify the original. The wonders of Waddesdon never cease. A Crown Jewel for sure.

Silbury Hill, Wiltshire

Silbury Hill is not a hill but a huge, flat-topped dome of earth, nearly forty metres tall and one hundred and sixty-five metres in diameter, like a fantastically enormous Christmas pudding. It is the largest Neolithic mound in Europe and the only one on this scale that is not a burial site.

Having sat placidly on what is now the verge of the A4 near Marlborough for more than four millennia, it started to come alive in the course of 2000: an alarming hole appeared in its crown, along with dents on its sides. The deep central hole could, at one level, be explained easily enough: it followed the line of a shaft sunk by the Duke of Northumberland in 1776. But where was the soil that had been displaced going? Archaeologists and engineers found that the answer was into tunnels, the largest dating to 1968 when Professor R.J.C. Atkinson undertook a dig sponsored by the BBC. The central chamber was big enough for the young Magnus Magnusson to present a television programme from it. When the BBC left, they closed the metal door to the tunnel, tucked the key underneath it, but failed to ensure that more than a few yards had been properly backfilled. As a result, the hill had been on the move.

Ideas about it were also in motion. Archaeologists now have a precise date for the hill's construction. Antlers that were used as tools to build it have been carbon-dated; because antlers grow new every year, they can be dated much more accurately than wood, which might come from a tree that is many scores of years old. Construction was under way around 2400 BC, during the florescence of monument-building in Wiltshire that included Phase II of Stonehenge. However, as at Stonehenge, work probably continued on the site several hundred years after that. Building went on in three stages, the earliest – Silbury I – being a small, relatively flat mound, made both of gravel and organic matter such as wood, leaves, moss and turf; the presence of the organic material suggests that it had ritual significance. Outside Silbury I was a ditch. The second phase of construction, Silbury II, built up to the edge of the ditch, creating a domed monument made of chalk. Silbury III absorbed the first ditch, and left the hillock that we see today, surrounded by a new ditch several metres below the level of the A4.

The Duke of Northumberland had assumed that such a large and important monument must have been the burial place of an ancient king, interred with fitting amounts of funerary treasure. Since antiquaries started to visit the site in the seventeenth century, other theories have been advanced, among them that Silbury was a platform for Druid sacrifices or an astronomical observatory. Today, we can be certain that nobody, king or otherwise, was buried underneath the mound, and the archaeologists who worked with engineers to stabilise the structure were able to shed light on its history. On the evidence of a piece of pottery that has been found cutting into it, Romans seem to have used the mound – perhaps they were digging for that fictional treasure. A large Roman settlement existed on the other side of the A4 (a Roman road), the foundations of which have just been revealed in a geophysical survey. Originally, the profile of the mound was rounded. The discovery of post holes and arrowheads shows that the top was flattened in the Norman period to build a fort. Silbury provided a formidable, ready-made motte.

Question: why was Silbury Hill built? Nobody knows, but perhaps constructing it brought its own rewards. Having so great a shared purpose would have helped the community to cohere. Why has Silbury been restored in the early twenty-first century? One answer might be: because, like the first builders, we are better for doing it.

London's sewers

In London, the summer of 1858 is remembered as the Great Stink, from the foul state of the sewage-infested River Thames. The nation's parliamentarians, sitting on the edge of the river at Westminster, suffered along with the rest of the population, their windows being hung with curtains soaked in disinfecting chloride of lime. This had one merit: it brought home the need for action. The newly formed Metropolitan Board of Works was charged with finding a remedy.

They already knew what had to be done. A number of Commissions had identified the problem of London's sewerage system, namely that much of it was discharged, untreated, into the Thames. Since the capital's drinking water was drawn from its river, cholera was a familiar evil, terrifying the rich as well as the poor. The degradation of the river was a relatively recent phenomenon. Fish had swum there until the 1820s. Until then, the conventional means of disposing of waste was by means of a cesspit dug under the house; this could be offensive to the occupants when it overflowed, and was hardly a joy to empty – though the contents had some value as manure. As the city grew, the price of manure necessarily fell, and the authorities allowed effluent to be drained into the streams and brooks that survived from the pre-urban landscape. These watercourses flowed into the Thames.

Joseph Bazalgette, the MBW's chief engineer, designed a new system: around eighty-three miles of 'interceptory' sewers, running roughly parallel to the Thames, would take the sewage away to a safe distance to the east of the city. From the heights of Hampstead the fall was sufficient to ensure a natural flow; but this was not the case in low-lying areas such as Westminster or along the south bank. Here the flow was maintained by four great pumping stations at Pimlico, Deptford, Crossness (where the great beam engines can still be seen, handsomely restored) and the 'cathedral of sewage', Abbey Mills. In addition, well over a thousand miles of smaller sewers were constructed of brick, and a visit on one of Thames Water's open days shows that, after more than a century of service, they have survived in remarkable condition complete with their original pointing. The works included the construction of the Albert, Victoria and Chelsea Embankments, where sewers were built in conjunction with underground railway tunnels.

Today the Thames is once again home to over a hundred species of fish, though on stormy days small quantities of raw sewage still reach the river via an overflow provision, which was acceptable in Bazalgette's day but which has escalated in proportion to London's size and population. Cue another public furore – and another engineering project has been launched. Tunnel Boring Machine Rachel and Tunnel Boring Machine Charlotte have been nosing their way through the clay and silt beneath the river to form a new twenty-five-kilometre relief sewer. How fabulous it looks in the photographs, how shiny and new

– but there is one thing that Bazalgette would have recognised: the millions of tons of waste soil being expelled by Rachel and Charlotte are removed by barge, saving thousands of lorry movements and big quantities of CO_2: another way in which life is coming back to the Thames.

Berwick-upon-Tweed,
Northumberland

The Royal Border Bridge at Berwick-upon-Tweed comes striding across the River Tweed on twenty-eight brick-and-masonry arches, part of it being a viaduct over the land; the engineer Robert Stephenson built this section first – then on it went, two thousand seven hundred navvies humping eight million cubic feet of stone and two and a half million bricks, to slam straight through the medieval walls of Berwick Castle. The Great Hall, where Edward I took oaths of allegiance from the Scottish nobility in 1296, went; its place is now taken by a railway platform. When the Victorians wanted to build, they built. Historical sentiment came a poor second.

But the Royal Border Bridge is a wonder, and so is Berwick. Should we regret the loss of the castle hall? Berwick's early history was grim. That oath-taking took place after Edward had slaughtered all the male inhabitants of the town. He was furious that the Scots, who had temporarily got hold of it, had refused to surrender. Thereafter, Berwick became an essential base for English operations whenever an army was sent into Scotland. In 1306, the Countess of Buchan, who had crowned Robert the Bruce, was imprisoned in a crown-shaped cage suspended from the castle walls. But it continued to occupy what was effectively a no-man's-land; in three centuries, it changed hands fourteen times. The guns were fired for the last time in celebration when James VI of Scotland passed through the town on his way to becoming King of England in 1603. Before that the inhabitants of Berwick must have found life confusing and precarious.

The architectural result of Berwick's many crises was the greatest system of fortifications in England. Until the Tudor period, it had been protected by tall, thick walls. After a short period of Scottish rule ending in 1482, the walls were lowered and backed by earth ramparts, providing a better defence against artillery. The appearance of French troops in Scotland in the 1520s, following the Scottish disaster at the Battle of Flodden, caused another bout of activity. Bulwarks were constructed, and in 1530 Henry VIII's Master of Ordnance began work on Lord's Mount – a massive two-tier artillery fortification, protecting a weak point in the walls. In the 1540s, the 'rough wooing' intended to precipitate a marriage between the infant Mary Queen of Scots and the future Edward VI re-emphasised Berwick's importance. The greatest period of activity, however, followed Mary I's loss of Calais in 1558, when France egged Scotland on to attack England. It had become impractical to retain the full two-mile length of the old walls; instead the town withdrew behind a series of massive ramparts, earthworks and bastions, their complex clean-edged geometry being carefully calculated to provide a clear range of fire for guns attacking from any angle.

No longer bellicose, this martial town continues to ponder what the Scots will do. An exodus of the Edinburgh middle classes after independence could make Berwick a little Morningside.

The Channel Tunnel

The physical symbol of Britain's new relationship with its continental neighbours is the Channel Tunnel. Previous generations may have celebrated England as a jewel 'set in a silver sea', whose waters had protected it from invasion since 1066; now it is a jewel attached to the Continent by the steel of a railway track and the great thirty-one-mile tube of *le Tunnel sous la Manche*. Huge, costly projects which demand international cooperation are, for obvious reasons, rare; this one deserves to be considered not just as a jewel but as a Crown Jewel. Britain may have left the European Union but it is physically tied to the Continent – plugged into the European rail network.

Visionaries had dreamed of connecting Britain and France by tunnel since the age of Napoleon. The more recent of them recalled that Britain had once been part of the same landmass as continental Europe, and had still been attached by a narrow isthmus as recently, in geological terms, as thirteen thousand years ago. An attempt at tunnelling had been made in 1880, when a boring machine began digging on either side of the Channel. In 1940, when Britain's high command waited daily for Hitler to launch a seaborne invasion, there was general relief that a tunnel did not exist. By the mid-1950s, however, it was deemed that the military objection to a tunnel was obsolete. Plans were drawn up in the 1960s and launched in 1973: the same year that Britain joined the Common Market, as the European Union was then known. It was not an auspicious time: the oil crisis – shortages caused by war in the Middle East, immediately followed by aggressive price rises by OPEC – threw the economy into confusion and the project was abandoned. A cross-Channel bridge, or Europont, was examined, but rejected on grounds of cost.

In 1984, the French and British governments at last showed that they were serious about a tunnel, though they wanted private money to pay for it. Eurotunnel made the successful bid, for two rail tunnels with a service tunnel linked to them in between. A decade and eight million cubic metres of soil later the Chunnel opened, and Britain felt itself to be a little less islandy than before. Suddenly, Paris and Brussels were, in time, closer to London than Liverpool or Truro. Among the many hitherto unnoticed qualities in the French to which British eyes have been opened is the superior state of their railway track, as passengers, contrasting the bullet-like speed of their train on the French side of the 'Chunnel' with its slow, spasmodic progress between Dover and Victoria

Station, remained all too acutely aware. Even that was improved with the line to St Pancras International.

British governments are by instinct parsimonious. They fight shy of *grands projets*. Very occasionally they will lift their eyes to the horizon and see that a big statement can boost national self-respect and add to the happiness of the country. Let us celebrate these times when they happen. Like certain types of bus, you never know when the next one will come along. HS2? Who can say.

Bridges over the Tyne

One of the high points of the railway journey between King's Cross and Edinburgh is the Tyne: the crossing is spectacular – in eighteenth-century terms, sublime. The present mainline railway bridge – the King Edward VII, built in 1902–6 – might have been engineered for the moment of drama when trains from the south draw into Newcastle-upon-Tyne Station. The bank of the river is steep at that point and passengers seem briefly to float over the roofs of the adjacent streets. Alighting, they will find themselves in one of the grandest of mid-nineteenth-century neo-Classical set pieces: the front is a Palladian conception of a *porte-cochère* and end pavilions adorned with giant Doric pilasters, designed by the North Eastern Railway company's architect, Thomas Prosser, in 1863. But oh, they will be standing on the site of medieval Newcastle, much of which was demolished by the railway promoters without a qualm; as at Berwick, they even smashed through the castle walls.

Look to the east. The Edward VII Bridge is only one of a series of six that cross the Tyne at this point, and not the most arresting to look at. Charles Harrison, the engineer for the North Eastern Railway, had originally planned to raise a bridge of only two spans, of lattice girder construction, but the discovery of old coal workings meant that he had to increase the number of piers. This is not evident from the train. Instead, passengers can enjoy the sequence of Newcastle's other bridges, starting with the Queen Elizabeth II Bridge, opened by H.M. the Queen in 1981; the ironwork is painted the ecclesiastical colour, light blue, but is otherwise unremarkable. Then comes Robert Stephenson's High Level Bridge of 1849, the first railway bridge doubling as a road bridge (costs were saved by putting the rail line above the roadway, to avoid increasing the breadth). The railway part is now used only as a turning loop.

At a lower level, jaunty in its livery of red girders and blue control-tower roof, is the Swing Bridge of 1868–76. It was designed by the armaments manufacturer Lord Armstrong – whose country house, Cragside, lies thirty miles to the north – and the Tyne Improvement Commission. When opened, it was the largest bridge of its kind in the world: necessary to allow big ships, previously impeded by a nine-arched bridge of 1781, to get upstream. The original hydraulic engines are still in use.

In the distance, behold the mighty arc of the Tyne Bridge, reminiscent of the contemporary Sydney Harbour Bridge if only a third of the length (the same consultant was used). A high-level bridge for the Great North Road had been mooted in 1860; its construction, more than eighty years later, was made possible by a government subsidy intended to relieve unemployment in the shipyards on Tyneside. A new way of building, being developed for Sydney, was used in the construction: the two halves of the arch were built out from each bank of the river by a cantilever system, using cables, cradles and cranes. They were pinned together in February 1928, after which the road deck was built. In 1929, the bridge was opened by George V and Queen Mary, crossing sedately in their Ascot landau; the King's speech was recorded by Movietone News.

Beyond soar the parabolic eyebrows of the Gateshead Millennium Bridge, built for pedestrians and cyclists in 2001; when the bridge pivots to allow shipping to pass, it looks as though it is winking. Bravo, designers Wilkinson Eyre, for continuing a great tradition; elegance and innovative technology hold hands.

The Thames Barrier

The greatest works of engineering are often beautiful. I could never condemn Concorde for its noisy engines when it flew over our London home, because the bass growl, which never became so familiar I ignored it, would made me look up – and there was the consummately elegant, sleek silver dart of an aeroplane glinting in the early evening sky. I cannot help experiencing a puzzled awe when I see offshore wind turbines, in their serried ranks, glittering on the horizon of the sea; I am told by campaigner friends they are an *ignis fatuus* and that the cost of maintenance will, over time, outweigh the green energy they produce. But the achievement of building these whirling giants – two hundred metres tall, in the case of those off Yorkshire – in the North Sea and elsewhere is phenomenal. So it is with the

Thames Barrier. It looks like a row of polished helmets, which, when the steel gates between them are raised, forms a shield. And unlike the other examples I have mentioned, there is no questioning its practical contribution to national well-being. We need it more and more.

I declare an interest. Around Christmas 2019, some neighbours received official texts warning them that they could be at risk of flooding. This is, in one sense, not entirely surprising, because our part of London used to be marshy; before it could be developed in the mid-nineteenth century, Thomas Cubitt dumped hundreds of barge loads of rubble, some from the excavations at St Katharine's Dock, onto the ground, to elevate it. The barges came in by the Grosvenor Canal, the basin of which would become the site of Victoria Station. But if Pimlico is low-lying, so are many other places along the length of the Thames, which, before the building of the embankments, dawdled sluggishly, looping as it went, in a broad, slow stream towards the estuary. So a flood for us would mean that Hammersmith, half of Southwark, Victoria Station, the Houses of Parliament, parts of the City, Canary Wharf, the Greenwich Peninsula and the Olympic Park could also be under water. We have only the Thames Barrier to protect us.

The Barrier spans a 520-metre-wide stretch of the river, nine and a half miles downstream from Parliament. Pairs of hydraulic rams lift ten steel gates from the riverbed to block the incoming flow of the Thames, generally at times of storm surge combined with high tide. If water threatened to overtop the gates, a gap would be opened at the bottom to allow a controlled 'underspill' . . . but this has not happened as yet. Indeed, since operations began in 1982, water has got no closer than two metres from the top of the gates. So far so good. But the number of times on which the gates have had to be closed has been increasing. And the average of five closures per year (a total of one hundred and eighty-six between 1982 and late 2019) masks spikes in activity: in the exceptionally wet year of 2014, the Barrier was closed fifty times. It is expected that the rate of closure will increase over coming decades as sea levels rise.

What is expected, of course, is not necessarily what happens, in the unpredictable maelstrom of climate change. Freak weather events are getting to be the new normal.

No need for panic. The Environment Agency's Thames Estuary 2100 plan has the situation under control. But my goodness, that Barrier is a Crown Jewel.

The Royal Botanic Gardens, Wakehurst

One of the less-sung wonders of Britain is the state of its botany. The gardening-mad British probably know more about the flora of their country than any other nation on earth. This is not quite such a big claim as it seems; because the British Isles were cut off from the Continent at the formation of the English Channel at the end of the last ice age, the flora are relatively restricted: many species never found their way here. Even so, the work of unpaid enthusiasts in recording species in their area – the country has been divided up into ten-kilometre squares – is phenomenal. And even that is exceeded by the systematic collection of seeds by the Royal Botanic Gardens. Its botanists have gathered, dried and catalogued the seeds of thousands of species from around the world, which have been deposited in specially built, temperature-controlled vaults, the size of thirty-seven double-decker buses, at the Royal Botanic Gardens' country estate of Wakehurst, in Sussex. The vaults contain more than a billion individual seeds.

The Millennium Seed Bank stands in a long tradition of collecting plants, begun in the eighteenth century. The Farmer

King, George III, was personally interested in botany, having been encouraged to develop his own gardens at Kew on scientific lines by his early and greatly loved mentor the Earl of Bute. Eventually Bute, who was briefly Prime Minister, fell out of favour; but by this time – the 1770s – Sir Joseph Banks had arrived within the royal orbit. Banks was already a celebrity. The son of a wealthy Lincolnshire landowner from whom he inherited at the age of twenty-one, he had accompanied Captain Cook on his voyages of exploration in the *Endeavour*. He was also a customer at Coutts, continuing the bank's association with seedsmen, plant collectors and botanists that had begun in 1757 when Minier and Mason, seedsmen on the Strand, opened an account. James Coutts bought from them. Intriguingly, there are references to packets and collections of seeds being sent out from the bank in the 1740s – then as now, presumably, gardeners loved to swap. This was an age in which the development of new strains and species was associated with agricultural improvement.

In expanding Kew Gardens, Banks was able to call upon the many scientific contacts he had made around the world. The King's name could be invoked to encourage ambassadors and the East India Company to help in collecting plants and seeds. Banks was a systematic man. Hoping to rival and surpass similar institutions in Paris and Vienna, he organised a programme of plant collecting that would be as comprehensive as possible. Gardeners from Kew were sent to South Africa, the Canaries, Australia, South America and elsewhere. They sent back not only plants but details of the soil they grew in and the conditions in which they flourished. Two gardeners from Kew were on the *Bounty* when Captain Bligh sailed to Tahiti in 1787 to collect breadfruit plants, to be raised and transplanted as a source of cheap food in the West Indies. Banks's instructions for the care of the plants on the cramped ship, which involved frequently moving and sponging them, may have contributed to the famous mutiny.

Kew Gardens may today serve both as a site of scientific research and a pleasure ground for Londoners, but George III's hope was that its botanical work would improve British farming. The Millennium Seed Bank has a similarly practical motive: to preserve species for applications that may as yet be undreamt of. The potential benefits over coming centuries are unquantifiable. Nobody can say what new uses humankind will derive from plants in the future. In the 1960s, the contraceptive pill was originally developed from a yam. How long will the seeds in storage remain viable to germinate? A long time, in some cases. Dr Roger Smith, the Kew biologist who began the project, cites pre-Colombian rattles made by inserting canna seeds into the soft, immature shells of growing walnuts. 'One that we know from carbon-dating the walnut shell to be 600 years old has been germinated.' As biodiversity comes to be increasingly threatened around the world, the Millennium Seed Bank offers the last hope that plant species can be saved from extinction.

The Victoria Line

It is generally admitted that the Victoria Line is the best line in London. All right, all right – full disclosure: we live a hundred yards from one of the stations and since my family and I use it nearly every day, we are partial. But it is, honestly, a miracle. Not only does it go to all the places you want of an Underground line – Green Park for the London Library, King's Cross and St Pancras for the overground to Ramsgate – but trains run at a rate of one every ninety seconds. This never ceases to astound those of us who remember the pitiful state of public transport a generation ago. Trains came infrequently, if at all, in the 1970s; there were often strikes; although, if memory serves, the seats may still have been upholstered in moquette fabrics designed by Marion Dorn before the Second World War, they had been impregnated with cigarette smoke (for, yes, smoking was permitted on the Tube). They carried only a fraction of today's passengers.

Hurrah for the London Underground. The very first stretch was opened by the Metropolitan Railway in 1863: the first underground railway in the world. It sought to answer the problem of a city congested by the volume of traffic generated by the new railway termini, which brought people and goods to the periphery of the city but then left them to battle their way across in a variety of horse-drawn conveyances. The traffic jams were horrendous. Early lines were built just below the surface of the city by a method called 'cut and cover'. Later, in order to push lines beneath London's densely built streets, the tunnelling system developed by Marc Brunel for the Thames Tunnel was adopted, but only when it was possible to power trains by electricity; deep tunnels had too little ventilation for steam trains. In the 1930s, art was brought to bear on the expanding network; under its chief executive Frank Pick, the London Underground adopted an improving mission, not unlike the Reithian BBC. Art-minded contemporaries likened Pick to Lorenzo the Magnificent in fifteenth-century Florence. He commissioned typefaces from Edward Johnston, posters from Laura Knight, Paul Nash and Graham Sutherland, and spotted the potential of the famous Tube map devised by an out-of-work signalling engineer, Harry Beck. The stations designed by Charles Holden played with Classical geometry but in an uncompromisingly Modern way.

The Victoria Line does not belong to this period of artistic flourishing. When it was opened between 1968 and '71, London Underground had lost its shine. Bad industrial relations combined with declining passenger numbers to create a mood of despair. The designers chose grey as their colour palette: grey tiles, aluminium trains; the 1970s would be a grey decade. A flicker of the Pick heritage emerged in a series of sixteen tile murals, one for each station, commissioned from artists such as Edward Bawden (Victoria and Tottenham Hale) and Tom Eckersley (Euston, King's Cross, Finsbury Park). Even so, it has never been a great aesthetic experience – not like the heroic new stations for the Jubilee Line, which have shades of the Moscow Underground or even Piranesi. But it works. Heavens, how it works – far harder than was envisaged in the 1960s.

Ten times more trains use the track, and most of them are pretty full; in rush hour, they are crammed. (I speak of the time before Coronavirus.) It would be impossible to run a greater frequency of service; more carriages cannot be added because the trains would be too long for the platforms; the size of the tunnel does not allow a double-decker. There are problems in the offing. Wheels squeal on the curved sections of the track. Not much can be done about it – no space for rubber wheels – beyond re-grinding the rails (a temporary expedient). Better fixings are possible on concrete sleepers but some of the sleepers are still wooden. These are weighty problems for the future.

How nice it would be, friends say, if we had a system such as Copenhagen or Vienna; but these are much smaller cities than London. New York would be a closer comparison. Beijing? That's new. I cannot help it, the Victoria Line leaves me in awe. Imagine what life would be like without it.

The Doddington Hall tapestries

Doddington Hall in Lincolnshire is one of those country houses you find only in Britain. The attics are full of old toys, military headgear, unwanted commodes and a giant figure of the White Rabbit, left over from an Alice in Wonderland-themed event. A collection of Roman antiquities, some found on the estate, is displayed in the downstairs lavatory, along with a child's pedal-operated aeroplane with patriotic RAF roundels. From the roof, you can see Lincoln Cathedral, on a good day. Built around 1600, Doddington has hardly been changed outside, and in half a millennium it has never been sold.

Best of all are the tapestries. Once, tapestries were valued far above paintings and furniture: this reflected the skill and time that it took to make them, as well as the precious metals that were woven through them to give a sparkle of luxury. They were versatile wall hangings, capable of being rolled up and carried from one palace to another, as the Tudor monarchs made their progresses around the country. In the seventeenth century, one of Charles I's greatest coups was to purchase the cartoons, or working drawings, that Raphael made for a series of tapestries on the subject of the Acts of the Apostles; he had a set of full-scale tapestries made from them at the Mortlake tapestry works established by his father James I. In the first decades of the eighteenth century, the Duke of Marlborough commissioned a series of tapestries to celebrate his victories against Louis XIV; they still hang in Blenheim Palace. But the vogue passed; gloomy old tapestries were entirely unsuited to the interiors of Robert Adam and his contemporaries, inspired by the Ancient World. Usually the bright colours had faded in the sunlight, leaving only a monochrome of silvery blue.

Doddington was one of the few houses where tapestries were still appreciated, due to the antiquarian tastes of its owner John Hussey Delaval. Delaval inherited the house, as a second son, in 1759. In time, he would also own the other family properties of Seaton Delaval and Ford Castle in Northumberland, doing work to all of them. At Doddington he began in 1760. He retained the Elizabethan walled gardens and courtyards at a time when Capability Brown's style was eliminating them elsewhere; and when remodelling the inside of the house, Sir John shunned the more delicate new styles that were coming in and sent drawings from London for distinctly old-fashioned detailing such as panelling, and a Gothic frieze for the chimneypiece of the Holly Room. And in bedrooms, Flemish tapestries dating from the 1620s (presumed to have hung in the Elizabethan Great Hall) were chopped up and nailed to the walls like wallpaper in a highly unusual scheme. In 1762 John Delaval's agent, William Portis, reported that he had had 'a tayler all this week mending the tapestry before we hung it up'. Use of tapestries in this way, covering every inch of the wall, is now very rare.

Made from wool, tapestries are vulnerable to damage from

UV light, coal dust, moth, damp, rot and being nibbled by rodents. Age is not generally kind to them, unless care is taken to keep them in trim. Remarkable for their use in Delaval's antiquarian scheme, the Doddington tapestries are not of the finest quality, such as the 'Four Seasons' tapestries at Hatfield House, finished by Ralph Sheldon at his factory in Warwickshire; nor as big as the Oudenaarde tapestries at Hardwick Hall (whose inferiority to Brussels tapestries can be seen from the traces of paint that have been identified: it was used to sharpen the colour). Doddington's tapestries are of a coarser type, more workaday – and vanishingly few of this grade of tapestries have survived as they were not cherished and cared for like the finest ones. Decorating the Holly Bedroom and the Yellow Bedroom, they come from two series depicting 'Scenes from Rural Life' and 'The Trojan Wars', mercilessly hacked about and tacked up. Heroes in armour vie with bagpipers and a sportsman smoking a pipe with his gun beside him.

Fortunately, with support from Lincolnshire County Council, the University of Lincoln, the Heritage Lottery Fund, the Country Houses Foundation, the Pilgrim Trust, the Mercers' Foundation, Dulverton Trust, Lincolnshire Community Foundation and many other donors, the Doddington Hall Conservation Charity was able to employ a team of conservators, who worked for five years patiently conserving the tapestries – to the intense interest of visitors – in the most fragile and beautiful of houses.

Things We Do Well

I am not a Pollyanna. Not everything in England is as good as it might be – far from it. But there are some things that we can be proud of doing well. Were some unimaginable Notre-Dame-like cataclysm to remove them, they would be specially mourned. We can hold them up as examples of excellence that we would like the rest of life to achieve.

I start with the Hospital of St Bartholomew, otherwise known as Barts: how amazing that after nine hundred years it still fulfils the charitable purpose for which it was founded by a courtier turned monk in the reign of Henry I. Only, rather better, given advances in medical science: it is now a flagship of the National Health Service and one of the great teaching hospitals of the world. We can clap for Barts. We can be proud of the excellence of the Royal Opera House, whether opera is our bag or not: opera is hugely complicated, as well as costly, to stage well, and all the effort and expense will be wasted if it fails to deliver the emotional punch that audiences expect. Covent Garden productions are knockouts, more often than not. Around the corner from the Royal Opera House is Neal's Yard Dairy, centre of the British cheese revival, which has defied all expectation by making a gastronomic desert bloom. Wimbledon Fortnight remains Wimbledon Fortnight despite all the pressures of commercial tennis. The BBC lives, it seems, to infuriate a proportion of its audience (me included); but how the nation would mourn it, should it ever go.

Market towns – even unsung ones like Louth – continue to offer an ideal of civilised existence. The hospitality offered by the celebrated George Hotel at Stamford deserves its fame. Time present and time past are both present in Little Gidding, as they were for T.S. Eliot and Charles I. The red kite is a phoenix that has arisen from the ashes of local extinction to excite anyone who sees this massive bird (whose name, I now realise, has nothing to do with the kite-shape of its tail feathers). The Elgin Marbles, a dazzling human achievement, are displayed in the most appropriate possible setting for such a work: a museum that brings together the cultures of the world to enrich the meanings of its holdings and provide inspiration to the nearly seven million people who visit it for free each year.

St Bartholomew's Hospital, Smithfield

Those three talismanic initials: NHS. How proud we are of them, and how in awe of its doctors, nurses, ambulance drivers, porters and other staff at a time of crisis, such as that of the Coronavirus pandemic. But hospitals have a history that pre-dates that of the National Health Service. St Bartholomew's Hospital in London's Smithfield, while still at the cutting edge of medical science, was founded nine hundred years ago. It is still on the same site. The very old institution and the very new in technology live harmoniously together, to the benefit of both. Today's health-care professionals – highly trained, technologically sophisticated – are proud of a tradition that dates from monastic times; the monks of the twelfth century were motivated by the same compassion as themselves.

The man who founded Barts, one Rahere, was a courtier of Henry I's who would have died on a pilgrimage to Rome, had he not been tended by monks attached to a church dedicated to St Bartholomew. Rahere vowed that, should he recover, he would found a hospital in London; on his way home, his intention was strengthened by a vision of St Bartholomew, who told him to build a church in his name at Smithfield, outside the city walls – a desolate area. Accordingly, in 1123, Rahere founded both a hospital and a priory; the Church of St Bartholomew the Great survives from the latter, although the priory was suppressed at the Dissolution of the Monasteries in 1539. The hospital might also have disappeared had the City authorities not petitioned Henry VIII; shortly before his death in 1547, the King granted the hospital to the City of London. It was in poor condition and the endowments did not cover its costs; the shortfall was met by donations. This started a tradition of philanthropy that continues to this day. The ground occupied by the hospital formed its own parish, served by the Church of St Bartholomew the Less.

In 1609 William Harvey, who would become the first person to describe the circulation of the blood, was appointed the hospital's physician. Since he also attended the court, finally becoming Charles I's personal physician in the 1630s, he could be criticised for his absences. Nevertheless, he laid down some practical rules for administering medicine at Barts, largely to ensure that junior doctors could not exercise their skills without the approval of colleagues. Very short, round-faced, swarthy, and with a peppery temper, a doctor's execrable handwriting and an alarming tendency to fiddle with a small dagger that hung by his side, Harvey would personally see patients once a week, seated at a table in the hall, flanked by his apothecary, steward and matron.

In 1729, plans were approved for a redevelopment that swept away the medieval street plan, replacing it with four handsome blocks around a courtyard. The architect was James Gibbs, famous for his churches, university buildings and country houses. Three of the blocks contained fourteen wards each, serving around five hundred patients. The North Wing contained offices and a Great Hall, whose walls are lined with the names of the donors who subscribed to the cost of building. William Hogarth gave his services as mural painter for free; his work comprises two huge oil paintings on the walls of the staircase leading up to the Great Hall, on the biblical themes of the Good Samaritan and the Pool of Bethesda, at which Christ healed the sick. While the grand ceremonial spaces of the North Wing added to the dignity of the hospital, surgeons such as Edward Nourse and Percivall Pott improved the practice of their profession; Nourse's anatomical lectures were the forerunner of what became, in the nineteenth century, the largest medical school in London.

Today, Barts is part of a National Health Service Trust that occupies several sites across London. The Barts Heart and Cancer Centres are both located in the King George V wing of the hospital, which replaced one range of Gibbs's quadrangle in 1937; recently this wing has been comprehensively refurbished. Innovative services include robotic surgery, complex electro-physiology, stem-cell transplantation and immunotherapy for cancer treatment. All this and history too. Fantastic.

Neal's Yard Dairy,
Covent Garden

I do not mean *just* the Neal's Yard Dairy. This entry could showcase the equally splendid Ripon's Cheese Stores in Pimlico (I have to say that; it's next to our home). Or any of the many excellent cheese shops that are now to be found in provincial cities. But Neal's Yard was in at the beginning, having been in what was still a scruffy part of London – yet to recover from the departure of the old Covent Garden fruit and vegetable market – in 1979. I remember those days well. At Cambridge, our meals in hall would end with the delectable offering of 'blue or white'. Cheese had become that generic. Although the nadir had yet to be plumbed; Lymeswold, a bland nothing of a cheese, with a fake name devised by marketeers, was not launched upon a long-suffering public until 1981. Valiantly, Neal's Yard took on the Blob and won.

But oh, they were dire times. Just as local breweries were being put out of business by industrial producers, using chemicals and steel kegs, so the big dairies thought they could get away with similar techniques to produce flavourless cheese. Shoppers were deemed to want convenience, not character. Taste buds degraded by Second World War rationing could not handle pungent flavours. Before Neal's Yard, the most exciting cheese sensation to which the ordinary person could aspire was Danish blue; Edam – Dickens's 'modest Dutchman' – was embraced with affection; the more characterful of French cheeses were, for most people, too smelly. Cheddar was as likely to come from Canada as Somerset.

So Lymeswold, created by the Milk Marketing Board which wanted to soak up an excess of milk, was greeted with a cautious enthusiasm. But then the public rebelled. In 1992, it went out of production and the fight-back by artisan cheese producers began. This crusade has now reached parts of the United Kingdom which never had much of a cheese tradition, such as Northern Ireland and Scotland. Top chefs – French ones – may complain that Britain lacks specialist *affineurs*, whose job is to bring on cheese so it can be served at the peak of condition. But such has been the power of the local-food movement that many of the best restaurants now serve nothing but British cheese.

In 1979, Neal's Yard was a revelation. Who in those days knew that cheese could be so good? And British cheese at that. This was an era when Britain's cuisine had yet to become the envy of the gastronomic world. The very mustiness that tingled the customer's nostrils entering the shop – and the waxy paper in which the cheese about to be bought was enfolded – those things promised a better world; a world of which most people could not even dream. But look at us now. 'How can you govern a country in which there are two hundred and forty-six kinds of cheese,' lamented Charles de Gaulle (although the precise number of *fromages* does vary, according to source, from two hundred and forty-six to four hundred). The British now make at least seven hundred – more, it is said, than the French. It would not surprise me if there were two hundred and forty-six varieties of farmhouse Cheddar alone. What a revolution . . . and yet civil order has been maintained.

Neal's Yard, take a bow; yours, more than anyone's, is the credit for this phenomenon. In the priestly calm of his Nottinghamshire dairy, Joe Schneider is making Stichelton – an unpasteurised cheese that resembles Stilton in every particular, except one: traditional Stilton has to be made from pasteurised milk. Stichelton was a brand developed in partnership with Randolph Hodgson, founder of the Neal's Yard Dairy. When Jonny Crickmore, son of a dairy farmer in Suffolk, wanted to move into cheese-making, he asked Hodgson's advice. 'Unpasteurised Brie,' came the answer. It cannot be called Brie – that is a protected name. Crickmore sells it as Baron Bigod, the Earl of Norfolk who ruled Suffolk in the twelfth century. Powerful name, powerful stuff. Neal's Yard Dairy is a Crown Jewel to mark a truth that must be self-evident to all. Life only gets better.

The market town of Louth

This is about local life. We are lucky in this country to have so many societies and clubs, usually voluntary and operating below the national radar; people give a lot of leisure time to running them and taking part. You know the kind of thing: a snapshot could be taken of all those village noticeboards that advertise yoga classes, lectures, litter-picking, amateur dramatics and the work of the Neighbourhood Forum, whose laborious job it is to prepare the Neighbourhood Plan. Nowhere I know better expresses this spirit than Louth, a beautiful, largely Georgian town with brick façades and sash windows – outwardly little changed from the days of Mrs Gaskell's *Cranford* and much in demand as a film set. This state of preservation can only reflect a strong local community. You sense this in the Louth Museum, whose central exhibit is a panorama of the town created in the 1840s. Every detail of the streets, gardens and local population is depicted, in what comes over today as a work of exceptional love.

Louth Museum reflects the spirit of the place in another way; it is owned by the Louth Naturalists', Antiquarian and Literary Society – the Nats and Ants as they are familiarly known. As the name suggests, it is a learned society of the type that – along with more recently founded amenity societies – does so much for the calibre of towns and villages across Britain, keeping them intellectually awake and fighting the ugliness that can accompany modern life.

That natural history should be yoked with antiquarianism and literature should not surprise us; the first two were viewed as part of the same province before 1900. After the formation of the Society of Antiquaries, now gloriously housed in London's Burlington House on Piccadilly, in 1707, the study of local history, geology, botany and wildlife became a fashionable activity for landowners and clergymen. With the rise of magazines devoted to these topics in the nineteenth century, it became practically an obsession for people eager to participate in the great debates of the era. There was a rage for collecting and classifying: butterflies, coins, fossils (they were rewriting the understanding of Creation, since the latter belonged to species not mentioned in Genesis), stuffed fish, Napoleon's breakfast service, wonders and curiosities, Egyptology – they are still displayed in the old-fashioned mahogany cases of the Wisbech and Fenland Museum, opened in 1849 to display the collections of the Wisbech Literary Society (founded 1781) and the Museum Society (1835). In 1873 a surveyor listed one hundred and sixty-nine local scientific societies in Great Britain and Ireland, most of them field clubs that had been formed since 1850.

Founded in 1884, the Nats and Ants is a relative latecomer to this party, but made up for it by opening a museum in 1910. For most of the next century this comprised a single gallery; there are now three, due largely to a Heritage Lottery Fund grant in the early twenty-first century. Truth to tell, the panorama owes less to the museum where it is now displayed than to the perilous state of the 295-foot spire of the parish church, built, we know from records, by the master mason John Cole and others in 1501–15. Lightning damage, the vibration from the bells and botched repairs meant that by 1844 it needed urgent attention, and that year scaffolding was erected. William Brown, a reporter and horse painter, was among those who went up. He may have penned the account of the 'very beautiful and extremely novel' view that appeared under the name of the rector's wife, Sarah Mantell: from the top of the spire, 'the gardens appear like the green plots on a topographical map; the hay stacks like beehives, the mansions of the gentry like robin houses, the carriages and homes like Dutch toys, and the inhabitants walking hither and thither in the street, neither exactly like human beings nor quite like the industrious ants of which they are atypical'. (Shades of Orson Welles on the Prater Park Ferris wheel in *The Third Man*.)

The description exactly matches Brown's 360-degree panorama, made in two halves. No other town in Britain possesses such a fine visual record. The detail of the early Victorian town gardens and the relationship of this well-ordered redbrick town to the prosperous countryside beyond are particularly fascinating; just outside the town can be seen the large medieval fish ponds that used to breed fish for a Cistercian abbey. We need more panoramas. We need more places like Louth.

The Royal Opera House

I accept that not everyone likes opera. You may be a fan, you may not be. However, I include the Royal Opera House, Covent Garden, on grounds of excellence. I have been going there, as often as I can afford, since about 1970. It has enabled me to witness an institution transform itself from being a rather British affair – patchy in the quality of its productions, not always hitting the high notes (in any sense), content to appeal to an audience who went because their families had always gone – to one that aspires to be the best in the world, across the board. In writing about it, superlatives fall from the keyboard. It attracts the world's greatest stars. The direction is superb, the orchestra fabulous, the chorus fantastic. In Antonio Pappano, in post since 2002, it has a musical director of genius.

There is ballet too, for those who like it. Following a dazzling architectural renewal by Stanton Williams, completed in 2018 – a project that had lasted for three hundred thousand working houses during which the main stage never closed, mounting nine hundred and ninety-six world-class performances – facilities backstage have been transfigured. A former rehearsal space has become a small theatre, the Linbury, for rare repertoire and contemporary works. Audiences now find that experiencing the building – which might involve taking a giant escalator up through the glass and cast-iron market building of the Floral Hall (now a bar), or looking out across Covent Garden piazza from a newly made terrace – is almost as dramatic as the action on stage. All of which was entirely funded by money raised from private philanthropists, whether individuals, organisations or trusts.

There is history to the Opera House – of course there is. It was founded as the Covent Garden Theatre, opening in 1732 with a performance of Congreve's *The Way of the World*. It was modelled on two existing London theatres, one (Drury Lane) possibly by Wren, the other (the Haymarket) by Vanbrugh. Since there were no purpose-built concert halls in London at this time, the Covent Garden Theatre was also used for musical performances, including – at great expense – the premiere of several Handel operas in the 1730s. The *Messiah* had its first performance here in 1743. But let us not detain ourselves too long with the first Covent Garden; it burnt down in 1808 (Wren's Drury Lane and Vanbrugh's Haymarket have also gone). It was rebuilt by Henry Holland on fireproofing principles. As *The World* reported, 'neither cloth, silk nor linen, is used in decorating the Boxes, and water colour is used instead of oil'; the surfaces were covered in thin board.

This theatre was transformed in 1847 to create the present auditorium. The prime movers in this enterprise were a group known as the Costamongers, after the Neapolitan conductor Michael Costa, who had fallen out with the management of Her Majesty's, the previous home of Italian opera. Costa chose a fellow Neapolitan to do the work: Benedetto Albano. Albano had fled Naples in the best operatic tradition, after being implicated in the assassination of a police chief; he arrived in England after some years working as an architect in France. Since, in comparison with France and Italy, opera in Britain was distinctly provincial, his reorganisation was much praised. There was a resemblance to La Scala; Holland's boards gave way to plaster decoration in a medium ('canabic') invented by Albano; and the Italian Domenico Ferri painted the shallow dome. Around 1900, the stage was completely remodelled by Edwin O. Sachs, introducing both electricity and the machinery needed for Wagnerian music drama.

After the Second World War, when Covent Garden market was nearly demolished for a road scheme, it seemed that the opera house was doomed. Now it faces another threat, along with other theatres that have been closed, due to Coronavirus. Cue transformation scene. Opera is all about sudden reverses of fortune. Audience despair will soon turn to joy when the doors reopen.

The All England Lawn Tennis and Croquet Club, Wimbledon

As an architectural ensemble, the All England Lawn Tennis and Croquet Club at Wimbledon has few redeeming features. The site used to be a landscape park designed by Capability Brown and it would have been better, aesthetically, if it had stayed that way. But nobody could deny that the spot is hallowed.

The Club moved to its present site, at the top of Wimbledon Hill, in 1922, when the Centre Court was built to the designs of the otherwise obscure Captain Stanley Peach. What would become the sacred turf was brought down from Cumberland and tended by fifteen groundsmen. Over the years, the original tennis-party atmosphere, epitomised by strawberries and cream, evolved into the stupendously money-generating fixture of today, with a staff of fifteen hundred dedicated to catering alone. Could anyone mourn the disappearance of the architecture if it were to be suddenly swept away? Not really. But without Wimbledon fortnight the world would be bereft.

Croquet had preceded tennis in popularity. It was in the offices of *The Field* magazine that the All England Croquet Club was founded in 1868. But another game was on the up, due to a series of technical innovations. The invention of the lawn mower in the mid-nineteenth century made it possible to cut grass shorter and more evenly than before, when scythes were generally used, and the vulcanisation of rubber, developed by the American Charles Goodyear in 1839, allowed the making of balls that would bounce on this smooth sward. The first experiments, with a game similar to racquets but played outside, took place in 1859. Initially, lawn tennis was regarded as portable – nets could be raised on empty roads, or even on frozen ponds. While this did not survive as an essential feature of the game, the professional classes were quick to realise that it could be played – more energetically than croquet – on a suburban lawn, without incurring the expense of shooting, hunting or polo. Non-players could still partake of the indispensable tennis tea, in which, from an early date, strawberries and cream could be expected to figure, along with the now extinct iced claret cup.

Rules had to be written, clubs formed. Like football, cricket, rugby, boxing, polo, cross-country riding, mountaineering and some types of Alpine skiing, tennis was one of the many sporting pastimes either that were invented in England, or whose rules were codified by Englishmen. The committee of the All England Croquet Club acquired four acres of lawn at the bottom of Wimbledon hill; some of the grass was turned over to tennis courts in 1875, and the words 'and Lawn Tennis' were added to the name of the Club. (They were later changed to 'Lawn Tennis and . . .'.) The world's first lawn tennis championship, using rubber balls covered in flannel, was held two years later.

Tennis quickly became a vogue; it was a social game, it allowed young people of both sexes to mingle decorously, and courts could be fitted into the large suburban gardens of the prosperous middle classes as easily as in the parks of country houses. The sexes would not seem, on the face of it, to be fairly matched. While the men could remove their dazzlingly striped blazers, perhaps tying a scarf around their midriffs to relieve the monotony of their white flannels and shirts, the ladies were unable to escape their highly restrictive costumes. Long skirts might be gathered up with a spare hand to stop the wearers from tripping up, but without showing ankles . . . All gone, all gone. Let's not talk about the present over-commercialised sport, pursued by monomaniacs to the exclusion of all else. Leave me to my dreams.

Little Gidding, Cambridgeshire

The adjective 'numinous' – I have already used it of Hexham Abbey and I confess myself stumped by Little Gidding. Does 'gnostic' do it? History seems to have imbued the place with an almost palpable sense of spirituality. T.S. Eliot, visiting on a spring afternoon in 1936, responded to it; afterwards he made 'Little Gidding' the title of the last of his great reflections on time and interconnectedness, *Four Quartets*.

The story of Little Gidding begins with a financial catastrophe. In 1624, the Virginia Company, which had founded the American colony of Virginia in 1607, was wound up by the King withdrawing its charter. It had been appallingly managed since its foundation. In the last few years John Ferrar, its deputy, had been trying to make what sense he could of its affairs, but now found himself embroiled in the disaster; he was on the point of being ruined. A solution was found which involved the purchase of the manor of Little Gidding by his widowed mother, Mary, from a bankrupt former partner. John, Mary and John's brilliant younger brother Nicholas decided to go and live there. They had had enough of London. They wanted to pursue a spiritual life. An outbreak of plague meant that they left London even sooner than they intended. They arrived at Little Gidding in 1626.

The manor had been all but abandoned. An Elizabethan owner had enclosed it, possibly evicting some of the inhabitants, whose numbers had already been reduced by plague. None of the houses was occupied, the church had not been used for sixty years, and only a shepherd was still living there, in a hut. Before anything else, Mary Ferrar cleaned the church and said prayers. The manor house was then put to rights, and the land let. Under Nicholas's leadership, the family followed a regime dedicated to a timetable of prayer. They lived austerely. John looked like a priest, and Nicholas went some way to becoming one, being ordained as a deacon by Charles I's Archbishop of Canterbury, William Laud. Although they worshipped according to the Book of Common Prayer, word got around that they were Papists.

When John, Nicholas and Mary Ferrar were joined by John and Nicholas's sister Susanna, with her husband John Collet and their family of many children, the household grew to forty people, from babies to ancients. They printed books, played and wrote music, and Nicholas, in the hours between the almost constant round of services and prayer, translated Latin texts. Medicines were dispensed to local people, and children taught. The little ones followed a dry curriculum consisting principally of Bible study, but it was not unkindly done; when they had recited a psalm they would be given a penny, and they were treated to lunch on Sundays. To make their learning more enjoyable, they were set the task of composing concordances, or harmonies; lines of the printed text of the Gospels were cut out and had to be pasted into a book in the correct order. The method encouraged them to memorise the story and make comparisons between the different Evangelists' accounts. It also helped improve their dexterity; the pages were decorated with appropriate prints.

In the spring of 1642 King Charles visited, astonished to find that the church was completely bare of ornament, let alone statues of saints. By this time Nicholas was dead. Charles would soon raise his standard at Nottingham, opening the Civil War. For now, he could delight in the community (he already owned two of their harmonies), while the young princes were fed with apple pie and cheesecakes in the buttery. He made a present of some money that he had won at cards. 'Little Gidding is a happy place,' he concluded. Other troubled spirits have felt so since. The farmhouse that replaced the manor house in the nineteenth century is now a retreat centre.

The George Hotel, Stamford

Around 1800, Stamford merchants saw the prosperity that the canal system was bringing to neighbouring Grantham; but they never succeeded in getting a connection to it. Half a century later, a subsequent generation was so overjoyed that a proposal to bring the railway was defeated – it went to Peterborough instead – that they rang the church bells. The future had been rejected; Stamford chose nostalgia instead. Peterborough grew, Stamford snoozed. Which is one reason that today, built from creamy Clipsham limestone and little changed since the Georgian period, it is such a beautiful town, and in hot demand as a setting for period dramas. But Stamford did not always miss the moment. It was an important place in the great days of coaching, as can be seen from the George Hotel. Stamford and that renowned coaching inn reached their zenith together, when the Great North Road – now the A1 – made both of them hum.

In 1724, Daniel Defoe 'stopp'd at the George out of curiosity, because it is reckoned one of the greatest Inns of England'. The next year it was graced – if that is the word – by an exceptionally large cockpit built by Brownslow, 9th Earl of Exeter. Not long afterwards the façade of the George was rebuilt and the sign, hung from what looks like a gallows, stretching all the way across High Street St Martin's, one of the main approaches to the town, was erected. Turnpike trusts continued to improve the roads throughout the rest of the century, enabling coaches to travel reliably and at speed. Dickens loved England's great coaching inns, already being eclipsed by the railways, for their bustle and life. In *The Pickwick Papers* he describes the speed – and attendant excitement –with which it was possible to change horses:

> Away ran the hostlers and the boys. The lanterns glimmered, as the men ran to and fro; the horses' hoofs clattered on the uneven paving of the yard; the chaise rumbled as it was drawn out of the coach-house; and all was noise and bustle.
>
> 'Now then! – is that chaise coming out to-night?' cried Wardle.
>
> 'Coming down the yard now, Sir,' replied the hostler.
>
> Out came the chaise – in went the horses – on sprang the boys – in got the travellers . . .
>
> 'Off with you!'
>
> The boys applied whip and spur, the waiters shouted, the hostlers cheered, and away they went, fast and furiously.

Worthwhile inns had good fires to warm travellers who had experienced the elements; and good food, served sufficiently promptly for customers to eat well before the coach left on its next stage. He would surely have found both at the George. Alas, Dickens never seems to have visited, but he would have loved the architecture; it was all of a muddle.

For despite its name, the George is far older than its Georgian heyday. Its origins lie in a hospital of the Knights of St John of Jerusalem, known as the Knights Hospitaller. The House of the Holy Sepulchre would not have served principally as a hospital, although the knights would have tended the sick; they supplied hospitality, in the sense of secure lodging at a time when inns were few, particularly for pilgrims. Part of the crypt survives under the present champagne bar. It is recorded that in 1189 the hospital was endowed with a meadow and an orchard, and an inn. As the inn expanded after the decline of the Hospitallers, parts of the medieval structure were incorporated into later works, as can still be seen in the courtyard. The George's standing in the late Middle Ages can be gathered from its fifteenth-century proprietor, John Dickens, who was three times Alderman of Stamford, and whose daughter Alice married one of King Henry VIII's sergeants-at-arms.

There were numerous coaching inns at Stamford during the eighteenth century – the Bull, the Bluebell, the Old Swan, the George and Angel: all of which have now gone. England's fattest man, Daniel Lambert, whose gargantuan dimensions are recorded on his tombstone in St Martin's churchyard – 'three Feet one Inch round the LEG, nine Feet four Inches round the BODY' – died at the Waggon and Horses in 1809. But the George ruled supreme, not only being rebuilt at the end of the eighteenth century at a cost of £1800 but surviving, in the finest of fettles, into the present day. Long may it thrive.

The British Museum

In 1816, the Elgin marbles were bought for the British nation from the 7th Earl of Elgin, who had removed them from the Parthenon in Athens. Elgin had spent heavily on securing the marbles, while ambassador to Turkey: Athens was then part of the Ottoman Empire. The British were in high favour after the expulsion of Napoleon from Egypt. Elgin's piracy, as it is now represented, had been undertaken with the approval of the authorities in charge of Athens at the time. As he and his family were returning from Constantinople, they fell into the hands of the French government, Elgin's release being offered in return for his archaeological hoard. This was not so as to return it to Athens: Napoleon's idea was to add it to the superb collection of antiquities, dubiously assembled from around Europe, in the Louvre. Elgin refused. The marbles went instead to the British Museum and have caused ripples – sometimes waves – of controversy ever since.

Today, admirably displayed to millions of visitors each year, they are one of innumerable wonders in the museum. Not only was this the first museum of its kind in the world – founded in conformity with the French encyclopaedist Diderot's belief that all human knowledge could be gathered together in one place, arranged according to subject – but the quality and scope of its holdings remain difficult to beat. It is a kind of Gaia-like cultural ecosystem, whose extraordinary collections create a whole that is different from and greater than the sum of its parts. Inevitably, museum-making involves the translocation of cultural artefacts, taking them from the places where they were made and showing and interpreting them in a new context – arguably to enhance their meaning through their proximity to other pieces. This idea has its critics but is widely accepted. Were the Elgin marbles to be returned to Greece, as campaigners demand, they would not be re-erected in their original position, on the Parthenon, but placed in another museum (without, incidentally, the BM's free entry). They would be nearer their place of origin but still alienated from the temple for which they were created. They would have moved from one museum context to another. They would remain deracinated. What would have been gained?

Enough of the marbles; the British Museum contains so many collections – not just antiquities. They amount to eight million objects, reflecting an intellectual curiosity that goes back to Sir Hans Sloane. Sloane's collection provided the foundation of the museum. An Irish doctor with a gargantuan and omnivorous appetite for collecting, he amassed the beautiful and the curious, the useful and the bizarre, the natural and the artificial, the incredibly old, the new but exquisite, as well as plants, fossils, zoological specimens, anatomical oddities, antiquities, prints, drawings, coins, books, manuscripts – or as Horace Walpole described, 'hippopotamuses, sharks with one ear, and spiders as big as geese'. On Sloane's death at the age of ninety-two in 1753, the collection, comprising some eighty thousand objects, was bought on behalf of the nation; a number of eminent libraries were added to it; and from 1759 it became known as the British Museum.

After the Battle of the Nile in 1798 and the Treaty of Alexandria of 1801, the British Museum received the Egyptian antiquities that Napoleon had been preparing to take back to France. The museum was then crammed into the seventeenth-century Duke of Montagu's town house and the arrival of these pieces, some of them massive, showed up the inadequacy of the arrangements: big sculptures had to be kept in sheds. In the 1830s, Montagu House was replaced by a new museum designed by Robert Smirke, with a gigantic portico of Ionic columns. The chaste Greek Revival style pays tribute to the Classical world, some of whose finest monuments were now to be found inside the museum: an assertion of their universal relevance. Where better to appreciate the Elgin marbles? We listen to Beethoven not only in Bonn or Vienna. The British Museum celebrates human civilisation as a property of the world. Remove the Elgin marbles and the idea totters.

Red kites over the M40

The M40 is one of the better motorways. Opened in the 1970s, it flows with the contours of the landscape – unlike the earlier M1, which is brutally and boringly straight. When it emerges from the high chalk sides of the Chilterns cutting and the Oxfordshire plain stretches before you, the heart lifts. Mine does, anyway – and I do not like driving. It may not be so much the topographical prospect that has this effect as the sight of something sublime. Wheeling above the motorway, on outstretched wings and extended pinions, are red kites. These birds are elegant but enormous: quite alarming if you happen to see one near your windscreen – they have a wingspan of six feet. When the M40 was built, they were almost extinct in Britain: a bird once common across the whole country had been reduced to a single breeding pair in Wales. However, a reintroduction programme, begun in 1989 at Stokenchurch – a name familiar to motorway drivers from the service station and landmark of the BT tower – has been so successful that they are almost always to be seen, and not just singly: a dozen or more may be in the air together.

Why kite? I have heard people say that the name derives from the bird's forked tail; in fact, according to Stefan Buczacki's invaluable *Fauna Britannica*, it is onomatopoeic, in imitation of the bird's long whistling call. A dialect name for the red kite was 'puddock'. The poet John Clare describes 'The sailing puddock's shrill "peelew"'. Clare was a great naturalist. 'Peelew' is more like the cry than kite. Although nobody seems to have eaten kite, in the manner they did rooks (in a pie), they supposedly had medicinal properties. 'The testicles pulverized being taken for a considerable time, cause fruitfulness,' wrote John K'eogh in his *Zoologia Medicinalis Hibernica: or, a Treatise of Birds, Fishes etc.*, of 1739. I would not know. Otherwise the red kite was regarded as vermin, although – perhaps paradoxically – its size and beauty were its undoing. It became a target for taxidermists and egg collectors. By the 1870s, it had retreated to a last redoubt in the Welsh mountains.

Red kites are now seen far from their point of release and seem to be on a mission to recolonise England. This is glorious to behold; at a time when songbirds are in decline and even house sparrows have become fewer, this magnificent creature, like other raptors, is staging a spectacular comeback. The kite is not without critics. It never has been. Unlike the fluttering kestrel – Gerard Manley Hopkins's 'windhover' – which is also often seen near motorways, it is a scavenger; and it is not looking for small mammals in the verges, but roadkill. References in Shakespeare suggest it was far from popular. In *The Winter's Tale*, Autolycus alludes to its partiality to old rags for building into its nests. Elsewhere, 'kite' is used as a term of abuse. 'Detested kite! Thou liest,' rages King Lear.

Today, disapproval among thoughtful country folk focuses on the sheer number of kites. Our love of avian splendour has led, quite rightly, to the protection of raptors and other 'top predators', such as the red kite; but as their numbers build, the consequences for mammals and birds lower down the food chain must be watched. The red kite may eat carrion when it can get it; but it will snack on small rodents and birds. There may come a day when a balance has to be struck and their numbers need to be controlled. From the perspective of a generation ago, that is a good problem to have. For the time being, let us simply enjoy the spectacle the red kite has brought back to our skies.

Tate Britain

I have thought about this one. I know that I should really make it Tate Modern; this is the great meeting place – and happening space – of the contemporary arts; somewhere for all ages, ethnicities and incomes, exemplifying the wonderful discovery, made by the British public in recent years, that they like doing things together (think also of the pedestrian shopping streets around England, the vogue for street food, the immense crowds – terrifying for some of us – that assemble for New Year's Eve firework displays and the like; or the carnival-like popularity, some years ago, of the Queen Mother's hundredth birthday parade). Which is doubly to be celebrated, given the countervailing tendency for us to interact intensively with our mobile devices and computer screens more than with other people. And triply so, at a time when Coronavirus has knocked it on the head. Furthermore, Tate Modern was created by Herzog & de Meuron – strange folk, I interviewed them – from, of all things, the impossibly huge brick bulk of a 1950s power station, which, in the days that it was working, used to float a plume of acidic smoke over St Paul's. So all good – but I would not be true to myself if I did not make Tate Britain the Crown Jewel. This undersung older sister of Tate Modern is, for my family and me, a source of constant delight.

Built in 1895–97, Tate Britain was a building of its time, with a giant portico and a dome. Domes were in the air, so to speak; they evoked the architecture of Rome – not the Rome of the Roman Catholic Church, still regarded with suspicion, if not horror, but that of the Roman Empire; which suited a country, Britain, that went Empire-mad at the turn of the twentieth century. Sir Henry Tate, who paid for the building, was himself an imperial figure. His company Tate & Lyle refined sugar grown in the West Indies at a works in Liverpool.

Tate offered a collection of sixty-five narrative, mostly Victorian, works to the nation; they included Sir John Everett Millais's *Ophelia*, John William Waterhouse's *The Lady of Shalott* and Sir Luke Fildes's *The Doctor*. It took several years and a change of government to come up with a site for the art gallery that was to house them – the choice alighting on an insalubrious spot on the north bank of the Thames, previously occupied by the Millbank Penitentiary. Externally the architecture may be rather ho-hum, but it rises to a sublime dignity inside, where John Russell Pope, W.H. Romaine-Walker (whom I like because he refused to speak on the telephone) and Gilbert Jenkins were responsible for the marble-lined Duveen Sculpture Galleries – a magnificent space, in the spirit of Pope's contemporaneous National Gallery of Art in Washington. It is magisterially, marmoreally Classical: not the sort of hall that you would have thought obviously appropriate to the huge, zany contemporary installations that are shown there, but the dialogue between architecture and artwork is effective.

This gallery is where Britain comes to burn incense before its great national masters: allegorised Elizabethans, debonair Cavaliers, Restoration beauties, horses by Stubbs, morals from Hogarth, conversation pieces, pre-Raphaelites, Sargent, Turner in all his profusion and glory. With a civilised Members' Room to recoup one's forces after so much looking, there is really nowhere I would rather be.

For all that, I do not pretend that our museums, Tate Britain included, are necessarily better than those in other countries – some are, some aren't. These merit inclusion in this section on Things We Do Well because they are free.

Unconditioned Stimuli

These are things that bring about an unconditioned response. You see them, you cannot help feeling an emotion – or so it is with me. The ancient buildings that survive at Ewelme in Oxfordshire, the legacy of a medieval palace, are moving as well as beautiful; it is wonderful that they continue in their original uses. Tears come to the eyes. In their completely different ways, the Foundling Hospital and the Cabinet War Rooms contain objects that evoke great human dramas, on the small scale and on the epic. Ramsgate Sands are childhood. (Sand is like that: children who have never seen a beach before know exactly how to play on it.) The London Library – please pause a minute while I genuflect before the wisdom that radiates not just from the rows of worn book spines but, yea, the metal floors that clank as readers walk over them, the leather armchairs in which readers have been known to fall asleep. The drone of the bumblebee brings with it deckchairs, Pimm's, dahlias – all summer is contained within that *Bombus* buzz.

The statue of Charles I at the top of Whitehall is rather under-sized for its position (appropriately enough: he was not a large man). It is delicate, not bombastic. The story of how it was rescued from destruction after the Civil War gives it an aura beyond its quality as a work of art. Buxton Opera House, like all Frank Matcham's theatres, lifts the spirits; as does, from sheer unexpectedness, the Halifax Piece Hall. The BBC does its best to exasperate those who would be its friends; I object to the profligacy with which it pays for stars and entertainment that do not enrich the nation's media diet and would be better broadcast by commercial stations. Call me old-fashioned, but surely the BBC exists to plug the gaps that the commercial sector leaves unfilled. And yet the sound of a news reader has the same effect as a British Airways pilot – unexcitable, unflappable, understated – and I breathe easily knowing a higher power is in control. However infuriating the organisation, you know, deep down, how much you would miss it. Like H.M. the Queen, some things are irreplaceable.

Ewelme, Oxfordshire

Ewelme is a species of English perfection, a mellow composition of brick and stone that seems to dream away time through the mist. Watercress grows in the clear waters of a stream, fed by the spring (*aewelme* in Old English) from which the village takes its name. Ewelme has a church, an almshouse and a school – institutions that survive, unusually, from the manorial arrangements of the Middle Ages; for Ewelme was once the site of a sumptuous house belonging to the Duke and Duchess of Suffolk, known as Ewelme Palace – 'so rich that I did never see the like', according to a traveller in 1574. No trace now remains of the house, but one of its occupants – Duchess Alice, granddaughter of the poet Geoffrey Chaucer – can be seen in the effigy on the alabaster tomb erected after her death in 1475, in the church that she and her husband had rebuilt; beautifully carved, she is shown in the long robes of what seems a religious nature (those of a woman who took nun-like vows but lived in the world), while the insignia of the Order of the Garter, which she was allowed to wear as a mark of royal favour, is wrapped around her wrist. Beneath is the horror death: behind a kind of tracery cage, the same lady as a cadaver – the only example in Britain of a female effigy to have such a memento mori.

Alice had been a rich widow when she married William de la Pole, then Earl (subsequently Duke) of Suffolk, who virtually ruled England, such was his influence over the indecisive Henry VI. Suffolk's badge was the clog and chain of a tame ape, from which he was known by the derisive sobriquet of Jackanapes. By 1450 a disastrous treaty, followed by war, had lost England most of its territories in France and the King was forced to commit Suffolk to exile. However, his ship was intercepted and his head summarily hacked off with a rusty sword.

Fortunately for the passage of the Suffolks' souls, there was the almshouse. Known as God's House, it provided for two chaplains and thirteen poor men retained not simply for charity but for a specific purpose: to say mass for the souls of the departed. Everyone who was rich enough in the late Middle Ages wanted to have people pray for them after death – and took trouble to ensure that they would, by endowing almshouses, colleges and, in churches and cathedrals, chantry chapels. The endowments paid for priests and paupers to conduct services, in accordance with the late medieval doctrine of Purgatory. Purgatory was viewed as a kind of waiting-room for the soul, before it was sent on its final journey towards Heaven or Hell. The length of time it spent there could be mitigated by prayer. No expense was spared on the architecture of God's House; it was built in the newly revived material of brick (there is a suggestion that the bricks could have been made by the same brickmakers as were employed at Eton College, a contemporary foundation where William de la Pole was an overseer and patron).

At God's House, begun in 1437, the schedule of devotion was almost continuous; an almsman's stipend was docked if he left the buildings for more than an hour at a time. The nature of the Suffolks' lives on earth may have made them feel they needed all the prayers they could buy. Today God's House, in proximity to the church and school, is a rare survival; in the fifteenth century it would have been commonplace.

The Cabinet War Rooms

The nerve centre of Britain's war effort during the Second World War was an overcrowded, smoke-filled, inadequately serviced basement under the New Government Offices, off Whitehall. They had been hurriedly fitted out as a temporary measure, finished just a week before war was declared in September 1939. Here, in a position conveniently near Downing Street and the House of Commons, the Prime Minister and his Cabinet could pursue their work sheltered, if not absolutely safe, beside the heads of the armed services. Since there is no reference to these underground war rooms in any German document, it seems that the enemy never knew of their existence. They seem almost to defy belief.

Ever since the First World War, it had been obvious that London would be a prime target for enemy aircraft in times of war, and planners predicted massive destruction and casualties. The nation's top decision-takers had to be protected, perhaps by removing them to deep tunnels dug in the suburbs. This proposal was rejected on the grounds that morale would suffer if Londoners thought their leaders were deserting them. Instead, it was decided to convert some old basement store-rooms in the traditional heart of government into offices and sleeping quarters. The arrangement suited the temperament of Winston Churchill, who became Prime Minister in May 1940. Throughout his career he had shown an appetite for risk, including risk to his personal safety, which he perpetuated by watching air raids from the top of the George Street building and making hazardous trips by plane and sea to visit other war leaders among the Allies. Initially, he was reluctant to abandon 10 Downing Street for the considerably less elegant underground war rooms but, when he realised that Downing Street could well be flattened, he understood the sense of the arrangement. Whether the underground rooms offered very much more protection to begin with is open to question. It was only in late 1940, after several Cabinet meetings had been held there, that a three-foot-thick concrete slab was laid over the top of the rooms as a protection against bombs. The space beneath the staircase hall was completely filled with concrete, through which a corridor had then to be tunnelled.

Churchill's habit of working late into the night made it particularly necessary that he should have a bedroom in these new quarters. Given the shortage of space, it had to double as an office, which suited his routine (he invariably worked in bed, and would carry on dictating from the bath). One wall was hung with an enormous map of Europe on which the deployment of forces was marked: curtains were drawn across it when visitors came. There was also the map room to chart the progress of the war – fighter scores during the Battle of Britain, the fate of convoys crossing the Atlantic, the advance of battlefronts across Europe, the toll on London taken by V1 and V2 rockets. A bank of telephones, colour-coded, allowed updates to be quickly relayed – an example of technology that veered between the futuristic and the homespun. The rooms were air-conditioned, and Churchill's own desk had been equipped by the BBC with microphones by means of which the Prime Minister could broadcast to the world. A small room – popularly supposed to contain the only lavatory – was equipped with a scrambler telephone that constituted a hotline to the President of the United States; a predecessor of modern digital technology, the scrambler mechanism was so big that it could not be contained in the war rooms but had to be outstationed in a basement under Selfridges in Oxford Street.

Conditions for typists, crammed into every available corner, were basic. Worse were the quarters for staff who slept on site, reached by a trap door. This was the spirit of stoic determination and make-do that won Britain the war.

Buxton Opera House

I t could be the Richmond Theatre, the Victoria Palace or the Tower Ballroom, Blackpool. Instead I give you the Buxton Opera House, my favourite work from the glorious oeuvre of Frank Matcham. Matchless Matcham, Magnificent Matcham, You can't Match 'im – Matcham's sobriquets reveal the position that he occupied as the king of theatre architects at the turn of the twentieth century. The buoyancy of his personality communicated itself both to his buildings and to his clients, and he was never daunted by the often awkward sites that the latter put before him, generally in London or the industrial towns. Buxton, the Derbyshire spa that had been developed by the Dukes of Devonshire, was a different proposition; the site, abutting the pioneering Winter Gardens of 1871 and overlooking the Pavilion

Gardens, was delicious. This was to be an Opera House, not a musical hall: a name rich in expectation for both management and clientele.

They wanted a jewel, quite small (it originally seated one thousand two hundred and fifty) but charmingly formed. And they got one. Although Matcham was incapable of being less than gutsy, the limited scale prevented coarseness. The effect of the bobble-hat domes (leaded and ribbed) above the entrance front, the cavalier use of the architectural orders and the ironwork canopy is irrepressibly jolly, without making too loud a guffaw. Inside, the shell canopies over the boxes, the trophies of musical instruments over the proscenium arch and the allegorical panels representing the arts (largely in a state of undress) are festive but intimate; no oompah-pah here.

Elsewhere, oompah-pah was just what was needed. For many people, life at the turn of the twentieth century was harsh. Working hours were long, and often physically demanding; the comforts of home might be meagre. Warmth and glitter as well as drink and company could be found in the richly ornamented, gas-lit gin palaces that by the mid-Victorian period had, in the cities, all but ousted the domesticity of old-fashioned pubs.

And out of the public house had grown another kind of escape: the music hall. By the 1890s shows no longer took place in front of diners seated at tables, as they had done at the old song-and-supper rooms, variety saloons and tavern concert rooms – although another antecedent of the music hall, the pleasure garden in the manner of Vauxhall in south London, had not quite died: the Rosherville Pleasure Gardens at Gravesend did not close until 1911. A boom in theatre building provided an alternative space

– opulent, swaggering, and, as the paintings of Walter Sickert reveal, conducive to a boisterous intimacy between the patrons watching the show and the performers. Between 1879 and 1912, Matcham designed more than a hundred and fifty theatres, knocking C.J. Phipps into a cocked hat; he could only manage seventy-two.

In contrast to bijou Buxton, the London Coliseum opened in 1904 as one of the mightiest of variety theatres, huge in scale and sumptuously decorated, with a terracotta façade and a rotating globe on top of a round tower supported by paired columns. The ambition was to attract middle-class family audiences with tea rooms and bars – amenities which combined 'the social advantages of the refined and elegant surroundings of a Club; the comfort and attractiveness of a Café, besides being the Theatre de Luxe of London and the pleasantest family resort imaginable'. In this incarnation the Coliseum was a complete failure, closing after two years. But Matcham's building proved irresistible; it survived, reinvented itself and is now home to the English National Opera. The Buxton Opera House hosts the annual Buxton Festival as well as a programme of popular shows throughout the year.

The London Library

When Charles Dickens was researching *A Tale of Two Cities*, his friend Thomas Carlyle picked a selection of books on the French Revolution from the shelves of the London Library and had them sent round in two carts. Decades later, when Arthur Ransome was in St Petersburg, he would flourish a letter demanding the return of some overdue books in front of whichever policeman, soldier or minor official was obstructing him; bearing both the Library's crest and the formidable signature of the chief librarian, it was 'far more useful than any other paper I possessed. At the sight of it opposition wilted.' Today, shards of glass are still occasionally to be picked out of the spines of books damaged by the bomb that hit a newly built tower of stacks during the Second World War, devastating Religion.

These are just a few of the stories of the London Library since it was founded in 1841. As a haunt of writers, as well as book-loving members of the general public, it has all the mystique that you would expect of a great literary institution, enriched through occasional appearances in the works of authors whom its shelves have nourished: several novels have used it as a setting. But the physical character of the Library, smiling on St James's Square from behind its quietly idiosyncratic front, hardly needs fiction to heighten its personality. August mahogany-panelled public spaces combine with book stacks that resemble the lower decks of a destroyer. Librarians are not now as intimidating as the portly Frederick Cox, a Jeeves-like fixture behind the issue desk during the post-Second World War years. (J.B. Priestley was among the writers too popular to meet the high standards required for his approval. Asked to repeat his name more loudly when signing out a book, the great littérateur did so. On which Cox enquired: 'Initials?') But the ghosts alone are enough to inspire awe.

And yet the stories tend to miss the point of the London Library. Arcane, even dotty though it may appear at times, it is – and always has been – as up-to-the-minute as any resource for the serious reader could be. At one level, the needs of today are oddly similar to that faced by Carlyle when he founded the Library – or to be more accurate, refounded a defunct eighteenth-century institution. While many public libraries have become a cross between a coffee shop and a computer suite, in which the printed word plays a declining part, the London Library continues to add half a mile of books to its collections every three years. While reference libraries only provide books during opening hours, nearly everything at the London Library can be taken out, to be read at home (books are posted to country members). Furthermore, readers can find books themselves, on open shelves, allowing them to roam at will through a whole subject category, finding treasures by serendipity.

In the nineteenth century, Carlyle's inspiration fired the literary colossi of the age, from Tennyson and Dickens to Gladstone and George Eliot. They and others gave money and collections to the point that the corner property that the Library had occupied in St James's Square since 1845 (the 'worst house in the square', as the biographer and antiquarian A.I. Dasent described it) became inadequate. During 1895–7 the house was rebuilt, with a stately reading room on the first floor lit by three tall, round-headed windows – a departure from the Georgian pediments elsewhere in the square. Leather armchairs, whose comfort is apt to overwhelm some members after lunch, preserve something of the domestic character of the previous house.

The architect of these works, James Osborne Smith, had previously refitted parts of the Bodleian Library in Oxford. Now obscure, his name deserves to be better known, because in one respect the new London Library was bold. Behind the reading room, the frame of the new structure was provided by the book stacks, made of cast iron. This must have seemed radical to readers, unused to clanking across what seem like cast-iron gangways, pierced to give views through to floors above and below. The use of this material saved space, always at a premium in the Library; and every inch between floor and ceiling was used to shelve the books.

Collections continued to grow, and the Library to expand. Piecemeal additions have created a warren of spaces, navigated by means of ancient finger signs pointing up and down the cast-iron staircases, and notes posted by librarians. If readers are occasionally baffled as they hunt to find where an alphabetical sequence of subjects is continued, most would probably not want it any other way. Some even relish the quiddity. But users are also grateful for the enhancements made by the architects Haworth Tompkins, executed in materials and colours that echo the Library's existing character, established largely in the 1890s and 1930s. More is planned.

The late Sir Roger Scruton, philosopher, controversialist and polymath, said that his favourite smell was that of the French Literature section of the London Library. Many readers will know how he felt.

Ramsgate Sands

We are at the seaside!

Britain is a collection of islands with a fretted coastline of Cornish coves, basalt outcrops, cliffs rich in fossils, colonies of puffins. For holidaymakers, though, it is the beaches that catch the eye. In this respect, if few others, Caithness resembles the Caribbean. Oh, the maritime glories of Northumberland, Anglesey, Pembrokeshire, Sussex – strands as lustrous as spun gold, soft as sugar and bobbing with the mysterious life of rockpools. But the beach of beaches must surely be Ramsgate Sands. I say nothing against Camber Sands, Grange-over-Sands or Sandbanks. None of them, though, was painted by William Powell Frith, whose *Ramsgate Sands* was – as the painter probably judged it might be – snapped up by Queen Victoria for the Royal Collection. Why? Because she had holidayed, happily, at Ramsgate as a girl. She did the town the honour of catching typhoid there in 1835.

Five miles to the east, connected by a continuous yellow carpet of sand, lies Margate, which developed as one of Britain's first seaside resorts in the mid-eighteenth century. Ramsgate didn't get into its stride until after the Napoleonic Wars, which ended in 1815 (one street is called Plains of Waterloo). By then, the Prince

Regent had given royal approval to the seaside by building his Marine Pavilion at Brighton. In 1821, as George IV, he took a ship from Ramsgate to visit Hanover – he was cross with Dover for supporting his wife, Queen Caroline, in the couple's tragi-comic divorce battle. An obelisk commemorates the event, as does the name of the Royal Harbour. A guidebook of 1846 pronounced that 'of the three watering places in the Isle of Thanet, Ramsgate is considered as the most fashionable'.

There were warm baths, in white marble surroundings, on the West Cliff. Out of the water, there were telescopes, donkey rides, a German band and all the activities depicted by Frith to distract the visitor. Until nightfall, that is, when Mr Fuller's 'famed marine library' came into its own – not only a repository of books but a music-hall, a bazaar and a very tame kind of casino, where a shilling stake might win you a cake of soap, a bottle of hair oil or a wooden spade. But the focus of activity – as the wooden spade suggests – was the famous sands.

Bathing had overtaken taking the waters at inland spas as a healthful activity. Lumbering wooden bathing machines with a deep canvas hood at one end and a horse at the other would be trundled into the water and turned around, while the drivers and horses splashed back to the beach; bathers then issued from beneath the canvas hood, which reached down to the sea. It was not foolproof as regards privacy. From the waterside it was 'just possible to catch a sly glance at the forms in dark dresses "bobbing around" and splashing each other, and to hear them giggling, as if they were up to all sorts of imaginable mischief', according to the witty *All About Ramsgate and Broadstairs*, published in 1864. Men had only the sea to preserve their modesty.

345

It would not do. Morals were getting caught up with everything, including health. Hear Dr Spenser Thomson, author of *Health Resorts of Britain and How to Profit by Them* (1860), inveigh against the 'almost heathen indecency of our bathing-places', where lookers-on equipped themselves with opera-glasses or telescopes to get a better view of the swimmers, with 'no more sense of decency than so many South-Sea Islanders'.

Things have changed since then, and one cannot deny that the English seaside has had its ups and downs. But Ramsgate has climbed out of the doldrums caused by cheap flights to the Mediterranean and the collapse of the British holiday industry. It is now the Portofino of Thanet. A recent triumph has been the restoration of the long-derelict Royal Pavilion, a handsome and interestingly Classical building of 1913, as the biggest Wetherspoons pub in the country. The beach can be as crowded and full of incident as it was in Frith's day. But it isn't always like that. Walk to Broadstairs on an autumn evening, with the cliffs of the French coast twinkling on the horizon, and you may have the sands to yourself. I treasure them.

The Foundling Museum, Bloomsbury

The Foundling Museum stands for philanthropy. Philanthropy built many institutions before the foundation of the Welfare State, and while our private donors may subsequently have been eclipsed by those of the United States, to the point that it is a habit we at times seem to have lost, we must still cherish it as an ambition. There are still many generous people around. Oxford and Cambridge may not be as well supported as Harvard and Yale, but money floods in for charitable causes such as disaster relief and children in need of operations. If ever there was a Crown Jewel, the Foundling Hospital – remembered in the Museum – is it.

Established by royal charter in 1739, the Hospital was a stepping stone on a journey about childhood. When Samuel Pepys found the Duke of York (the future James II) playing with his little daughters in the 1660s, it was a matter for comment. The idea of childhood as a period of special importance to the development of the individual hardly existed before the late eighteenth century: until then, children were regarded essentially as miniature adults, whose work and suffering they often shared.

Unwanted babies were often abandoned. The sight horrified Captain Thomas Coram when he returned to London after having made a fortune as a sailor and shipbuilder in the New World.

Childless himself, Coram wanted to create a refuge for such children, and enlisted the help of his friend the artist William Hogarth, another man without children, to do so. From this flowed one of the most remarkable artistic as well as charitable endeavours of the age. For in order to raise money for the Hospital, Hogarth persuaded his artist friends to contribute their talents for nothing. They were joined by the composer Handel, whose 'Music for the Royal Fireworks' had just received a rapturous reception at its first performances, and who was pioneering the new musical form of the oratorio. Handel gave the first of a series of benefit concerts for the Hospital in 1749, and became a governor, like Hogarth, the next year. This association with the arts made the Foundling Hospital a fashionable cause: a definite achievement in itself, given polite society's horror of the fallen women who were often the mothers of the unwanted babies. As a fund-raising technique, it is the ancestor of the work of so many charity ball committees today. It was previously unheard of.

The Hospital was built on a site north of Lamb's Conduit Street. When it sold its London estate in 1926 and moved to the country, the old hospital was demolished, except for the forecourt, and a new headquarters built on Brunswick Square by J M Sheppard, on the site of the former gardens. But the old Court Room, created in 1746, had been dismantled and was installed in this building. It has Rococo plasterwork, a chimneypiece by the Flemish sculptor John Michael Rysbrack and a series of paintings on the theme of charity and children masterminded by Hogarth. In a landmark of

English portraiture, Hogarth painted Coram, rough-hewn and unwigged, as well as giving his *March of the Guards to Finchley*, a satire lampooning the disreputable behaviour of His Majesty's troops, to the Hospital as a raffle prize. Perhaps not surprisingly, George II had not wanted it when it was offered to him; when it came to be raffled all but a hundred and fifty-seven of two thousand tickets were sold. No one can have been astonished to find that the winning ticket was one of the unsold ones, as a result of which the painting remained in the Hospital.

Some of the most moving objects in the Hospital's collection were not, however, works of art, but humble everyday items such as buttons, locks of hair, scraps of material and labels from bottles. They were left by mothers as a means of identifying their offspring, should they ever come back to reclaim them. Babies were chosen, or not, by a kind of lottery, each mother reaching into a leather bag containing three balls. If she lifted out a white ball, her baby was accepted; a red ball meant it would go on the waiting list; a black ball signified rejection. Tough though this system seems, it marked the dawn of a more enlightened age.

Bumblebees

It is a sunny afternoon. There is a deckchair on the lawn. A tall glass tinkling with ice cubes stands beside it. What is the aural background to this scene? Inevitably, it's the vibrating, bassoon-like note of the gloriously named *Bombus* doing her rounds – we thank the French entomologist Pierre André Latreille for bestowing the name in 1802; it's the Latin word for buzz or hum. Its 'drowsy tone', to quote the American thinker Ralph Waldo Emerson's poem 'The Humble-bee', evokes summer days, when nothing much can go wrong, or would not matter if it did:

> Wiser far than human seer,
> Yellow-breeched philosopher!

Emerson was writing after having lost a useful part of his income in the banking panic of 1837. Today brings its own challenges, but the fascinating bumblebee still has the power to console.

Now, here is something to amaze you. There is only one insect capable of pollinating tomato plants, and that's the bumblebee. Tomatoes keep their pollen tightly stored in anthers that other flying creatures cannot open. But bumblebees are big, burly things (even the girls). They can dislocate their wings, push their muscly thoraxes up to the anther and shiver; this is something they also do – being (another unexpected fact) warm-blooded – to warm up. The vibration occurs at exactly the frequency needed for the anther to spring open, leaving the bumblebee to fly off dusted all over in yellow pollen.

If bumblebees did not exist, tomato-growers would have to tickle the anthers by hand, using a slender wand; it is a time-consuming business. To save the tedium and labour costs, large glasshouses import thousands of boxes of bumblebee nests each year from France and Belgium, where our *Bombus* friends are farmed in hangars. No tomato tastes as good as one pollinated by a bumblebee.

Large and slow-moving, undisturbed by human company, unlikely to sting unless trodden upon – the males have no sting at all – the bumblebee is a genial garden companion. It is not only the tomato that benefits from her attention. Her long tongue can reach to the back of tube-shaped flowers whose anthers are beyond the reach of other bees. She isn't related to the honeybee or the many different types of solitary bee – ones who do not live in communal nests – which are of the order Hymenoptera. *Bombus* is a genus of its own, with twenty-four species in the UK. And how remarkable she is.

You will have noticed the gender: it is not accidental. Bumblebees are always female in spring. The boys don't come out until later, which is all too typical of the male of this genus, who 'stays out all night, gets drunk on nectar and looks for sex', according to Gill Perkins of the wonderful Bumblebee Conservation Trust.

The first brave queens stagger out of hibernation in February. These Big Berthas have to feed voraciously, making the flowers of pussy willow droop beneath their weight. They already have a supply of sperm, saved from a brief mating tryst with a male (now dead) the previous year. Having fattened up, they will look for a new site, zigzagging low over the ground to identify suitable holes (though some species nest in hollows of trees, others in long grass).

Once she has arranged her new home, the queen will begin the process of reproduction. This – and I promise you I'm not making it up – begins with her making a little cup, shaped like a thimble; she does this from wax excreted from her body which she moulds with her legs. The cup is filled with honey (concentrated nectar), and to accompany it will be a selection of pollen balls, rolled up and stuck together – with honey. Her larder completed, the queen is ready to lay her eggs and fertilise them with last year's sperm. The nectar cup and pollen balls will see her through the incubation period, during which she'll sit on the eggs like a bird. The first eggs to hatch will emerge as girls – good housekeepers: they gather food and look after the queen. Boys appear in high summer. Once they have left the nest they will not return.

Our twenty-four bumblebee species are not easy to distinguish. White-tailed bumblebees have, not surprisingly, a white tail – but then so do some buff-tailed bumblebees. The Great Yellow is difficult to miss – 'They're like big fat flying ping-pong balls,' says Gill – although you won't see her at all outside Caithness, Sutherland and the Orkneys. You may have noticed from the Emerson reference above that *Bombus* does not only occur in Britain; but we can claim some sub-species as our own. Like *Bombus terrestris audax*, the only bumblebee with a buff-coloured tail – and one or two others, but here it gets really complicated. It doesn't matter. This is the most lovable of insects, wherever it occurs.

But threatened. All insect numbers have crashed since the Second World War. We have only 3 per cent of the hay meadows that existed before tractors and silage came on the scene. Intensive agriculture has destroyed habitats and uses pesticides. Things may improve when the rulebook for agricultural support is rewritten following Britain's departure from the European Union. Garden owners can plant old-fashioned flower species and make habitats, although a word of caution: don't bother with a bumblebee nest box as sold by garden centres. They rarely work.

Charles I's statue, Whitehall

At the bottom of Trafalgar Square in London, looking down Whitehall, is a statue of a man on a horse. Many of the crowds who swirl around the piazza probably do not notice it, much less remember its story; but to those who know, it evokes a key moment in English history, both as regards the individual depicted and what happened to the statue after it was set in position. For the subject is Charles I. As a work of art, it seems somewhat constrained: the scale is small, the modelling too delicate for the position that the statue occupies, in the middle of a big and busy urban space. That is because it was commissioned not as a work of public art but for a private setting: the garden of the Lord Treasurer Sir Richard Weston, future Lord Portland's, house at Roehampton, to the west of the capital. The sculptor was one of the many artists that Charles had brought to the English court: the Frenchman Hubert le Sueur.

Le Sueur was the son of a master-armourer in Paris, and skilled as a foundryman as much as a sculptor. He first came to London in 1625. Since Charles had a French queen, Henrietta-Maria, cultural contacts between France and England were unusually strong. On arrival, Le Sueur's first job was to work with Inigo Jones on the temple-like funerary catafalque for Charles's recently deceased father, James I. The assassination of the unpopular royal favourite the Duke of Buckingham in 1628 provided another commission.

Weston began to think of ordering his equestrian statue of Charles I in the last weeks of 1629; in January the next year, a scrivener was instructed to draw up a contact between him and Le Sueur for 'the casting of a horse in Brasse bigger than a great Horse by a foot; and the figure of his Maj: King Charles proportionable full six foot, which the aforesaid Hubert Le Sueur is to perform with all the skill and workmanship as lieth in his power'. A great horse was the type used in the equestrian discipline of *haute école*, in which Charles excelled. Le Sueur was instructed to 'take advice of his Maj[esty's] Ridders of greate Horses' to make sure he got the details right – although there was nothing new about the form of the statue, which belongs to a tradition going back to that of the Roman Emperor Marcus Aurelius on the Capitoline Hill in Rome.

Purely as a sculpture, Le Sueur's work might not qualify as one of the absolute must-haves to save from a general conflagration. But the Stuarts – 'Wrong but Romantic', as *1066 and All That* memorably described the Cavalier side of the Civil War

– belonged to a line made for Hollywood: Mary Queen of Scots, Charles II (after the Battle of Worcester) and Bonnie Prince Charlie all inspired glorious acts of devotion on the part of their followers, in circumstances that were highly picturesque. So it was even with this statue of Charles I. After the Civil War, Parliament ordered it to be sold to the brazier John Rivett, on the strict instruction that it would be broken up. Out of loyalty, Rivett buried it, while keeping up a hammering noise in his workshop to pretend that it was being destroyed. This resulted, according to one writer, in 'a brisk trade in knives and forks, with bronze handles, which he pretended were made out of the obnoxious statue. He clearly must have made a good thing out of the knives and forks which he manufactured in bronze for sale, since the Royalists no doubt eagerly bought them as relics of their unfortunate and lamented sovereign, whilst the Puritans and Roundheads would be equally glad to secure them as trophies of the downfall of a despot.' Returned to Portland's family, the statue was sold to Charles II by the widow of the 2nd Earl in 1675.

Looking proudly down Whitehall, Charles's eyes rest on the Banqueting House, out of which he walked to his execution. Long live romance. The stone pedestal was made by Joshua Marshall from a design by Sir Christopher Wren.

The Halifax Piece Hall

The Halifax Piece Hall is Britain's Plaza Mayor, its St Mark's Square . . . not quite. It is much smaller than the Plaza Mayor, unless we mean the one in Salamanca as opposed to Madrid; it cannot boast the glory of St Mark's Basilica as a component part. All the same, it is an extraordinary space to find in Halifax, an industrial town in West Yorkshire. Bigger than the Piazza del Campidoglio in Rome or the main square in Bergamo. Italian comparisons come to mind because of the architecture; the Piece Hall, two hundred and thirty feet by two hundred and eighty-eight, is lined with stone columns in two tiers; since the site slopes, parts of these colonnades are supported on a rusticated basement arcade. All this, not as the centre of a great scheme of urbanism but for the benefit of handloom weavers, who came together here to trade 'pieces' of cloth. Each piece was a length of about thirty yards. The arcade and the colonnades protected the cloth from the glare of the sun, which would have faded the colours.

An inscription over the entrance gate declares the date on which the Piece Hall was opened: 1 January 1779. It marked the zenith of weaving as a cottage industry. Here, in three hundred and fifteen rooms that served as shops, accessible from either the courtyard or the colonnades, craftsmen could trade their wares. Weaving had taken place here since the Middle Ages but it was a competitive business. Halifax had been losing ground to other West Riding towns such as Leeds, Huddersfield, Bradford and Wakefield, which had already built themselves cloth halls – in the case of Leeds, two. To ensure fair competition, a porter enforced strict rules, allowing no merchant to enter the Piece Hall or buy cloth before ten o'clock and closing business at noon.

In the 1770s, Halifax was not a backwater. Local merchants were building Classical houses and one of them, Samuel Hill, employed scores of weavers in his enterprise, whose orders came from as far away as Persia. The scale of Hill's enterprise seems now to have foretold the end of the independent weaver: it looked forward to the mill factories that would soon supersede them. The Piece Hall belongs to a different generation; it was a cooperative and partly philanthropic venture, undertaken by the Piece Hall Committee, which met in the Talbot Inn. The landowner had given the site free, along with £840 towards the cost of construction. The rest of the money was raised by subscription.

There is some doubt as to the architect; one candidate is a very young local man called Thomas Bradley, but the little-known John Hope of Liverpool may have been name-checked in the song sung at the opening ceremony:

> Now our desires are crown'd by HOPE
> We'll be no longer seen
> Dispers'd around in ev'ry street
> As heretofore we've been

> But to a HALL whose Beauty vies
> With Palaces of old;
> Our Handy-work shall now be brought
> And straight be turn'd to Gold.

The reference to 'Palaces of old' suggests the ambition of the Committee. Their Hall, built for commerce, may be more rustic than Bedford Square and the other London squares then being built by great noblemen, but it stands comparison.

Sadly, not even the Piece Hall could rescue the handweavers. A decade after it was built, Edmund Cartwright invented his power loom. It became financially unattractive for merchants to buy small lengths from numerous hand-loom weavers when they could source more cheaply in bulk from one or two factories. Having been overtaken by commercial change, the Piece Hall fell into decline. It became a fish and vegetable market in 1863. From this fate it was rescued in the 1970s, when it was restored as an industrial museum, art gallery and antique shops. A further campaign of restoration began in 2014, and the Piece Hall reopened in splendour five years later.

W1A 1AA

It has been said that Poland is less a country than an idea, because its boundaries have shifted so often. A similar quip could be made of the BBC. It is no longer the monolith of the 1930s but an organisation that provides entertainment, as well as high-minded programmes, across as many platforms as it can straddle – internet, television, old-fashioned steam radio. And as it morphs, so it comes under mounting fire from a political establishment that resents its persistent refusal to toe the party line . . . whatever the party happens to be. The peculiar funding mechanism of the licence fee, payable by all British owners of a television set, looks increasingly shaky in an age when young people hardly ever seem to watch 'television programmes' on a TV, having a multiplicity of other screens at their disposal. It is a regressive tax. The poor pay the same as the rich.

To some, the BBC stands in an uncomfortable position, with one foot in the clear stream of public service and the other in the bog of private enterprise; the licence fee income is supplemented by selling programmes around the world and other services. And even when it is not in commercial competition with its rivals, it can behave as though it is, paying tens of millions of pounds for programmes such as *The Great British Bake Off* that have been a proven success elsewhere. Yet it serves also as a crucible for talent, whose creativity is then snapped up and exploited, to great financial advantage, by the commercial sector; and the poor old radio services succeed in struggling on, despite the barest of financial larders, as a paragon of journalistic excellence (Radio 4) or cultural value (Radio 3). Meanwhile, new service providers such as Netflix, Amazon and Sky compete for audiences, leaving the BBC – and the politicians who ultimately control its budget – to wonder what its role is. Provider of public service content that could not be made elsewhere? Echo chamber for the woke? Producer of blockbuster content that will sell around the world? Oh dear, it was so much simpler in the old days.

Or was it? When in 1922 the engineer John Reith applied for the job of managing director of the British Broadcasting Company, then in formation by a group of radio manufacturers, broadcasting was a mystery to most people, including him. The first government committee into 'the whole question of broadcasting' sat in 1923. A few years later, the BBC was given a royal charter and Reith was knighted. For decades, the quality of its programmes seemed better than that offered by commercial channels, whether in Britain or overseas, because budgets were not directly dependent on size of audience. Opened in 1932, Broadcasting House, that ocean liner in Portland stone, was in every sense the Corporation's flagship – retaining a symbolic authority, even though the television programmes are now broadcast from Salford, White City and numerous regional studios.

Designed by the otherwise little-known G. Val Myer, Broadcasting House reflected the Reithian mission to improve the taste and education of the nation, by bringing 'the best of everything to the greatest number of homes'. The interiors were designed by Raymond McGrath and other sophisticated Modernists, The very un-Reithian figure of Eric Gill carved a relief of Prospero and Ariel above the entrance to Broadcasting House: the size of Ariel's manhood was a source of worry to the governors, while passers-by suffered exposure to Gill's own virility, as he worked at the top of his ladder, clad only in the smock-like robe that he habitually wore, without – as they had occasion to realise – anything underneath.

In 2002, the 1932 building was remodelled and given a new east wing by MacCormac Jamieson Prichard: a project that brilliantly showed how a much-loved building can be brought up to date without loss of original character. Let us hope that the BBC as a whole can be given a similar makeover. With the NHS, it is, with all its faults, unique to Britain and perceived as a key part of our identity around the world.

Afterword

This book has been a journey of the mind, visiting places of outstanding qualities, which are often special to England and its history. Is there a conclusion to be drawn from it? I think so. England has extraordinary riches, some of which can be found here and nowhere else. We have our own way of doing things, our own distinctive aesthetic. This mosaic of different landscapes has been inhabited by people for a very, very long time, during which monuments have been raised, cities built and human ingenuity displayed. The past informs the present. It tugs at our emotions. England is that sort of place.

Change is all about us, and the pace accelerates – or has until now. Coronavirus turned the motor off, temporarily. It has forced the nation to stay at home and re-evaluate itself, in a general, unbidden period of introspection. This is a time to take stock. It could be that, post-pandemic, globalisation won't proceed at quite the hectic rate it has done in recent decades, but the homogenising tendency of the twenty-first century has already blitzed much of the individuality and distinctiveness of places to a bland and uniform purée. Where do we go from here? What do we have to build on? Is anything left?

Yes, I would say to the last question, as a result of considering my Crown Jewels. There are still many places of beauty and inspiration. Places that are special to this country, with a savour all their own; places to stir pride in what this nation does well. At a time of deep anxiety, they can give hope.

In the great national and international effort to rebuild the economy after the shock of 2020, let us remember that the unique things, the things of wonder, loveliness and creative genius, have a value beyond the balance sheet. As the world readjusts to a new normal, with more expensive air travel and less exuberant consumerism, it may be that they have an even greater role to play in our well-being than before.

Acknowledgements

I must acknowledge debts to many people: the list should really be longer than it is because I got to know some of these Crown Jewels a long time ago and I'm not sure I can dredge the lake of memory to the extent of remembering everyone who has helped me over the many years. I'm grateful to all. Of those who stand out from recent times I would like to thank my friends at Plantlife, particularly Trevor Dines, as well as those at the Woodland Trust. John Goodall and Mary Miers at *Country Life* have been a constant source of fun and encouragement. Some Crown Jewels have been adapted from pieces originally written for that magazine, for which I must thank the editor, Mark Hedges. Tracey Lovering introduced me to lichens. Nigel Farndale helped me with Yorkshire. James and Claire Birch opened the doors of Doddington. Orlando Rock let me into the story of the Heaven Room at Burghley. Gill Perkins of the Bumblebee Conservation Trust shared the mysteries and marvels of *Bombus*. Will Palin showed me St Bartholomew's Hospital. Martin Lutyens and Rebecca Lilley of the Lutyens Trust preside over Goddards. Philip Merricks is the *genius loci* at Elmley. Andrew Sanders discussed Durham. Thanks also go to James Stourton, Anna Keay, Ross

Murray, Michael Macgregor, Audrey Hoare, Tim Knox, Todd Longstaffe-Gowan and Jeremy Musson. I owe the idea for the book to my agent Adrian Sington of Kruger Cowne and to Andreas Campomar of Little, Brown. I am grateful to Claire Chesser for editing the book. My wife Naomi and sons William, Johnny and Charlie have contributed in so many ways, most obviously by their suggestions and encouragement. Since we have travelled together to many of these Crown Jewels at different times, I hope the book stirs memories.